Business Sustainability

Performance, Compliance, Accountability
and Integrated Reporting

BUSINESS SUSTAINABILITY

Performance, Compliance, Accountability and Integrated Reporting

ZABIHOLLAH REZAEE

Routledge
Taylor & Francis Group

LONDON AND NEW YORK

First published 2015 by Greenleaf Publishing Limited

Published 2017 by Routledge
2 Park Square, Milton Park, Abingdon, Oxon OX14 4RN
711 Third Avenue, New York, NY 10017, USA

Routledge is an imprint of the Taylor & Francis Group, an informa business

Copyright © 2015 Taylor & Francis

Cover by Sadie Gornall-Jones

British Library Cataloguing in Publication Data:
    A catalogue record for this book is available from the British Library

    ISBN-13: 978-1-78353-490-6 [hbk]
    ISBN-13: 978-1-78353-504-0 [pbk]

To the loving memory of my mother and father,
Fatemeh and Fazlollah Rezaee.
To my wife, Soheila, my daughter, Rose, and my son, Nick.
Also, thanks to my graduate assistant, Rob Palmer,
for his help in editing this book.

Contents

Figures

Tables

Preface

In today's business environment, global businesses are under close scrutiny and profound pressure from lawmakers, regulators, the investment community, and their diverse stakeholders to focus on sustainability and accept accountability and responsibility for their multiple bottom lines (MBL) of economic, governance, social, ethical, and environmental (EGSEE) performance. More than 6,000 public companies worldwide are issuing sustainability reports on some or all five EGSEE dimensions of sustainability performance, and this trend is expected to continue. Investors demand more relevant financial and nonfinancial sustainability information, regulators in several countries require disclosure of sustainability performance information, and public companies provide such information. However, proper determination of sustainability performance as well as accurate and reliable reporting of sustainability remains a major challenge for organizations of all types and sizes. This book offers guidance to organizations for proper measurement, recognition, and reporting of all five EGSEE dimensions of sustainability performance. In this book, business sustainability refers to the ongoing process of promoting, measuring, recognizing, enforcing, reporting, and auditing sustainability performance in the five areas of EGSEE. Traditionally, business organizations have reported their performance on economic affairs. In recent years, stakeholders, global organizations, and the public have increasingly demanded information on both financial and nonfinancial key performance indicators (KPIs) regarding all five dimensions of sustainability performance.

Sustainability performance and accountability reporting have gained a new interest in the aftermath of the 2007–2009 global financial crises and subsequent global economic meltdown, resulting in widening concerns about whether big businesses (banks and car-makers) are sustainable in the long term in contributing to the economic growth and prosperity of the nation. The ever-increasing erosion of public trust and investor confidence in sustainability of large businesses, the widening concern about social responsibility and environmental matters, overconsumption of natural resources, the global government bailout of big businesses, and the perception that government cannot solve all problems of businesses underscore the importance of keen focus on sustainability performance, compliance, and accountability reporting. This book examines business sustainability and accountability reporting and their integration into strategy, governance, risk assessment, performance management, and the reporting process of disclosing governance, ethics, social, environmental, and economic sustainability performance. This book also highlights how people, businesses, and resources collaborate in a business sustainability and accountability model.

There are four themes in this book. First, business sustainability is driven by and built on the stakeholder theory, which suggests that the primary purpose of business sustainability is to create stakeholder value with a keen focus on achieving long-term and enduring financial and nonfinancial performance for all corporate constituencies from shareholders to creditors, employees, customers, suppliers, society, and the environment. The second theme implies that the main goal and objective function for business organizations is to maximize firm value. The goal of firm value maximization under business sustainability can be achieved when the interests of all stakeholders are considered. It is highlighted in the book that creating stakeholder value is not the same as maximizing short-term profits and confusing sustainability performance with short-term profit maximization can put both shareholder value creation and stakeholder interest protection at risk. The main focus is on long-term shareholder value creation and maximization while considering trade-offs among other apparently competing and often conflicting interests of society, creditors, employees, and the environment. Business sustainability focuses on the achievement of long-term firm value maximization by creating value for shareholders and meeting the claims and interests of other stakeholders. The third theme is the time-horizon of balancing short-term and long-term performance, with a keen focus on long-term performance. Business sustainability focuses on the achievement of long-term and enduring performance and enables corporations to focus on maximizing long-term performance instead of meeting quarterly financial targets. The final theme is the multi-dimensional nature of sustainability performance in all EGSEE areas. The multi-dimensional EGSEE sustainability performance is interrelated. The relative importance of the dimensions with respect to each other and their contribution to the firm's overall long-term value maximization is affected by whether these EGSEE dimensions are viewed as competing, conflicting, or complementing with each other. One view is that these EGSEE dimensions are complementary because a firm that is governed effectively, adheres to ethical principles, and is committed to corporate social responsibility (CSR) and environmental obligations is also enabled to be sustainable in generating long-term financial performance. Another view is that corporations must do well financially in the long term to be able to do well in terms of CSR and environmental activities.

Purpose of the book

The primary theme of this book is the discussion of business sustainability and accountability reporting and their integration into strategy, governance, risk assessment, and performance management to create stakeholder value. To that end, this book covers many topics in this area, including the following important topics:

- Introduction to business sustainability performance
- Five EGSEE dimensions of sustainability performance
- Integrated accountability/sustainability reporting
- Measurement, recognition, and disclosure of sustainable financial and nonfinancial KPIs
- Roles and responsibilities of key players in accountability/sustainability reporting
- Laws, regulations, rules, and standards governing integrated accountability/sustainability reporting
- Best practices of sustainability performance, reporting, and assurance
- Current status of and future trends in sustainability performance, reporting, and assurance

Globalization and economic, social, and technological developments in the 21st century demand a new type of corporate accountability reporting, reflecting KPIs on both financial and nonfinancial information. It appears that public companies and their gatekeepers are not effectively fulfilling their fiduciary duties and professional responsibility to promote accountability, compliance, and transparency. An effective sustainability performance and accountability reporting model reflecting all aspects of business (e.g., economic, social, environmental, ethical, governance) in addressing the interests of all stakeholders is the bedrock of the capital market. Significant opportunities exist for businesses to improve the value relevance of their corporate reporting to better meet the needs of global investors and enhance investors' understanding of their sustainable performance. For these reasons, this book will appeal to all participants in the corporate reporting process, including the following:

- **Policy-makers, regulators, and standard-setters.** Policy-makers, regulators, and standard-setters should find the discussion in this book useful as we are moving toward mandatory reporting and assurance on all five EGSEE dimensions of sustainability performance.

- **Auditors.** Internal and external auditors should find the chapter materials relevant, useful, and suitable to their audit functions, as they are now encouraged (and soon will be required) to provide assurance on all five EGSEE dimensions of sustainability performance.

- **Corporations, their boards of directors, executives, and legal counsel.** The business sustainability performance dimensions, sustainability reporting, and assurance guidelines and best practices discussed throughout the book should help public companies and their boards of directors, executives, and legal counsel effectively discharge their responsibilities in integrating sustainability performance and reporting into corporate reporting.

- **Business schools and training programs.** Sustainability performance, reporting, and assurance presented in this book can also be easily used in educational and training programs of business schools and professional organizations. Other professionals, such as management accountants, internal auditors, corporate legal counsel, financial institutions, and financial analysts who provide accounting, auditing, legal, and financial services to corporations should find this book relevant and helpful to their professional services and activities.

- **International practitioners and students.** Discussion of sustainability performance and reporting with a keen focus on global corporate governance and convergence in financial reporting and auditing standards makes the book attractive to corporations, business schools, and professionals worldwide. Notable coverage includes discussion of corporate governance models throughout the world, international integrated reporting, and international auditing and assurance standards on sustainability reporting.

Highlights of the book

This book offers guidance to organizations for proper measurement, recognition, and reporting of all five economic, governance, social, ethical, and environmental (EGSEE) dimensions of sustainability performance as well as proper reporting and assurance on sustainability performance. This book supplements a few existing books on corporate sustainability in several ways:

- It focuses on key performance indicators (KPIs) in areas of economic, governance, social, ethical, and environmental matters. Two of these areas, governance and ethical issues, are not addressed in the related books.

- It presents business sustainability as a strategic imperative designed to improve operational efficiency, financial reporting quality, and compliance with all applicable laws, rules, regulations, and standards.

- It adopts a holistic approach to corporate reporting (including integrated reporting) and assurance.

- It addresses the value relevance of sustainability/integrated reporting to investors and capital markets and their significance for global corporations.

- It presents sustainability strategies to create innovation in new products, services, energy efficiency, environmental facilities, and green initiatives.

- It examines the roles and responsibilities of all participants in the corporate reporting process, including directors, officers, internal auditors, external auditors, legal counsel, and investors.

- It discusses emerging initiatives in corporate reporting, including the use of the XBRL platform, convergence to a set of global accounting standards, and convergence in corporate governance.

- It presents ways to improve public trust, investor confidence, business reputation, employee satisfaction, corporate culture, social responsibility, and environmental performance.

More than 6,000 European companies will have to disclose their environmental, social, governance, and diversity sustainability performance in 2017 financial reports. Several professional organizations currently promote integrated sustainability reporting and thus influence sustainability development, performance, reporting, and assurance. Examples of these global organizations are the International Federation of Accountants, the Global Reporting Initiative, the International Integrated Reporting Council, and the Sustainability Accounting Standards Board. This book presents an integrated model for business sustainability to underscore the important role of business in society in promoting responsible business behavior. This integrated sustainability model enables business organizations to be responsible stewards in creating stakeholder value by contributing to wealth creation for shareholders as well as contributing to the well-being of customers, employees, society, and the environment. Sustainability performance refers to the process of focusing on the achievement of economic sustainability performance in creating shareholder value while recognizing the importance of environmental, social, ethical, and governance performance in protecting interests of other stakeholders (under stakeholder theory). Both financial and non-financial dimensions of sustainability performance are important and they complement each other. The expected benefits of focusing on all EGSEE dimensions of sustainability performance are generation of earnings supported by cash flows, enhancement of market performance and growth, effectiveness and efficiency of operations, reduction of environmental liability and litigation costs, cost savings resulting from a sustainable supply chain, improved product quality and customer satisfaction, enhanced reputation and regulatory approvals, and improved employee loyalty, competency, integrity, and productivity. Business sustainability has advanced from greenwashing and branding to a business imperative, as very recently stakeholders (including shareholders) demand, regulators require, and companies report their sustainability performance in all five dimensions: economic, governance, social, ethical, and environmental. A decade ago, less than 50 companies released sustainability reports. Now, more than 7,000 global public companies disclose sustainability performance information. It is expected that business sustainability will gain further momentum as investors continue to demand, regulators continue to require, and companies continue to disclose sustainability performance information.

1
Introduction to business sustainability performance, reporting, and assurance

In today's business environment, global businesses face close scrutiny and profound pressure from lawmakers, regulators, the investment community, and their various stakeholders to focus on sustainability measures and accept accountability and responsibility for their multiple bottom lines (MBL) of economic, governance, social, ethical, and environmental (EGSEE) performance. Organizations worldwide recognize the importance of sustainability performance in creating stakeholder value. Over 6,000 public companies worldwide issue sustainability reports on some or all five EGSEE dimensions of sustainability performance, and this trend is expected to continue well into the future. More than 6,000 European companies will be required to disclose their environmental, social and governance sustainability as well as diversity information for their 2017 financial reporting and onward. However, proper measurement of sustainability performance, as well as accurate and reliable reporting of sustainability performance, remains a major challenge for organizations of all types and sizes. This chapter offers guidance to organizations to properly integrate sustainability into their business models and strategic plans and practices. It also provides guidelines for complete and accurate measurement, recognition, and disclosure of all five EGSEE dimensions of sustainability performance in an integrated reporting model.

1.1 **Introduction**

Sustainability or sustainable development was first defined in the 1987 Brundtland Report as "… development that meets the needs of the present without compromising the ability of future generations to meet their own needs."[1] This definition has been criticized for not being adequately specific about whose or which needs should be considered, and it appears to primarily focus on environmental sustainability whereas other dimensions of sustainability performance such as economic and social should be also considered.[2] Business sustainability, however, is a relatively new concept which has been defined as a process of focusing on the achievement of all five (economic, governance, social, ethical, and environmental (EGSEE)) dimensions of sustainability performance.[3] In this context, sustainability focuses on activities that generate financial (long-term earnings, growth, and return on investment) and nonfinancial sustainability performance (environmental, social, ethical, and governance) that concern all stakeholders. The terms business sustainability, corporate social responsibility (CSR), and triple bottom line (focusing on environmental, social and governance (ESG)) have been used interchangeably in the literature and authoritative reports. However, business sustainability is regarded as much broader than CSR and even ESG and has recently gained more acceptance.[4] Business sustainability has advanced from a main focus on CSR to integration into corporate culture, mission, strategy, business model, and management processes.[5] A recent research study conducted by *MIT Sloan Management Review*, the Boston Consulting Group, and the United Nations Global Compact (UNGC) suggests that business sustainability is moving away from isolated and opportunistic efforts with the main focus on CSR and toward a more integrated, holistic, and strategic approach of embracing all dimensions of sustainability performance and engaging diverse stakeholders.[6] Business sustainability for organizations means not only providing products and services that satisfy the customer without jeopardizing the environment, but also operating in a socially responsible manner and presenting reliable and transparent sustainability reports.

1   World Commission on Environment and Development, 1987, p. 43.
2   Starik and Kanashiro, 2013.
3   Brockett and Rezaee, 2012a.
4   United Nations Global Compact, 2013.
5   Global Reporting Initiative, 2013a.
6   Kiron *et al.*, 2015.

In this chapter, business sustainability refers to the ongoing process of promoting, measuring, recognizing, enforcing, reporting, and auditing sustainability performance in the five areas of economic, governance, social, ethical, and environmental (EGSEE).[7] Traditionally, organizations have reported their performance on economic affairs. Their sole focus on financial results has become complicated and irrelevant. In recent years, stakeholders, investors, regulators, global organizations, and the public at large have increasingly demanded information on both financial and nonfinancial key performance indicators (KPIs) in this platform of MBL accountability and sustainability reporting. Sustainability performance and accountability reporting have gained a new interest during the recent financial crises and resulting global economic meltdown which has sparked widening concerns about whether or not big businesses (e.g., banks and car-makers) are sustainable in the long-term in contributing to the economic growth and prosperity of the nation. The ever-increasing erosion of public trust and investor confidence in the sustainability of large businesses, the widening concern about social responsibility and environmental matters, the overconsumption of natural resources, the global government bailout of big businesses, and the perception that the government cannot solve all problems in the business world underscore the importance of having a keen focus on sustainability performance and accountability reporting. The United Nations Global Compact, in its 2013 Global Corporate Sustainability Report, while underscoring the importance of business sustainability, calls on corporations worldwide to integrate ten principles of sustainability pertaining to environment, human rights, fair labor, and anticorruption into their strategies and operations.[8]

There are four primary themes in this book that present a framework for the five dimensions of business sustainability performance (EGSEE) and ten sustainability principles as discussed in this chapter. First, the business sustainability framework is driven by and built on the stakeholder theory, which is the process of protecting the interests of all stakeholders, with a keen focus on achieving long-term and enduring financial and nonfinancial performance for all corporate constituencies from shareholders to creditors, employees, customers, suppliers, society, and the environment. The stakeholder theory implies that business organizations have obligations to a number of constituencies and thus should add value for

---

7   Brockett and Rezaee, 2012a.
8   United Nations Global Compact, 2013.

all stakeholders, as listed above.[9] This stakeholder view of business organizations and business sustainability is supported by researchers, regulators, and the business and investment community. For example, ISO 26000 takes into account all aspects of the triple bottom line (TBL) key financial and nonfinancial performance relevant to the planet, people, and profit.[10] In the past several years, more than 21 U.S. states, including Delaware, New York, New Jersey, and California, have enacted laws creating a new hybrid type of corporation designated as a "Benefit Corporation" for businesses that want to simultaneously pursue profit and benefit society.[11] The justification for B-corporations is that existing laws prevent boards of directors from considering the impact of corporate decisions on other stakeholders, the environment, or society at large. Boards of directors of B-corporations are required to consider the impact of their decisions on specific corporate constituencies, including shareholders, employees, suppliers, the community, and on the local and global environment.

Second, the main goal and objective function for business organizations is to maximize firm value. The goal of firm value maximization under business sustainability can be achieved when the interests of all stakeholders are considered. The main focus is on long-term shareholder value creation and maximization while considering trade-offs among other apparently competing and often conflicting interests of society, creditors, employees, and the environment. Business sustainability focuses on the achievement of long-term firm value maximization by creating value for shareholders and meeting the claims and interests of other stakeholders.

The third theme is the time-horizon of balancing short-term and long-term performance, with a keen focus on long-term performance. Business sustainability focuses on the achievement of long-term and enduring performance and enables corporations to focus on maximizing long-term performance instead of meeting quarterly financial targets. Businesses can no longer focus on short-term earnings performance. Achievement of this level of sustainable performance can take ten or more years.

The final theme is the multi-dimensional nature of sustainability performance in all EGSEE areas. The multi-dimensional EGSEE sustainability performance is interrelated. The relative importance of the dimensions with respect to each other and their contribution to the firm's overall long-term

9 Jensen, 2001.
10 International Organization for Standardization (ISO), 2011.
11 Delaware Law Series, 2013.

value maximization is affected by whether these EGSEE dimensions are viewed as competing, conflicting, or complementing. One view is that these EGSEE dimensions are complementary because a firm that is governed effectively adheres to ethical principles and commits to corporate social responsibility (CSR) and environmental obligations, enabling sustainable generation of long-term financial performance. Another view is that corporations must do well financially in the long term to be able to do well in terms of CSR and environmental activities. On one hand, corporations that are managed ethically, governed effectively, and are socially and environmentally responsible are expected to produce sustainable performance, create shareholder value, and gain public trust and investor confidence. On the other hand, more economically profitable and viable corporations are in better positions and have more resources to create jobs and wealth and better fulfill their social and environmental responsibilities.

1.2 Definition of business sustainability and multiple bottom line (MBL)

Business sustainability is the practice of creating stakeholder value by focusing on the achievement of financial performance that nurtures both long-term growth and profitability and nonfinancial performance that promotes corporate governance effectiveness, ethical conduct, and social and environmental responsibilities. Business sustainability is different from CSR insofar that CSR addresses one of the five EGSEE dimensions of sustainability performance and recognizes nonfinancial sustainability issues in the past, while business sustainability is a more comprehensive and integrated approach of focusing on both futuristic and forward-looking financial and nonfinancial KPIs. The European Commission has long promoted CSR and its integration into corporate strategic decisions by defining CSR as "a concept whereby companies integrate social and environmental concerns in their business"[12] This definition of CSR suggests companies take social actions above and beyond their mandatory requirements toward society and environment. Business sustainability with a keen focus on CSR can "bring benefits in terms of risk management, cost savings, access to capital, customer relationships, human resource management, and innovation

12 European Commission, 2011.

capacity"[13] Thus, disclosure of such information promotes interaction with all stakeholders on important nonfinancial ESG sustainability performance. Disclosure of nonfinancial ESG sustainability performance demonstrates companies' commitment and move toward achieving the European Union's treaty objectives of "the Europe 2020 strategy for smart, sustainable and inclusive growth, including the 75% employment target".[14] It also facilitates engagement with stakeholders regarding sustainable growth and risks in building trust in the company and shareholders regarding allocation of capital and achievement of long-term investment goals.

Companies should strive to maintain good CSR in their everyday practices to minimize information asymmetry to all of their stakeholders. If a company withholds information about its practices, whether intentionally in efforts to minimize its effect on the bottom line or unintentionally as a result of not performing due diligence in its processes, this may result in increased perceived risk of the venture, decreased share price, concerns regarding management's ability to lead the company, or even so-called "Black swan" events: unforeseen events that have a major, and usually negative, impact on the company and usually could be seen clearly in hindsight if more attention had been paid. Thus, good CSR is important for a company to have in the short run to ensure viability in the ever-changing marketplace. However, to build a strong company in the long run, business sustainability must be put into practice to prepare for the future and mitigate the unforeseen or inescapable events that may occur even when a company follows CSR principles rigorously. One of the key features of putting business sustainability into practice is that when faced with problems from multiple stakeholders, a sustainable company can pivot its position to answer to the problem in the best manner possible.

The CSR program is designed to maximize corporate social benefits while minimizing the conflicts between corporations and society caused by differences between private and social costs and benefits and to align corporate goals with those of society. Examples of potential conflicts between corporations and society are many, and some can be related to environmental issues (e.g., pollution, acid rain, global warming), child labor in developing countries, and wages paid by multinational corporations in poor countries. Business sustainability measures, which include rules, regulations, and best practices of CSR programs, can raise companies' awareness of the

13   European Commission, 2011.
14   European Commission, 2011.

social costs and benefits of their business activities. The Organisation for Economic Co-operation and Development (OECD) defines the purpose of a CSR program as "to encourage the positive contributions that multinational enterprises can make to economics, environmental and social progress and to minimize the difficulties to which their various operations may give rise".[15] This definition focuses on two important aspects of a CSR program, namely the creation of social value through corporate activities (social value-added activities) and the avoidance of conflicts between corporate goals and societal goals (societal consensus). These two aspects of CSR programs should be integrated into business sustainability strategies, decisions, and performance.

The concept of sustainability development first gained popularity and arrived at the worldwide agenda through the Brundtland report "Our Common Future" in 1987, which primarily focused on the environment and poverty.[16] According to the report, sustainable development is "development that meets the needs of the present without compromising the ability of future generations to meet their own needs".[17] A business that is sustainable takes into account its impact on the environment, community, society, and economy. In other words, the business strives to meet the criteria of multiple bottom lines (MBL). Business success traditionally was measured in correlation with financial achievements, wherein higher profits accounted for bigger success. The triple bottom line (TBL) was coined in 1994 by John Elkington, extending the measures of success in a business to include the three P's – people, planet, profit. The International Organization for Standardization (ISO) issued ISO 26000 in 2011, covering a broad range of organizational activities ranging from economic to social, governance, ethics, and environmental issues to assist organizations in achieving their triple bottom line.[18] ISO 26000 is a globally accepted guidance document for social responsibility which assists organizations worldwide in fulfilling their CSR. The social responsibility performance promoted in ISO 26000 is conceptually and practically associated with the development of achieving sustainable performance because the fulfillment of social responsibility necessitates and ensures sustainability development. ISO 26000 goes beyond profit maximization by providing a framework for organizations to contribute to sustainable development and the welfare of society. The core

15   Organisation for Economic Co-operation and Development, 2003.
16   Brockett and Rezaee, 2012a.
17   United Nations, 1987, p. 41.
18   International Organization for Standardization (ISO), 2011.

subject areas of ISO 26000 take into account all of the aspects of the triple bottom line (TBL) key financial and nonfinancial performance relevant to the three P's. Brockett and Rezaee provide a comprehensive definition by introducing new dimensions of sustainability performance. The multiple bottom line, as defined by Brockett and Rezaee, includes economic, governance, social, ethical, and environmental (EGSEE) dimensions.[19]

MBL is a useful tool for businesses, as it affords them the opportunity to see the impacts of their business practices in those various dimensions and how they relate to each other. When in the past companies could rely solely on the bottom line for reporting the results of operations, companies increasingly must report their results based on MBL if they wish to foster business sustainability. Though certain externalities may decrease what was the bottom line in the past, building the "true" cost of these externalities into the bottom line will result in more steady costs and stock prices as investors have more information about the company and fewer reservations for black swan events. Business sustainability has advanced from a singular focus on CSR to integration into management processes and corporate culture. Achievement of sustainable business sustainability has recently garnered the attention of corporate directors and executives, as evidenced by the recent research conducted by *MIT Sloan Management Review*, the Boston Consulting Group, and the United Nations Global Compact (UNGC), where a high majority (87%) of 3,795 surveyed managers agreed that boards should play a strong role in sustainability development, whereas only 42% reported that their boards actually were engaged in business sustainability and 90% agree that executives should address sustainability challenges.[20] Business sustainability demands integrated efforts by management and changes in managerial mind-set of focus on short-termism of the tangible quick wins to the achievement of long-term, sustainable, and nonfinancial performance.

1.3 Dimensions of sustainability performance

Business sustainability can be beneficial to both internal and external stakeholders. Stakeholders are those who have vested interests in a firm through their investments in the form of financial capital (shareholders), human

19   Brockett and Rezaee, 2012a.
20   Kiron *et al.*, 2015.

capital (employees), physical capital (customers and suppliers), social capital (the society), environmental capital (environment), and regulatory capital (government). Stakeholders have a reciprocal relation and interaction with a firm in the sense that they contribute to firm value creation and their wellbeing is also affected by the firm. Two attributes of business sustainability are sustainability performance and sustainability disclosures, and both are important to all stakeholders. The sustainability performance attribute underscores that firms that focus on their nonfinancial performance (including social and environmental performance) and are managed more effectively with good corporate governance are more financially sustainable. The voluntary disclosure attribute of sustainability performance posits that "good type" firms that focus on nonfinancial (environmental, social and governance, ESG) and sustainable financial performance have more incentives to disclose information to differentiate themselves from "bad type" firms that do not focus on ESG and financial sustainability in order to avoid bad reputation. Disclosure of voluntary ESG sustainability may signal management's commitment to transparency of both financial and nonfinancial performance and thus can affect information asymmetry and firm value. This section addresses sustainability performance, and the next section focuses on sustainability reporting and disclosure.

Sustainability performance is typically classified into financial and nonfinancial performance and grouped into five dimensions of Economic (E), Governance (G), Social (S), Ethical (E), and Environmental (E), abbreviated as EGSEE.[21] Although business sustainability continues to evolve, several dimensions of sustainability performance pertaining to social and environmental initiatives have gained widespread global acceptance. These initiatives include an ethical workplace, customer satisfaction, just and safe working conditions, non-discriminatory fair wages, workplace diversity, environmental preservation, clear air and water, minimum age for child labor, safe and quality products, concern for the environment, and fair and transparent business practices. Each industry has its own applicable set of sustainability financial and nonfinancial KPIs. Each business organization must carefully identify its own social and environmental responsibilities given the context of the business culture in which it operates. The list of financial and nonfinancial sustainability KPIs depends on a variety of factors: industry, legal regimes, cultural diversity, corporate mission and strategy, corporate culture, political infrastructure, and managerial philosophy.

21   Brockett and Rezaee, 2012a.

Despite these disparate sustainability performance dimensions and their KPIs, sustainability has become an integral component of business. This section describes each of the EGSEE sustainability performance dimensions and their related KPIs.

1.3.1 Economic sustainability performance

The most important and commonly accepted dimension of sustainability is "economic performance." The primary goal of any business organization is to create shareholder value through generating sustainable economic performance. Business organizations should focus on activities that generate long-term corporate profitability rather than short-term performance. The economic dimension of sustainability performance can be achieved when business organizations focus on long-term sustainability performance and improved effectiveness, efficiency, and productivity. Long-term economic sustainability performance should be communicated to shareholders through the preparation of high-quality financial reports. In a broader term and in compliance with G4 of the Global Reporting Initiative (GRI) Guidelines, the economic dimension of sustainability should reflect the financial strengths and concerns and an organization's economic impacts on its stakeholders and society by showing how the economic status of stakeholders changes in response to the organization's activities.[22] Economic sustainability performance can be measured directly through financial activities between an organization and its stakeholders or indirectly through nonfinancial costs and benefits of economic relations and their effects on stakeholders.

The KPMG 2013 Audit Committee Roundtable Report highlights the importance of long-term sustainable performance by suggesting that focusing on quarterly earnings can undermine a firm's long-term sustainable performance.[23] The KPMG report suggests the use of financial and nonfinancial key performance indicators (KPIs) and drivers of sustainable performance of operational efficiency, customer satisfaction, talent management, and innovation.[24] Although the conventional measures of cash flows, earnings, and return on investment are essential in evaluating financial performance, they don't reflect sustainable performance and future growth. The 2013 KPMG report identifies the key measures of sustainable performance

22   Global Reporting Initiative, 2013b.
23   KPMG, 2013a.
24   KPMG, 2013a.

as operational efficiency, customer satisfaction, talent management, and innovation that should be derived from internal factors of strategy, risk profile, strengths and weaknesses, and corporate culture as well as external factors of reputation, technology, completion, globalization, and utilization of natural resources.[25] Business sustainability demands an integrated effort by management and a change in managerial focus on the short-termism of the tangible quick wins to the achievement of long-term, sustainable non-financial performance. Sustaining sustainability requires understanding of both performance and risks and their integration into the corporate culture as well as management strategies, decisions, and actions. This integrated approach to sustaining business sustainability enables management to effectively compete in the global marketplace.

1.3.2 Governance dimension of sustainability performance

The corporate governance landscape has changed significantly in the aftermath of the global 2007–2009 financial crises. The lack of effective corporate governance has been mentioned frequently as an overriding contributing factor in the global financial crises. Internal and external corporate governance measures have been established by policy-makers, regulators, and corporations to improve the quality of corporate governance and thus stakeholder trust and investor confidence in corporate sustainable performance and reporting. Regulatory reforms in the U.S.A. such as the Sarbanes-Oxley Act of 2002[26] and the Dodd-Frank Act of 2010[27] are designed to improve the quality and effectiveness of corporate governance. Effective corporate governance promotes accountability for the board of directors and executives, enhances sustainable operational and financial performance, improves the reliability and quality of financial information, and strengthens the integrity and efficiency of the capital market, which results in economic growth and prosperity for the nation. The governance dimension of sustainability performance is affected by legal, regulatory, internal and external mechanisms, and best practices to create shareholder value while protecting the interests of other stakeholders. A rising trend in corporate governance is the matter of "say on pay." As businesses become more transparent in regard to their inner workings (not to mention the stark realization of the income gap

25   KPMG, 2013a.
26   Sarbanes-Oxley Act, 2002.
27   Dodd-Frank Act, 2010.

brought to light throughout the Great Recession), shareholders are asking for more say in how companies reward their executives.

1.3.3 Social dimension of sustainability performance

The social dimension of sustainability performance reflects the transformation of social goals into practices that benefit an organization's stakeholders. Social performance measures an organization's social mission and its alignment with the interests of society. The social dimension of sustainability performance ranges from ensuring the high quality of products and services, better customer satisfaction, and improved employee health and wellbeing to adding a positive contribution to the sustainability of the planet and the quality of life for future generations.

Socially responsible investment (SRI) is becoming an increasingly important part of business these days. Though the mantra of business has long been to increase shareholders' profits, the advent of benefit corporations (or B-corporations) has brought with it a chance for shareholders to affect businesses' methods of doing business to increase their own desire for social change, not personal enrichment. The United Nations Principles of Responsible Investing (PRI) were initiated in 2005 to encourage global investors to integrate ESG into their investment decisions.[28] Recently, under sustainable and socially responsible investing ("SRI") principles, investors consider various sustainability issues in their investment analyses, since SRI increased by more than 22% to $3.74 trillion in managed assets during the 2010–12 period.[29]

A prime example of this is the recently rebranded CVS Health®. Eschewing $2 billion in annual sales of tobacco products, CVS decided that it was in their long-term interest to promote the health of their customer base and terminate the sale of tobacco products in their stores. The company cited a study performed in San Francisco and Boston, both of which banned retail pharmacies from selling tobacco products, which indicated that there was a 13% decrease in the number of people buying tobacco products upon the ban.[30] Time will tell whether the expansion of the healthcare sector of CVS' business will ultimately lead to higher economic return for the company versus the revenue from its "unhealthy" products.

28   United Nations Environment Programme Finance Initiative, 2005.
29   US SIF Foundation, 2012.
30   Ziobro, 2014.

1.3.4 Ethical dimension of sustainability performance

An organization's ethical culture can play an important role in ensuring the achievement of goals and sustainability. The effectiveness of ethical sustainability performance depends on a corporate culture of integrity and competence and an appropriate tone at the top. Characteristics of an ethical organization's culture are codes of conduct for directors, officers, and employees, a system of responsibility and accountability, and a workplace that promotes honesty, mutual respect, and freedom to raise concerns.

There are myriad examples of poor ethics negatively affecting companies or even industries (simply look at how Walmart, BP, and lawyers are portrayed in the media) that have been dealt with in great detail elsewhere. The positive effects of good, ethical decisions by companies are less visible, but are increasingly apparent in the ways that companies do business. An example of this is the Google Green initiative, wherein the company plans on spending $1 billion on "green energy" and reducing energy consumption both by the company and by its clients. Those who utilize Google's services on the whole would continue to use these services even without this initiative, but this initiative is done in response to the fact that the company does indeed have many hidden environmental impacts from its data centers and online/offline footprints. And it makes good business sense to boot. Though the goodwill likely will not pay the bills for this initiative, the research driven by this group will decrease Google's astronomic electricity costs as well as provide them with the potential for moving into new markets, as evidenced already by their move into driverless cars. Even if this initiative is a net loss for Google monetarily, it is an ethical gain for the company because they must account for the vast amounts of resources that they use to provide their services.

1.3.5 Environmental dimension of sustainability performance

Stakeholders demand clearer and more transparent information about the impacts of an organization's activities and operations on the environment beyond what is legislated by law. The environmental dimension of sustainability performance includes creating a better work environment, reducing the carbon footprint, improving air and water quality, and maximizing the positive effects of an organization on natural resources and the environment. The Coalition for Environmentally Responsible Economies (CERES) and the U.N. Environment Program, in collaboration with the U.N. Global Compact, promote environmental initiatives.

Worldwide, governments are instituting measures to ensure that the environment is better protected by the behest of society at large. For example, the Chilean government recently canceled a $10 billion dam project in Patagonia due in part to inadequate environmental impact assessments, and in part to pressure from citizens who did not want the natural beauty and usability of their land to be devastated. In this case, the government decided to forego the economic benefits of the project in consideration not only of the current impact it would have on the environment, but also in light of future known and unknown ramifications. Patricio Segura of the Patagonian NGO CODESA reports that "This is a tremendous victory for citizens […] in building a fairer and more sustainable Chile that protects our natural legacy for future generations."[31]

1.4 Value relevance of sustainability performance

Integration of the five EGSEE dimensions of sustainability performance into managerial strategies and practices enables companies to conserve scarce resources, optimize production processes, identify product innovations, achieve cost efficiency and effectiveness, increase productivity, and promote corporate reputation. The 2013 *Global Corporate Sustainability Report* released by the United Nations Global Compact addresses the state of corporate sustainability today and presents the actions taken by companies worldwide in integrating sustainability into their strategies, operations and culture.[32] The report encourages companies to engage their suppliers in the establishment of more sustainable practices and integration of sustainability into their supply chain processes. In the context of shareholder wealth maximization and stakeholder welfare maximization, nonfinancial environmental, ethical, social and governance (EESG) sustainability activities can create both synergies and conflicts. The stakeholder theory suggests that sustainability activities and performance enhance the long-term value of the firm by fulfilling the firms' social responsibilities, meeting their environmental obligations, and improving their reputation. However, these sustainability activities may require considerable resource allocation that could conflict with shareholder wealth maximization objectives and force

---

31　Hill, 2014.
32　United Nations Global Compact, 2013.

management to solely invest in sustainability initiatives that would result in long-term financial sustainability.

Theoretically, management engagement in nonfinancial ESG sustainability activities, performance, and disclosure can be viewed as value-increasing or value-decreasing for investors. On one hand, companies that effectively manage their business sustainability improve ESG performance, enhance their reputation, fulfill their social responsibility, and promote a corporate culture of integrity and competence. On the other hand, companies can only survive and generate sustainable performance when they continue to generate profits and create shareholder value. Nonetheless, financial and nonfinancial EESG sustainability performance and disclosures supplement each other and are not mutually exclusive. Companies with effective governance, social and environmental responsibility, and high standards of ethics are expected to produce sustainable performance, create shareholder value, and gain investor confidence and public trust. Sustainability has gained the attention of global financial institutions and investors as they began to consider how EESG risks affect their investment portfolio value. For example, CalSTRS, in its *2013 Corporate Governance Annual Report*, indicates that it integrates the exposure to sustainability-related risks into its investment portfolio.[33] In focusing on EESG risk, the purpose is to ensure that firms manage their EESG risk and do not sacrifice long-term gains for short-term profits. A 2012 survey conducted by the *MIT Sloan Management Review*-Boston Consulting Group indicates that 31% of surveyed companies report that sustainability contributes to their profits, whereas 70% consider sustainability permanently on their management agenda.[34]

The 2013 United Nations study suggests that nonfinancial ESG dimensions of sustainability performance are value-relevant to investors by presenting new risks and opportunities that are fundamental factors in performance analyses and portfolio investment valuations.[35] The study argues that ESG performance information enables investors to conduct economic and industry analyses of ESG nonfinancial information including trends, externalities, and industry competitiveness effects of ESG that may affect shareholder value creation as well as assessment of the company's sustainability strategies and practices that may change the traditional investment valuation parameters and assumptions.[36] Proper understanding of

33   California State Teachers' Retirement System, 2013.
34   Boston Consulting Group, 2012.
35   United Nations Environment Programme Finance Initiative, 2013.
36   United Nations Environment Programme Finance Initiative, 2013.

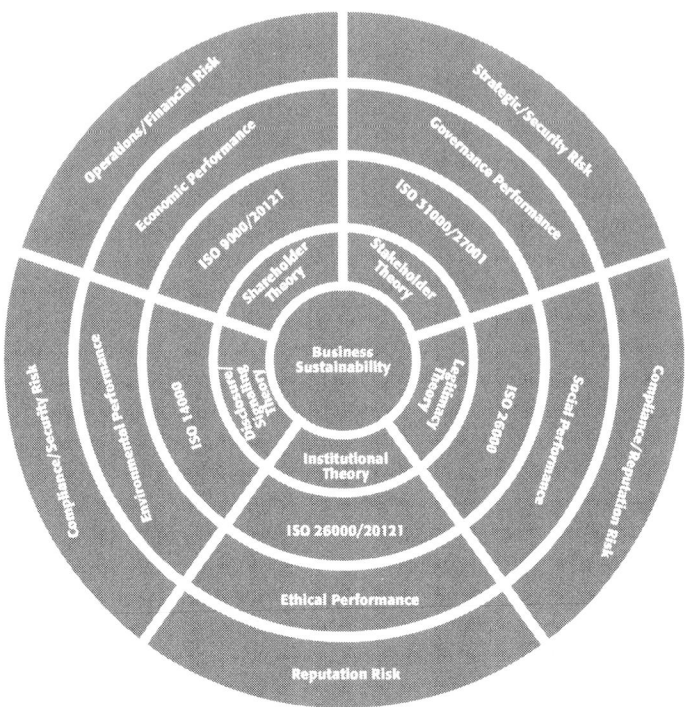

FIGURE 1.1   Sustainability theories, standards, performance and risks

sustainability theories, standards, risk assessment, and performance has been a major challenge for companies in measuring, recognizing, and disclosing the five EGSEE dimensions of their sustainability performance and for corporate stakeholders (including shareholders) in effectively using sustainability performance information in their investment valuations and portfolio analyses. This book provides stakeholders (including investors) with an integrated framework consisting of sustainability theories, standards, risks, and performance (as depicted in Figure 1.1 and thoroughly discussed in the next seven chapters) to obtain both long-term financial and nonfinancial sustainability information in making sound and informed investment decisions.

A 2014 survey of investors conducted by PwC finds that about 80% of responding investors said they considered nonfinancial EESG sustainability issues in their investment decisions when they were voting proxies and making investment portfolios in the past year. Among the top sustainability issues considered by investors are climate changes, resource scarcity, CSR, and good citizenship. Investors' primary drivers for considering sustainability issues in the order of performance are: risk reduction (73%), avoiding firms with unethical conduct (55%), performance enhancement (52%), cost reduction (36%), attracting new capital (30%), improving capability to create value (30%), and being responsive to interest groups (21%).[37] A 2014 survey of institutional investors reveals that the primary driver for investors in considering ESG sustainability issues is mitigating risk, as about three-quarters of responding investors believe that consideration of ESG sustainability issues reduces investment risk. Secondary drivers include enhancing performance and avoiding firms with unethical conduct.[38] Investors are often (and significantly more) dissatisfied than satisfied with sustainability information provided by firms regarding the following topics (in the order of the level of dissatisfaction): identification and disclosure of material sustainability risk and opportunities (82%); comparability of sustainability reporting between firms in the same industry (79%); relevance and implications of sustainability risks (74%); the impacts of social and environmental issues on supply chain (69%); Sustainability KPIs (68%); sustainability strategy that is linked to business strategy (68%); internal governance of sustainability issues (62); and processes used to identify material sustainability issues (57%).[39] More than 89% of the surveyed investors reported that they are very likely to request more ESG sustainability information from the firms in which they invest and about 80% said they will seek a meeting with the firms' boards or management regarding sustainability issues.[40]

Business sustainability enables management to focus on long-term and enduring financial and nonfinancial performance and disclose high-value and forward-looking information to all stakeholders. With business sustainability management has the opportunity to gather and use relevant financial and nonfinancial information for planning and forecasting and the related metrics that drive the business. Through business sustainability, management can better focus on sustainable value-deriving activities and use sustainability information to effectively communicate the company's sustainability performance that creates value for stakeholders. Business sustainability promotes business strategy, planning and decision-making, supply chain, and financial and nonfinancial management. It is important to communicate sustainability performance information regarding business

37   PricewaterhouseCoopers, 2014a.
38   PricewaterhouseCoopers, 2014a.
39   PricewaterhouseCoopers, 2014a.
40   PricewaterhouseCoopers, 2014a.

profit, processes, people, and planet (the environment) to all stakeholders in an integrated sustainability report. The next section presents how all five EGSEE dimensions of sustainability performance can be disclosed in an integrated sustainability report that benefits all stakeholders.

1.5 Sustainability reporting

The role of corporations in our society has evolved from profit maximization to creating shareholder value and, in recent years, to protecting the interests of all stakeholders. In today's business environment, global businesses face close scrutiny and profound pressure from lawmakers, regulators, the investment community, and their various stakeholders to focus on sustainability performance. Corporate disclosures, either mandatory or voluntary, are the backbone of financial markets worldwide. Public companies are required to disclose a set of financial information as long as their securities are held by the public. The primary purpose of corporate disclosures is to provide economic agents (e.g., shareholders, creditors) with adequate information to make appropriate decisions. Mandatory corporate reporting (including financial reports disseminated to investors and filed with regulators) is designed to provide investors with relevant, useful, and reliable information in making sound investment decisions. A moral hazard occurs in the presence of information asymmetry when management knows more about its actions and their effects on the financial reports and chooses to withhold proper financial information from investors.

Voluntary sustainability reports usually include any disclosures outside of financial statements that are not mandatory by regulators and standard-setters. Until the late 1990s, sustainability reports have been largely voluntary as part of the firm's supplementary disclosures. In recent years, many countries have adopted sustainability reports including Australia, Austria, Canada, Denmark, France, Germany, Malaysia, Netherlands, Sweden, Hong Kong, and the U.K. Regulators in other countries are expected to follow suit. Many global regulators, standard-setters, and other organizations, including the Sustainability Accounting Standards Board (SASB), Global Reporting Initiative (GRI), and International Integrated Reporting Council (IIRC), now promote and suggest guidelines for Integrated/Sustainability Reporting and Assurance. Business sustainability requires organizations to focus on achieving all five EGSEE dimensions of sustainability performance by taking initiatives to advance some social good beyond their own interests (e.g., compliance with applicable regulations and enhancement of shareholder wealth). Simply stated, business sustainability means enhancing corporations' positive impacts and minimizing their negative effects on society and the environment while creating value for stakeholders. The true measure of success for corporations should be determined not only by their reported earnings, but also by their governance, social responsibility, ethical behavior, and environmental performance. Business sustainability has received considerable attention from policy-makers, regulators, and the business and investment community over the past decade, and is expected to remain the main theme for decades to come. Sustainability theories, standards, policies, programs, activities, risk management, and best practices presented in this book should assist business organizations worldwide in integration of the five EGSEE dimensions of sustainability performance into their management processes in order to improve their KPIs as well as the quality of financial and nonfinancial sustainability information disseminated to their stakeholders.

The concept of sustainability performance suggests that management must extend its focus beyond maximizing short-term shareholder profit by considering the impact of its operation and entire value chain on all stakeholders including the community, society, and the environment. Disclosure of EGSEE dimensions of sustainability performance, while signaling management's commitment to sustainability and establishing legitimacy with all constituencies, poses a cost–benefit trade-off with implications for investors and business organizations. In creating stakeholder value, management should identify potential social, environmental, governance, and ethical issues of concern and integrate them into their strategic planning and managerial processes. There are many reasons and justifications of why management should integrate sustainability performance into its processes and practices, including the pressure of the labor movement, development of moral values and social standards, and the change in public opinion about the role of businesses in environmental matters, governance, and ethical scandals. Companies which are or aspire to be leaders in sustainability are challenged by rising public expectations, ever-increasing innovation, continuous quality improvement, effective governance measures, high standards of ethics and integrity, and heightened social and environmental problems. Thus, management should develop and maintain proper sustainability programs that provide a common framework for the integration of all five EGSEE dimensions of sustainability into their management processes, consisting of:

- Integration of financial and nonfinancial sustainability KPIs into the business and investment analysis, supply chain management, and decision-making process.

- Communication of the company's management sustainability strategies, practices, and expectations to major stakeholders including suppliers and customers to mitigate risks and foster corporate values and culture.

- Continuous assessment of the company's sustainability initiatives and related managerial processes to monitor and improve sustainability performance and identify challenging areas and risks that need further improvements.

- Promotion of product innovation and quality, customer retention and attraction, employee satisfaction and talent attraction, and productivity through management sustainability processes.

- Development of the environmental, social, ethical, and governance initiatives that will impact the company's ability to generate sustainable financial performance for shareholders and create value for all stakeholders.

- Establishment of financial and nonfinancial KPIs relevant to all five EGSEE dimensions of sustainability performance that support management strategic decisions and actions.

- Development of integrated sustainability reports to ensure that relevant financial and nonfinancial sustainability performance information is disclosed to all stakeholders.

- Periodic certifications of both financial and nonfinancial sustainability KPIs, issuance of integrated sustainability reports, and securing external assurance reports on all five EGSEE dimensions of sustainability performance.

The ever-increasing interest in sustainability reporting on nonfinancial information is a natural response to stakeholders' search for more information from businesses on governance, environmental, and social matters. Customers are more aware and make decisions based on how environmentally friendly a company is. Investors demand sustainability information when assessing companies' cost-effectiveness, efficiency, and long-term survival. Integration of the five EGSEE dimensions of sustainability performance into the corporate infrastructure, business model, and management processes enables companies to conserve scarce resources, optimize production processes, identify product innovations, achieve cost efficiency and effectiveness, increase productivity, and promote corporate reputation. Other benefits of sustainability reporting include an improved reputation, increased employee loyalty, and higher customer satisfaction. However, there are several sustainability challenges that, if not addressed properly, threaten business value, but they can be turned into business opportunities in the right hands. Taken together, the persistent challenges of sustaining sustainability have been the proper identification, measurement, recognition, reporting, and assurance of financial and nonfinancial KPIs.

Examples of these challenges according to a 2015 report by the Corporate Economic Forum are:[41]

- **Operational resources.** Integration of business sustainability into the company's supply chain management is challenging when dealing with price volatility and availability of scarce resources.

- **Government regulation.** Management faces the challenge of effective compliance with all sustainability regulations rules and standards, which has increased the cost of said compliance.

- **Mergers and acquisitions.** Business sustainability generates and promotes merger and acquisition activities and can cause companies to add or divest assets. Management should recognize the sustainability impact of these changes and make proper decisions.

- **Major investors.** Institutional and socially responsible investors have recently shown much interest in business sustainability. Thus, management should recognize this continuing interest in sustainability and its possible impact on the cost of capital.

- **Activist shareholders.** Shareholders are more actively involved with sustainability activities, and many shareholder resolutions in recent years are related to the environment and society. Management should address these resolutions to avoid reputational or financial damages.

---

41   Nidumolu *et al.*, 2015.

- **Reporting requirements.** Financial and nonfinancial sustainability information is more popular and is demanded by external stake-holders. Management should recognize such continuous interest in sustainability information and integrate it into corporate reporting.

- **Talent acquisition.** Employees are interested in business sustainability, shown by their interest in working in environmentally friendly, diverse, and socially responsible companies. Thus, management should demonstrate commitments to sustainability in attracting and maintaining talented employees.

1.6 Principles of business sustainability

Business sustainability has been promoted in response to demands by investors, necessary compliance with requirements of regulators, and voluntary initiatives by corporations in light of interdependences between global financial markets, the business community, and investors in advancing sustainable performance. More than 8,000 companies in 140 countries have adopted the ten sustainability principles established by the United Nations Global Compact and integrated these principles into their strategic planning and operations.[42] These ten sustainability principles are classified into four general categories of human rights, labor, environment, and anticorruption and relate to three dimensions (social, environmental, and ethical) of sustainability performance as explained in the prior section and presented in Table 1.1. The 2013 sustainability report of the United Nations (UN) Global Compact suggests two ways for companies to achieve business sustainability by:

1.   Integrating the ten principles into their strategies and operations

2.   Taking actions that support continuous improvements in sustainability performance[43]

The UN Global Compact report also provides the Global Compact Management Model as a practical tool for companies to improve their sustainability performance.[44] The suggested model consists of six managerial processes

---

42   United Nations Global Compact, 2013.
43   United Nations Global Compact, 2013.
44   United Nations Global Compact, 2013.

Principle	Description	Categories	Sustainability performance
1	The protection of international human rights should be respected and supported	Human rights	Social
2	Businesses shall not take part in the abuse of human rights		
3	Freedom of association and the right to collective bargaining should be supported	Labor	
4	Forced and compulsory labor should be eliminated		
5	Child labor should be effectively eradicated		
6	Discrimination in employment and occupation should be abolished		
7	Businesses should take safety measures against environmental challenges	Environment	Environmental
8	Greater environmental responsibility should be promoted		
9	The advances and distribution of environmentally friendly technology should be encouraged by business		
10	Businesses should combat extortion, bribery, and all forms of corruption	Anticorruption	Ethical

TABLE 1.1   United Nations ten Global Compact principles and sustainability performance

Source: United Nations Global Compact, 2013.

of committing to, assessing, defining, implementing, measuring, and communicating sustainability strategies, operations, and performance in ensuring alignment with the ten principles and compliance with applicable laws, rules, and regulations.[45]

1.7 Status of sustainability performance, reporting, and assurance

Over the last couple of years, companies have begun to stray away from the mind-set of "profit only" to one that recognizes that building and maintaining sustainable business practices is a good strategy for their companies.

45   United Nations Global Compact, 2013.

The 2013 Global Corporate Sustainability Report released by the United Nations Global Compact presents the current state of business sustainability by reviewing the actions taken by companies worldwide in advancing their business sustainability.[46] The report uses ten principles of sustainability and processes in its suggested model as benchmarks in assessing corporate sustainability actions and performance. The report presents responses of 2,000 companies in 113 countries regarding their sustainability progress and challenges. The key findings of the 2013 sustainability report are:

- Companies are taking proper actions to achieve sustainability performance as evident by 65% of signatories committing to sustainability at the CEO level, whereas about 35% train their managers to integrate sustainability into their strategies and operations.

- Large companies are leading the way toward sustainability performance and integrated reporting while medium-sized enterprises (SMEs) still face challenges to achieve sustainability.

- Supply chains are a roadblock to the achievement of improved sustainability performance.

- Companies are moving forward with a focus on the achievement of all dimensions of sustainability performance from education to poverty eradication, employment growth, and climate change.[47]

In a conversation between Desiré Carroll (Senior Technical Manager of IFRS and Sustainability expert for the American Institute of CPAs) and Steve Leffin (Director of Sustainability for UPS), Steve revealed that by shifting between ground and rail efficiently, UPS was able to consume less fuel, preserve the environment, and save on costs.[48] This is one of many examples of business sustainability practices.

An accountability assurance principle means conducting business in an ethical and socially responsible manner. A proper assurance process requires timely and deliberate planning, bold action, effective implementation, enforceable accountability, continuous monitoring, and an independent third-party assurance on sustainability reports. The performance enhancement principle indicates achievement of sustainable EGSEE

---

46   United Nations Global Compact, 2013.
47   United Nations Global Compact, 2013.
48   Carroll, 2014.

performance by enhancing corporations' positive impacts and minimizing negative effects on society and environment.

Many countries have and are adopting laws and regulations that make sustainability reporting mandatory for large companies. The European Commission, on September 29, 2014, endorsed the adoption by the Council of the Directive on disclosure of nonfinancial sustainability information for more than 6,000 companies for their financial year 2017.[49] According to the Global Reporting Initiative (GRI), the number of organizations releasing stand-alone sustainability reports grew from 44 firms in 2000 to 1,973 in 2013.[50] This number is expected to rise as more and more companies realize the potential that is paramount in the reporting of their practices.

The GRI was launched in 1997 to bring consistency and global standardization to sustainability reporting. GRI initially focused on incorporating environmental performance into corporate reporting with its "Sustainability Reporting Guidelines," which were published in 2000, 2002, 2006, 2011, and 2013. GRI is now considered the sole global standard-setter in sustainability reporting. The current version, the "G4 Guidelines," was issued in May 2013. In addition to including more data points in the disclosures from the previous version 3.1, G4 adds in a good number of disclosures in most aspects, particularly by adding the "Ethics and Integrity" element and substantially strengthening "Corporate Governance" measures.[51]

Sustainability reporting can be promoted in three ways:

1. Through market forces of the demand for and interest in EGSEE performance reporting by investors and financial markets.

2. Through mandatory sustainability reporting by regulators and listing standards of stock exchanges[52] and European Parliament Directives to require large public companies in Europe to report on their social, governance, environmental, and diversity initiatives.

3. Through a combination of mandatory and voluntary initiatives.

Many public companies now voluntarily manage, measure, recognize, and disclose their commitments, events, and transactions relevant to EGSEE. More than 6,000 companies worldwide currently disclose sustainability reports according to the GRI. According to the GRI, in 2000, fewer

---

49   European Commission, 2014.
50   Global Reporting Initiative, 2013b.
51   Global Reporting Initiative, 2013b.
52   Singapore Exchange, 2011.

than 50 companies worldwide disclosed some sustainability information on various dimensions of sustainability performance on a voluntary basis. By 2005, this number increased to 300 companies, 1,500 companies in 2009, over 2,000 in 2010, and more than 6,000 in 2014, and the pace is growing.[53]

The move toward the issuance of mandatory sustainability reporting has (predictably) moved at a snail's pace. For example, in 2009, the Social Investment Forum (SIF) requested that the Obama Administration take initiatives to restore investor confidence by strengthening corporate responsibility of mandatory reporting on corporate environmental, social, and governance issues. The SIF has developed a proposal requesting the SEC to require public companies to:

- Report annually their sustainability information in compliance with the GRI guidelines.

- Disclose their short-term and long-term sustainability risks in the Management Discussion and Analysis (MD&A) section of their 10-K reports.[54]

Many countries (France, Malaysia, Sweden, the U.K., and Singapore) are modernizing their corporate reporting systems to include environmental, social, and governance (ESG) factors in compliance with GRI guidelines. The European Commission (EC) recently started considering whether to require disclosure of nonfinancial (ESG) information. The European Commission, on September 29, 2014, endorsed the adoption by the Council of the Directive on disclosure of nonfinancial sustainability information for more than 6,000 companies for their financial year 2017.[55] The Directive provides nonbinding guidelines to facilitate the disclosure of nonfinancial information by large public companies, and their stakeholders (including investors and society at large) are intended to benefit from this increased transparency of nonfinancial sustainability information. The Directive also provides large companies with significant flexibility to disclose nonfinancial information either as a separate report or an integrated report along with financial information.

There is no mandatory guidance at this time for sustainability reporting. However, there are several voluntary guidelines for sustainability reporting, including the reporting frameworks released by the GRI, the Connected

---

53   Global Reporting Initiative (2014).
54   Woll, 2009.
55   European Commission, 2014.

Reporting Framework, and the reporting publications of AccountAbility. An alternative mandatory sustainability report should be considered to accomplish the following:

- Standardize dispersed sustainability reports that are currently issued.

- Establish a globally accepted reporting framework for sustainability information.

- Create uniformity in objectively reporting all five dimensions of EGSEE performance.

- Ensure that a wide range of users, including investors, have access to uniform and comparable sustainability reports.

- Facilitate uniform sustainability assurance.

- Unlike audit reports on financial statements, assurance reports on sustainability information are not standardized, regulated, or licensed.

- IFAC released its revised "International Standard on Assurance Engagements Other Than Audits or Reviews of Historical Financial Information," 3000 (ISAE 3000).[56] Specifically, ISAE 3410 deals with assurance engagements for an organization reporting greenhouse gas (GHG) statements.

- GRI also recommends that assurance be provided on sustainability reports by external assurance providers, which can be designated with a "+" added to the application level declared. Alternatively, GRI can examine the content of detailed sustainability reports and express an opinion on the extent of compliance with GRI guidelines, but not the quality and/or reliability of disclosed sustainability information.[57]

Currently, sustainability reports are voluntary and (normally) not audited by external auditors. Existing sustainability reports bear different names (green reporting, corporate social responsibility reporting), serve different stakeholders in achieving a variety of purposes, and vary in terms of content, structure, format, accuracy, and assurance. A more standardized,

---

56   International Federation of Accountants, 2011.
57   Global Reporting Initiative, 2013a.

integrated, and audited process is required to make sustainability reports on EGSEE performance comparable, commonly acceptable, and relevant to all corporate stakeholders. Recently, Global Reporting Initiatives provided a comprehensive Sustainability Reporting Framework to enable greater organizational transparency.[58] In 2013, the International Integrated Reporting Council (IIRC) developed the International Integrated Reporting Framework, which provides guidelines for companies to integrate financial and nonfinancial performance information to benefit all stakeholders.[59] The European Parliament, on May 15, 2014, issued a new directive that would require listed companies to disclose information on their environmental, social, and diversity impacts, in addition to financial information on economic performance.[60] It is expected that companies in other countries will follow suit and thus in the near future sustainability reports will reflect both financial and nonfinancial information relevant to all five EGSEE dimensions of sustainability performance, and assurance will be provided on these reports to enhance their credibility and reliability.

Assurance providers play an important role in providing assurance on sustainability reports reflecting all five EGSEE dimensions of sustainability performance. Objectivity, reliability, transparency, credibility, and usefulness of sustainability reports are important to both internal and external users of reports and can be enhanced by providing assurance on sustainability reports. Sustainability assurance can be provided internally by internal auditors or external assurance providers. While internal auditors are well qualified to assist management in the preparation and assurance of sustainability reports, external users of sustainability reports may demand more independent and objective assurance on sustainability reports. This type of assurance can be provided by certified public accountants (CPAs), professional assurance providers, or equivalent accredited individuals, groups, or bodies. Current auditing standards are intended to provide reasonable assurance on financial and internal control reports prepared by management. However, the degree of reliance placed on nonfinancial information such as sustainability reporting is not clear. Assurance standards on different dimensions of sustainability performance reports vary in terms of rigorousness and general acceptability. For example, auditing standards governing reporting and assurance on economic activities presented in the

58   Global Reporting Initiative, 2013a.
59   International Integrated Reporting Council, 2013a.
60   European Commission, 2014.

financial statements are well established, widely accepted, and practiced. Assurance standards on other dimensions of sustainability including governance, ethics, social, and environmental standards are yet to be fully developed and globally accepted.

An integrated model for assurance on all five EGSEE dimensions of sustainability performance reporting is desirable and will be discussed in detail in future chapters. In order to audit financial statements and internal controls over financial reporting attention, this model considers a standard published by the Public Company Accounting Oversight Board (PCAOB) and applies it to the economic dimension. Two recent standards released by the International Auditing and Assurance Standards Board (IAASB), namely the International Standard on Assurance Engagements, "Other Than Audits or Reviews of Historical Financial Information," 3000 (ISAE 3000) and ISAE 3410 (Assurance Engagements on Greenhouse Gas Statements) assurance practice will be used for each dimension of EGSEE sustainability.[61] This integrated model provides the policy, practical, and educational implications of employing EGSEE reporting and auditing. The growth of sustainability reporting use and its potential to raise important assurance issues related to sustainability reporting will be very important in the future.

Recognition of the growing number of assurance services seems apparent from the issuance of assurance practice guidance statements in recent years by influential bodies such as AccountAbility,[62] the Global Reporting Initiative[63] and the European Federation of Accountants.[64] Two important sources of guidance on the assurance of sustainability reporting, each released in 2003, are provided by AccountAbility's AA1000 and the IAASB's International Standard on Assurance Engagement (ISAE) 3000. The AA1000 assurance standard provides guidance for an assurance engagement for assurance providers from outside the accounting profession, while ISAE 3000 provides guidance for an assurance engagement for members of the accounting profession. The International Standards on Assurance Engagements (ISAE) 3000 (issued by the IAAS Board in 2004), the AICPA's Attestation Standards (AT Section 101), CICA section 5025 and AA1000 Assurance Standards (AS) (issued in 2008 by AccountAbility (AA)), provide guidance for assurance on nonfinancial dimensions of sustainability.[65]

---

61   International Federation of Accountants, 2011.
62   AccountAbility, 2003.
63   Global Reporting Initiative, 2002.
64   Fedération des Experts Comptables Européens, 2002.
65   Brockett and Rezaee, 2012a.

In April 2001, the Global Reporting Initiative released its working paper entitled "Overarching Principles for Providing Independent Assurance on Sustainability Reports." The standard was developed by an international and interdisciplinary multi-stakeholder working group headed by Canadian Alan Willis, a Chartered Accountant. Their standard is divided into five general principles:

1. **Business case for independent assurance.** Discusses the need for companies to evaluate the business case for engaging an assurance provider for their sustainability report. Included in the evaluation are: the need to ensure clarity of goals and expectations; definition of scope; definition of objectives; and determination of benefits and costs.

2. **Prerequisite conditions for assurance engagements.** Sets out the primary requirements for a successful assurance engagement, including: evidence to support reported information, criteria against which to evaluate the evidence, resources to carry out the assignment, and cooperation in carrying out the assignment.

3. **Approaches and procedures.** Discusses, at a high level, the planning and execution of the assurance engagement, including: determining the approach and work plan, obtaining and evaluating evidence, and documenting the assignment.

4. **Communication of results.** Provides guidance on the reporting stage of the engagement, specifically: communicating the results of the assignment and providing comments and recommendations.

5. **Attributes of assurance providers.** Focuses on the assurance providers themselves and discusses: independence, integrity, due care, confidentiality, competence, and accountability.[66]

External assurance is an important part of Integrated Reporting, as assurance providers verify the information contained in the reports and publish those conclusions so that others, generally less experienced in the particular dimensions in which said assurance providers have expertise, may be assured that the practices faithfully confirm the statements made by management. The G4 Guidelines state that assurance providers must:

66   Global Reporting Initiative, 2002, p. 25.

- Be independent from the organization and therefore able to reach and publish an objective and impartial opinion or conclusions on the report.

- Be demonstrably competent in both the subject matter and assurance practices.

- Apply quality control procedures to the assurance engagement.

- Conduct the engagement in a manner that is systematic, documented, evidence-based, and characterized by defined procedures.

- Assess whether the report provides a reasonable and balanced presentation of performance, taking into consideration the veracity of the data in the report as well as the overall selection of content.

- Assess the extent to which the report preparer has applied the Guidelines in the course of reaching his conclusions.

- Issue a written report that is publicly available and includes an opinion or set of conclusions, a description of the responsibilities of the report preparer and the assurance provider, and a summary of the work performed to explain the nature of the assurance conveyed by the assurance report.[67]

These reports by external assurance providers should allay concerns that stakeholders have about the company and its practices, as well as provide institutions with evidence should any appearance of malfeasance manifest from investigations. Thus, it is necessary for the G4 Guidelines to include incentives and castigations, as reported on in the "Carrots and Sticks" publications made by UNEP, GRI, KPMG, and the Centre for Corporate Governance in Africa. The first edition, entitled *Carrots and Sticks for Starters*,[68] explains the different sides of voluntary and mandatory reporting, arguing that there is not a dichotomy, but instead should be a balance between the two, allowing companies to report not only what is required, but their individual corporate decisions as well. The second edition, released in 2010,[69] provides an updated examination of the voluntary versus mandatory reporting discussion and addresses the evolution of regulatory measures around the world.

---

67   Global Reporting Initiative, 2013c.
68   KPMG and United Nations Environment Programme, 2006.
69   KPMG *et al.*, 2010.

Numerous bodies have developed methodologies and standards for external assurance for global, regional, and country-specific audiences. Many of these bodies come in the form of trade associations of accountants, engineers, and other professionals who come together to write standards that will raise the quality of their respective industries as a whole.[70] As reporting becomes more nuanced, there will be somewhat of a reckoning for companies. Those which have not been disclosing their issues well may see a downtick in their equity capital as investors realize there are more liabilities than previously thought. Conversely, those which receive good marks from external assurance providers may see an uptick in their value as investors find that there is less risk than previously perceived. One of the greatest benefits of having external assurance is that companies will be forced to deal with issues previously unforeseen (perhaps even by the companies themselves) and improve their procedures accordingly. Those which use this as an opportunity to grow will, in general, be rewarded accordingly, while those which do not will suffer. From an overall marketplace view, this will help the market become more efficient and, all else being equal, more profitable to those with the best practices.

1.8 Professional organizations influencing sustainability development, reporting, and assurance

Business sustainability promotes long-term profitability and competitive advantages, helps maintain the wellbeing of the society, the planet, and people, and creates value for all stakeholders. Global authoritative standard-setters, including the International Federation of Accountants (IFAC), the Global Reporting Initiative (GRI), International Integrated Reporting Council (IIRC), and the Sustainability Accounting Standards Board (SASB) now promote Integrated/Sustainability Reporting. Sustainability reporting measures, recognizes, and discloses five EGSEE dimensions of sustainability performance. More than 6,000 companies worldwide are reporting their various EGSEE sustainability performance and many global exchanges either require or promote their listed companies to disclose sustainability information. The goal of long-term firm value maximization under business sustainability can be achieved when the interests of

---

70 KPMG *et al.*, 2013.

all stakeholders including shareholders are considered. Regulators, investors, and companies throughout the world continue to value a firm's sustainability performance.

It is expected that Integrated Reporting will play an important role in future corporate reporting and in rebuilding investor trust and confidence in public financial information. Trust in public company financial reporting has eroded in recent years, and there is concern about the short-term focus on only financial information and the lack of attention given to non-financial ESG performance information. Conventional corporate reporting, based on historical financial information, predominantly focuses on the economic dimension of sustainability performance and short-term value drivers, but does not recognize the increasing importance of nonfinancial ESG dimensions of sustainability performance. Integrated Reporting provides an opportunity to go beyond this short-term focus on financial performance and enable companies to pay attention to both financial and nonfinancial KPIs in demonstrating more clearly their stewardship and social utility, environmental initiatives, and, simultaneously, economic value. Integrated reporting is a vehicle by which public companies communicate their value creation strategies, decisions, and actions through short, medium, and long-term performance in all five EGSEE sustainability performance metrics to all stakeholders. Integrated reporting enables business organizations to integrate EGSEE sustainability performance reporting into the mainstream corporate reporting process.

The evolution of GRI guidelines began with an initial focus on incorporating environmental performance into corporate reporting with its first publication, *Sustainability Reporting Guidelines*, in 2000. The GRI, in its G3 (initially) and G4 guidelines (released in May 2013) promotes sustainability reporting as a standard practice of disclosing sustainability-related issues relevant to businesses and stakeholders.[71] The goal of long-term value maximization can be achieved when all stakeholders' interests are considered. The main focus is on long-term shareholder value creation and maximization while considering trade-offs among other apparently competing and often conflicting interests of society, creditors, employees, and the environment. The various dimensions of sustainability performance are inter-related. The relative importance of the dimensions with respect to each other and their contribution to the overall firm's long-term value maximization is affected by whether economic and other sustainability

71   Global Reporting Initiative, 2013b.

dimensions are viewed as competing, conflicting, or complementing. The economic and other sustainability performance dimensions are complementary because a firm that is effectively governed, behaves ethically, and commits to social and environmental initiatives is also sustainable while generating long-term financial performance. Although the primary goal of many corporations will continue to be enhancing shareholder value by producing sustainable economic performance, they must also effectively deal with ESG issues to ensure value is added for their shareholders and other stakeholders.

Important principles of Integrated Reporting are:[72]

- Ensuring that corporate strategy is articulated well as a core part of the report

- Connecting all parts of the business as a whole

- Making information concise and easily readable

- Being future-oriented and inclusive of multiple stakeholders

- Taking care to provide materiality, value, and assurance to the audience of the report

These principles should help companies see the importance of Integrated Reporting and its effect on their business. More can and will be added in due time as the IIRC works with companies to further develop best practices. The fourth generation (G4) of GRI's guidelines covers economic, governance, social, and environmental performance.[73] The GRI reporting process enables organizations to disclose self-declared sustainability information based on one of three application levels (A, B, or C) depending on the extent of information provided. The GRI initially focused on a triple bottom line of economic, social, and environmental performance with Version 3.1 (G3) of its sustainability framework. In its G4 guidelines (released in May 2013) the GRI promotes sustainability reporting as a standard practice of disclosing sustainability-related issues relevant to companies business and their stakeholders.[74] The G4 Guidelines present Reporting Principles, Standard Disclosures, and an Implementation Manual for sustainability reporting on

---

72   Adams, 2013; International Integrated Reporting Council, 2011.
73   Global Reporting Initiative, 2013a.
74   Global Reporting Initiative, 2013a.

economic, environmental, social, and governance performance (EESG) by all organizations regardless of their type, size, sector, or location.[75]

The Sustainability Accounting Standards Board (SASB) establishes and creates sustainability accounting standards suitable for developing measures to disclose material sustainability issues for 88 industries in ten sectors, suggests the process for mandatory filings to the Securities and Exchange Commission (SEC), such as the Form 10-K and 20-F, through the first quarter of 2015. The SASB's primary concern is creating standards that enable peer-to-peer comparison between companies, which can be useful for investment decisions and allocation of capital.[76] In June 2011, the Global Initiative for Sustainability Ratings (GISR) developed Environmental, Social, and Governance (ESG) ratings standards with an eye toward maximum harmonization with leading complementary standard-setters, most notably the Global Reporting Initiative (GRI), the International Integrated Reporting Council (IIRC),[77] the Carbon Disclosure Project (CDP), and SASB.[78] Harmonizing SASB standards with existing disclosure standards avoids additional costs for companies and aligns the SASB's work with global corporate transparency efforts. In April 2013, the International Integrated Reporting Council (IIRC) released the draft of its framework consultation on integrated reporting intended to provide guidelines on communication with stakeholders.[79] The IIRC's proposed framework addresses fundamental concepts of integrated reporting and its guiding principles on an organization's strategy, governance, performance, and prospects. The products of the SASB, GRI, and IIRC can be used in complementary ways for the development of a sustainability report for investors and all stakeholders. The SASB provides standards for mandatory filings, whereas GRI and IIRC provide frameworks for voluntary reporting.

---

75   Global Reporting Initiative, 2013a.
76   Sustainability Accounting Standards Board, 2013.
77   International Integrated Reporting Council, 2013a.
78   CDP Worldwide, 2013.
79   International Integrated Reporting Council, 2013a.

1.9 Best practices of sustainability performance, reporting and assurance

Sustainability performance, reporting, and assurance evolves as investors demand more relevant sustainability disclosures, regulators require more extensive sustainability reports, and business organizations integrate sustainability into their strategic decisions, actions, and performance. Best practices of sustainability performance, reporting, and assurance are also being developed. According to GreenBiz and UPS, there are five ways to convey the vital importance of sustainability to senior executives:[80]

1. Sustainability enables cost reduction and efficiency improvement

2. Sustainability incentivizes organizations to focus on risk assessment, management, and mitigations (financial, operational, compliance, strategic, and reputation risks)

3. Sustainability creates new competitive and revenue-generating opportunities

4. Sustainability encourages innovation

5. Sustainability promotes talented employee recruiting development and retention

Best practices of sustainability performance, reporting, and assurance (presented in Table 1.2) suggest that:

- Sustainability strategies should be integrated into corporate decision-making processes in promoting the achievement of all five EGSEE dimensions of sustainability performance

- Companies should use a principles-based approach in integrating both financial and nonfinancial sustainability information into their corporate reporting

- Companies should assess sustainability risks in all aspects of strategy, operations, compliance, finance, and reputation and minimize their impacts on EGSEE sustainability performance

- Companies should provide assurance on their sustainability reports to gain credibility, investor confidence, and public trust

---

80   Kuehn, 2010.

A recent report by the Conference Board presents many cases in which nonfinancial EESG sustainability actions and performance have a positive impact on financial performance.[81] The report also highlights the importance of establishing the link between financial and nonfinancial EESG sustainability using KPIs. Sustainability information on EESG is typically considered as an externality beyond disclosure of economic performance, which can be viewed positively or negatively by market participants. Examples of positive externalities are board independence and diversity, majority voting, environmental initiatives regarding climate change, customer satisfaction, job creation, and fair employment. Examples of negative externalities are CEO duality, natural resource depletion, pollution, and human rights abuses. In disclosing their externalities in terms of strengths and concerns, firms have a tendency to overemphasize positive externalities and underemphasize concerns as incorporated into the ESG scores. A 2013 joint study by the Investor Responsibility Research Center Institute (IRRCI) and the Sustainable Investments Institute (Si2) reports that only 1.4% of the S&P companies (seven firms) issued a stand-alone sustainability report by mentioning sustainability reporting in their regulatory filing of 10-K reports, whereas almost all S&P companies (499) disclosed at least one piece of sustainability information, 74% placed monetary value on their sustainability-related disclosures, and about 44% of the companies linked their executive compensation to some type of sustainability criteria.[82]

These best practices of sustainability performance, reporting, and assurance are gaining global acceptance. A 2014 survey of investors conducted by PwC finds that about 80% of responding investors said they considered ESG sustainability issues in their investment decisions when they were voting proxies and making investment portfolios in the past year.[83] Among the top sustainability issues considered by investors are climate changes, resource scarcity, CSR, and good citizenship. Investors' primary drivers for considering sustainability issues, in the order of performance, are risk reduction (73%), avoiding firms with unethical conduct (55%), performance enhancement (52%), cost reduction (36%), attracting new capital (30%), improving capability to create value (30%), and being responsive to interest groups (21%).[84] Investors are typically more dissatisfied than satisfied with

---

81   Bertoneche and van der Lugt, 2013.
82   IRRC Institute and Sustainable Investments Institute, 2013.
83   PricewaterhouseCoopers, 2014a.
84   PricewaterhouseCoopers, 2014a.

Company	Link	Country	Industry	Example of sustainability initiative
Westpac Banking Corporation	westpac.com.au	Australia	Banks	First bank in Australia to publish an environmental policy, 1992
Biogen Idec, Inc.	biogenidec.com	U.S.A.	Pharmaceuticals and biotechnology	Has created a series of initiatives to encourage STEM research among youth
Outotec OYJ	outec.com	Finland	Capital goods	Promotes and undertakes worldwide seminars and initiatives to educate and help customers and locals
Statoil ASA	statoil.com	Norway	Energy	Discloses all revenues and payments in the countries in which they operate.
Dassault Systèmes SA	3ds.com	France	Software and services	Introduced SolidWorks Sustainability software to gauge the environmental impact of customers' designs
Neste Oil OYJ	nesteoil.com	Finland	Energy	Committed to responsible sourcing of fuel stock and non-deforestation
Novo Nordisk A/S	novonordisk.com	Denmark	Pharmaceuticals and biotechnology	Creates Blueprints for Change to measure the linkage between the company's Triple Bottom Line and value created for the company and society
Adidas AG	adidas-group.com	Germany	Consumer durables and apparel	Adopts so-called "Fair Play," pillars of sustainability vis-à-vis People, Product, Planet, and Partnership
Umicore SA	umicore.com	Belgium	Materials	Has created an interactive report wherein stakeholders can tailor the data received to their particular interests
Schneider Electric SA	schneider-electric.com	France	Capital goods	Develops solutions to give off-grid communities access to mobile electricity producers
Cisco Systems, Inc.	cisco.com	U.S.A.	Technology hardware and equipment	Runs a product trade-in program wherein Cisco reuses old products to create new ones, saving environmental cost of new production and of disposal
BASF SE	basf.com	Germany	Materials	Has created AgBalance to evaluate sustainable practices across the entire value chain

BMW	bmw.com	Germany	Automobiles and components	Perform analyses to determine the matrix of sustainability matters most important to stakeholders and to the company at large
Aeroports de Paris	aeroportsdeparis.fr	France	Transportation	Exceeds federal guidelines on environmental protection of all land the group owns
ASML Holding IV	asml.com	Netherlands	Semiconductors and semiconductor equipment	Despite using much less water than most competitors, still strives to reduce water consumption significantly

TABLE 1.2   Top 15 sustainable companies

Source: Sustainability Accounting Standards Board (2013).

sustainability information provided by firms relevant to sustainability risk, challenges, opportunities, and sustainability performance dimensions.

1.10 Conclusions

Business sustainability enables organizations to focus on achieving both financial and nonfinancial key performance indicators (KPIs) to create value for shareholders and protect the interests of other stakeholders, including employers, creditors, suppliers, governments, the environment, and society at large. Business sustainability (as presented in this chapter) is a framework for organizations to achieve their desired performance in all areas of economic, governance, social, ethics, and environmental (EGSEE) sustainability dimensions. This chapter presented a framework for business sustainability performance, reporting, and assurance. Although many business organizations will continue primarily to maximize financial performance to create shareholder value, they must also effectively deal with nonfinancial performance issues to ensure that they add value for all stakeholders.

1.11 Action points

- Recognize the importance of full commitments from the board of directors and top executives in promoting business sustainability, focusing on both financial and nonfinancial KPIs to create value for shareholders while protecting the interests of other stakeholders

- Develop business sustainability strategies that focus on the achievement of all five EGSEE dimensions of sustainability performance

- Identify main sources and key drivers of business sustainability initiatives, development, and performance

- Integrate sustainability initiatives and developments into all facets of business planning, strategies, decisions, and actions

- Adopt the Integrated Reporting Framework in communicating all five dimensions of sustainability performance with stakeholders

- Provide assurance on all five EGSEE dimensions of sustainability performance reports
- Present holistic, concise, and integrated sets of both financial and nonfinancial KPIs

2
Relevance and importance of business sustainability for corporations

Business organizations play important roles in society by interacting with a variety of constituencies in creating value for all stakeholders. Public companies are increasingly focusing on business sustainability as highlighted in Chapter 1 and making progress on setting expectations for their suppliers to integrate sustainability into their strategies and practices. Proper communication of sustainability performance is important in disclosing commitments to create stakeholder value. Corporate reporting is a process by which public companies disclose their mandatory financial and voluntary nonfinancial information on economic, social, ethical, governance, and environmental activities to all stakeholders. Corporations report their economic activities and performance in compliance with regulatory requirements and contractual covenants to satisfy financial information demands by investors. Corporations also voluntarily disclose their nonfinancial information on corporate governance, social, and environmental matters for a variety of reasons, including the demand by stakeholders as a means of avoiding the attention of regulatory bodies where sanctions for non-compliance are imminent and to comply with industrial codes and best practices. This chapter presents corporate reporting consisting of both financial on economic sustainability performance and nonfinancial information on ethical, social, governance, and environmental sustainability performance. Business organizations produce financial and nonfinancial information to satisfy the needs and demands of all of their stakeholders including investors, creditors, customers, employees, suppliers, government, and society as discussed in this chapter.

2.1 Introduction

The past decade has witnessed widening attention on accountability and social responsibilities of corporations caused by a wave of global financial scandals at the turn of the 21st century and has led to the growing demand for corporate accountability on issues ranging from economic to social responsibilities. The demand for more transparent corporate reporting reflecting economic, social, governance, ethical, and environmental sustainable performance is increasing in the context of sustainability reporting. Corporate sustainability reporting originally focused on environmental and corporate social responsibility (CSR) matters and gradually emerged as presenting all multiple bottom line (MBL) issues. Corporate reporting is often referred to as sustainability reporting, corporate social responsibility, or "multiple bottom line" reporting and reflects the role of corporations in society. Corporate reporting focuses on both financial and nonfinancial key performance indicators (KPIs) to ensure corporations are held accountable to all stakeholders and fulfilling their responsibility in managing their affairs in a fair and transparent fashion.

2.2 The role of corporations in society

The role of business corporations in our society has evolved from profit maximization to creating shareholder value to protecting the interests of all stakeholders. Thus, there has been a widening growth and interest in corporate accountability in response to the reported rash of corporate scandals at the turn of the 21st century and the global 2007–2009 financial crisis. Figure 2.1 shows a two-way communication and interaction between corporations and all of their stakeholders.

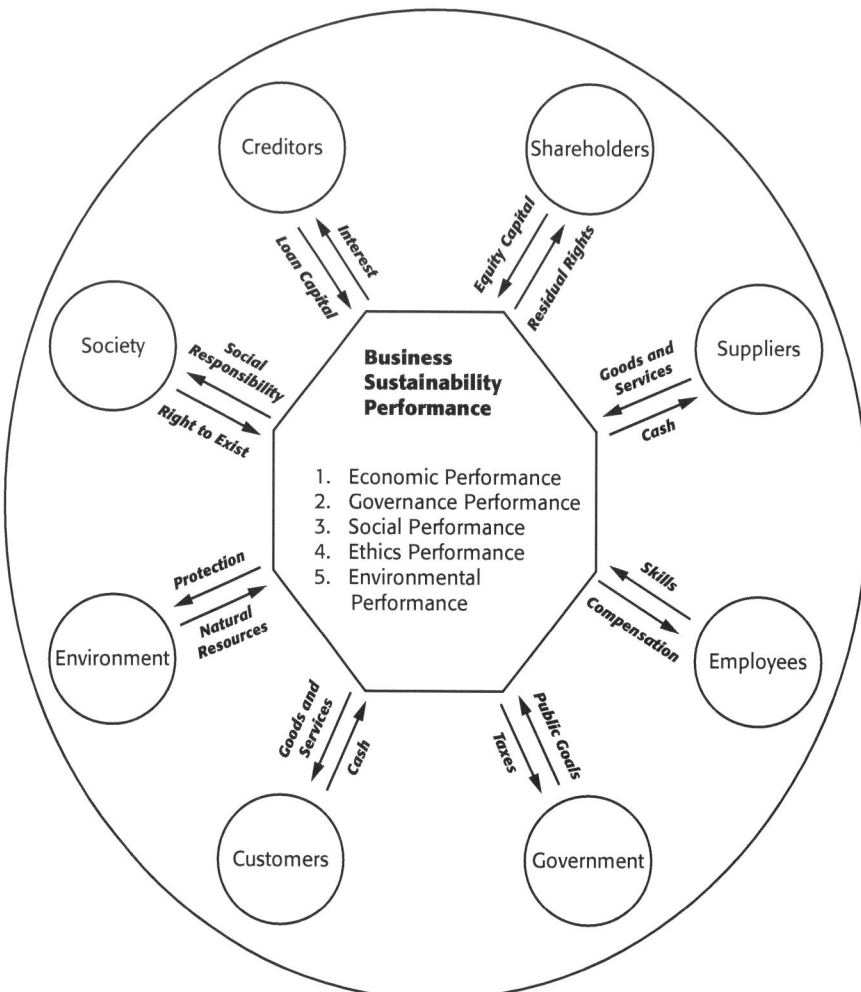

FIGURE 2.1   Role of corporation in society

Source: Brockett and Rezaee (2012a).

As seen in this diagram, a corporation has many stakeholders, and there is always a two-way path between them. The next section identifies and describes corporate key stakeholders.

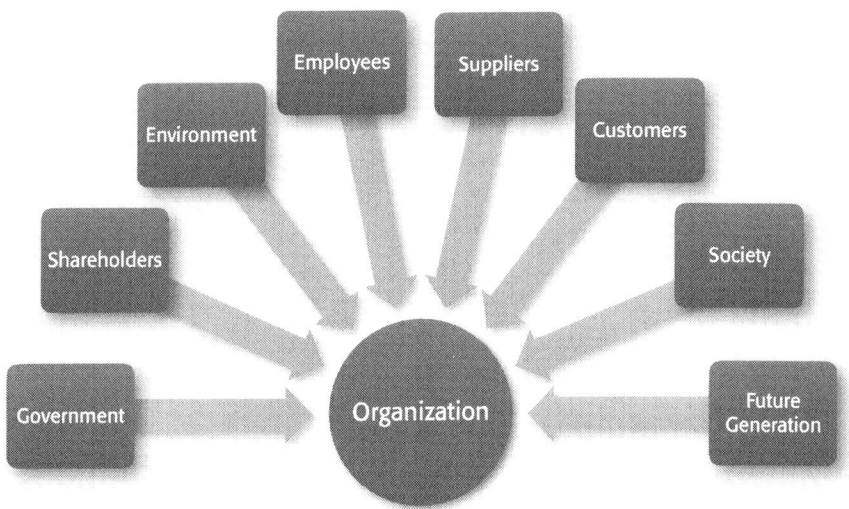

FIGURE 2.2   Stakeholders

2.3 Corporate key stakeholders

Figure 2.2 depicts key stakeholders in a business organization including shareholders, creditors, employees, customers, suppliers, government, the environment, and society.

2.3.1 Shareholders

Shareholders provide capital to the corporation through purchasing shares in the company with the expectation of having future returns on said capital through dividends and stock appreciation (capital gains) caused by increased value of the company. Corporations raised funds from investing public by issuing shares of their common and preferred stocks. The initial outlay of capital is unidirectional as the company starts its operations, but in order to be sustainable, the corporation must give its shareholders residual rights. As partial owners of the company, shareholders hold proportional rights to company earnings, claims on company assets, and rights to dividends issued by the company. Shareholders are considered the primary stakeholders who bear the risk of unsustainable earnings and thus corporate failures.

The direct model of shareholders in it most simplistic form involves investors conducting research on the activities of an organization or its industry to purchase specific securities through their analysis. Attending shareholder meetings offers greater insight to the direction of management's intent, and coupled with basic research they can invest and either gain or lose on such decisions.[1] However, today this example would be of a majority shareholder, not the everyday trader who buys and sells for various reasons (attractiveness of company, cyclical trades, short term) or invests in mutual funds or other derivatives where the role of management and the relative disconnect between the large shareholder base can distort the view management takes on increasing shareholder value. The board of directors, as the representative of the shareholders, have a fiduciary duty of monitoring and overseeing management functions in accurately disclosing relevant stakeholder information, e.g. financial, social or environmental. The shareholder will still be after a reasonable rate of return based on the organizations' practices, but is tied to a larger group of stakeholders that will drive the organization to incorporate a MBL. Shareholders are very much interested in receiving and utilizing both financial and nonfinancial ESG information as evident by a survey of investors conducted by PricewaterhouseCoopers where more than 89% of the surveyed investors reported that they are very likely to request more ESG sustainability information from the firms in which they invest and about 80% said they seek a meeting with the firms' boards or management regarding sustainability issues.[2]

2.3.2 Suppliers

Suppliers provide the goods and services that the company needs to carry out its business. These include everything from durable materials to custom goods to intellectual property. In return, a sustainable company supports its suppliers through reliable, steady streams of cash. Mutually agreed and shared beneficial interaction between the company and its suppliers can have enduring and sustainable effects on the profitability and solvency of the company. The supply chain is arguably one of the most important aspects of an organization. A competent supply chain management system can yield significant competitive advantages. Walmart, Costco, GE, McDonald's, and others have superior supply chains and therefore have significant influence over their supply chains. Ensuring that the company facilitating their supply chain is environmentally sustainable can be measured through systems such as ISO 14000 or other compliant measures that are

---

1   Spurgin, 2001.
2   PricewaterhouseCoopers, 2014a.

discussed in detail in Chapter 5. However, clearly documenting and influencing a whole supply chain to be environmentally sustainable following the same practices as the parent company is difficult. Large organizations wield purchasing power and can influence directly quality control, timing, amounts, and even environmental impact on a supplier causing a trickle-down effect. An industry that is comprised of a few large players such as the telecom industry or the public utility industry (which have to adopt particular environmental standards) have greater adoption rates by their suppliers whereas a more fragmented market will not.[3] Moreover, direct pressures from stakeholders (regulators, suppliers, industry associations, etc.) have the most influence on an organization persuing some form of environmental certification.[4] Other pressures that will influence an organization and its supply chain are the whole industry's attitude and current position toward environmental sustainability and other corporate governance issues.

2.3.3 Employees

A sustainable company values its employees and ensures that they are compensated adequately for their services through salaries, benefits, good work environments, and bonuses. Employees reciprocate this compensation by providing their skills to the best of their abilities and strive to better their skills as their tenure increases. Employees' contributions to sustainable earnings and business sustainability are often ignored even though in many industries human capital is more important than physical capital. Employees are an integral part of an organization. They are the laborers and provide the fruits of capitalism. Healthy and happy employees that are entrenched into the organization's cultural norms as well as management's missions and goals are crucial. Furthermore, employees with this mind-set tend to stay with their job for a longer period of time (reducing turnover) and can help the organization acquire top industry talent. If the organization is not complying with regulations (e.g. environmental) or not staying on the forefront of their business ethics, employees will leave and look for better positions. Internal mechanisms, policies, procedures, practices, principles, goals, missions, and visions are essential to maintaining a healthy working environment and retaining employees. With the advent of the Internet, one disgruntled employee can reach far more people than

---

3   Delmas and Toffel, 2004.
4   Kollman and Prakash, 2002.

in the past. Organizations are consistently battling with developing a MBL to ensure they are building a sustainable company and keeping a healthy workforce.

2.3.4 Government

The Government, through laws, regulations, and standards, develops a regulatory and compliance framework for companies within which they can operate and create sustainable performance. These laws, regulations, and standards should be proactive, effective, cost-efficient, and scalable to ensure proper compliance, effective enforcement, and robust consequences. In return, the company pays taxes so that the infrastructure can be maintained. Perhaps the most influential stakeholder, yet also the one most difficult to please, is the Government. The Government offers the company an analysis of their needs and wants so that the company can then know how to and how much to provide, as well as the means to work within the system to provide these.

One of the most obvious stakeholders that will permanently affect an organization's environmental policies is regulatory bodies. Governmental influence is coercive power through legislation or other mandates. Governments globally have different regulations and laws regarding environmental practices and are changing with influences from national conferences such as the Copenhagen accord. Common ways to see the relative performance of a plant or an organization would be to look at the number of environmental compliance violations and enforcement actions taken by regulators to correct non-compliance.[5] Organizations now and in the coming years are facing the effects of globalization, which takes an organization's practices out of the local scope and brings them into the world's playing field. Organizations that have international operations will have to abide to the specific countries; regulations which will affect how the parent company visualizes its global vision toward environmental sustainability.

2.3.5 Customers

The end recipients of all commercial operations are customers, whether the company supplies goods and services to end customers (consumer market) or to other businesses (B2B, or business-to-business). The company distributes its goods and services to its customers who pay cash in return for said

5   Kassinis and Vafeas, 2002; Khanna and Anton, 2002.

same offerings. Customer satisfaction and reputation, as well as production of safe and good quality products and services, are the keys to the sustainability of corporations.

Customers give direct feedback to organizations on products and have been demanding products that are recyclable, reliable, user friendly, environmentally friendly, have a long life expectancy, and are backed up through warranties. This implies that consumers of goods and services apply more pressure on organizations to conform to a MBL in the short and long term than other market participants such as commercial customers. As the world's economies flatten out and become one, intertwined global market customers will have more of an impact on international fronts. For example, U.S. customers have been able to influence Chinese companies to adopt and conform to environmental practices such as ISO 14000.[6] This is a coercive power, and one that should not be trifled with. Customers have purchasing power; if no one will buy finished goods then the business tends to fail. Customers shape the future of products by giving critical feedback to organizations. Environmental sustainability has become inherent in many industries such as the automotive industry, where car manufacturers have been pressured to engineer more fuel-efficient vehicles, fuel diverse vehicles, and alternative propulsion systems such as pure electric and fuel cell vehicles. Some of these changes come from regulatory bodies, pushed by society demanding healthy living environments. As the end-user of finished goods, customers have unlimited power through collective establishments, e.g., voting, joining environmental groups, and acting on an individual level in becoming environmentally sustainable.

2.3.6 Environment

The Environment is one of the more contentious stakeholders with which a company must deal. The Environment provides companies with the natural resources necessary to do their work, while sustainable companies must protect the environment to ensure its viability. On a macroscopic level, every company has to deal with the environment in some manner, some more or less than others. For instance, a mining company that pollutes the local water supply should endeavor to clean up the supply during and after operations, while a small paperless office may just need to offset the fuel burnt from its electricity use. At the minimum, companies should minimize

6   Christmann and Taylor, 2001.

their negative impacts on the environment and strive to preserve a better environment for the next generations.

Today humanity is vulnerable to extreme weather changes due to the persistently expanding population. The movement into less hospitable areas and the growing dependence on high-yield food production is increasing the damage to the environment, while simultaneously deepening mankind's dependence on a large-scale transportation scheme of goods. The expanding industry racing to meet the needs of an ever-increasing population may tilt the delicate balance irrevocably toward catastrophe. Emissions and population continue to grow exponentially. Carbon dioxide (CO_2) is the principal greenhouse gas emitted as a result of human activity (e.g., burning of coal, oil, and natural gas). Increasing globalization and development in second- and third-world countries has meant that the seasonal and annual amounts of carbon dioxide (CO_2) have increased in the atmosphere since the late 1950s.[7]

Today's global society relies heavily on the smooth transfer of goods, commodities, and food around the world without interference from natural weather phenomenon. Corporations move further away, creating a shipping industry that relies on a complex network of interdependence. The increase in greenhouse gasses can disrupt this delicate network by destabilizing long-distance infrastructure. Increasing volatility in climatic patterns will increase uncertainty about future demand, supply chain, and infrastructure stability. About a third of the U.S. GDP is sensitive to weather changes.[8] The natural environment is the climate, which our daily lives and business transactions take place in. If the natural environment is degraded to the point of exhaustion, businesses and society will suffer the tragedies. Business sustainability coupled with accurate documentation and implementation of voluntary and regulatory environmental practices will ensure that future generations will prosper.

2.3.7 Society

Society provides companies with their right to exist, while companies are accountable to society to be responsible to their demands. As opposed to the government stakeholder, Society by itself encompasses the notion that a company has no natural right to exist and depends on the whims of society. Conversely, a sustainable company uses its social responsibility to become

---

7   See http://www.esrl.noaa.gov/gmd/ccgg/trends/.
8   Lazo *et al.*, 2011.

an integral part of Society at large. Corporations should minimize their negative effects and maximize their positive effects on society.

Society is the broad umbrella, the collective efforts of many, that can develop voluntary standards such as the ISO series (9000, 14000, and 26000), LEED, sustainability indicators, and deeper awareness of the intimate relationship humans have with the environment and the impact this will have on future generations. Global Warming is becoming a global issue and has brought environmental sustainability into the headlines. Nations are being affected by its consequences and have made strides through regulation or voluntary actions to help mitigate current and long-term effects of climate change. Local communities have the power to put pressure on organizations through voting on local and national ballet measures (elected officials) and can be involved with environmental activist groups, and non-governmental organizations (NGOs). Moreover, lawsuits can restrict proposed projects by organizations or collect damages from unlawful practices. Communities that claim to have an interest in environmental practices tend to use these actions to lobby for organizations to follow local views and regulations.[9] This can be measured using indicators such as regulations drafted and put in place, attitude, demographics, and actions taken to increase the local community's environmental sustainability.[10]

2.3.8 Creditors

In line with shareholders, creditors also provide capital to the company, although with more restrictions. Whereas shareholders have no intrinsic right to the money invested in the company (on liquidation, shareholders are generally the last to be paid), creditors have more tangible rights to company assets and receive regular interest payments commensurate with the riskiness of the investment. The terms of the interest payments are finite, and once they are done, then there is no relationship between the company and its creditors. However, this is seldom the case in the real world, as debt is generally cheaper than equity, so sustainable companies must endeavor to keep current with their interest payments if they wish to have the influx of capital from Creditors.

9   Maxwell *et al.*, 2000.
10   Delmas and Toffel, 2004.

2.4 Stakeholder value creation

Business sustainability can be viewed from the stakeholder perspective as a process of meeting the needs and protecting the interests of all stakeholders now and in the future. Thus, business sustainability is driven by and built on the stakeholder theory with a keen focus on achieving long-term and enduring financial and nonfinancial performance. The stakeholder theory implies that business organizations have obligations to a number of constituencies and thus should add value for all stakeholders, including shareholders, creditors, suppliers, customers, employees, government, environment, and society.[11] Conventional shareholder theory, however, implies that the primary goal of a corporation is to create shareholder value in a single objective function of maximizing financial performance.[12] Business sustainability promotes the application of stakeholder theory in protecting interests of all stakeholders while determining trade-offs among these apparently competing and often conflicting interests. Thus, the main goal of value maximization for all stakeholders under business sustainability can be achieved when the interests of all stakeholders are considered. Jensen (2001) offers an enlightened stakeholder theory which promotes long-term enlightened value maximization as a firm's objective to protect the interests of all stakeholders.[13] Business sustainability is a process which enables corporations to design and implement strategies that contribute to enduring performance in all EGSEE areas. This definition of business sustainability is consistent with Jensen's enlightened stakeholder theory in the sense that it too promotes "maximization of the long-term value of the firm as the criterion for making the requisite trade-offs among its stakeholders."[14] Business sustainability, by focusing on the achievement of long-term economic performance to maximize firm value, not only ensures long-term profitability and competitive advantages, but also helps in maintaining the wellbeing of the society, the planet, and people. Corporations and their directors and executives have many incentives to engage in business sustainability, including maximizing long-term profit and firm value, fulfilling their corporate social responsibilities, meeting their environmental obligations, and improving their image and reputation.

11   Jensen, 2001.
12   Jensen, 2001.
13   Jensen, 2001.
14   Jensen, 2001, p. 9.

With all this being said, there is no guarantee that a company that follows all of these guidelines and seeks to serve all of its stakeholders in the most ideal combination of factors for its structure will ultimately be benefited by these EGSEE measures. Robert Reich, U.S. Secretary of Labor under President Bill Clinton, writes in his paper entitled "The Case Against Corporate Social Responsibility" that the extent to which companies, particularly large firms, do not have the practical ability to decrease their financial profit by increasing their commitment to EGSEE measures.[15] In his view, with abnormal profits driven out of the marketplace by extreme competition, there is little that companies can do to affect extraneous EGSEE changes unless:

- They are willing to lose profits to gain market share, or
- Those changes are regulated for the entire industry and must be followed by all peer companies

While companies may make decisions to enact EGSEE changes that do in fact help society and nonfinancial stakeholders, in the end Reich states that any of these changes that companies in a super-competitive environment make are in fact financial decisions. Reich writes, "Dow Chemical reduces its carbon emissions so it can lower its energy costs. Alcoa estimates annual savings of about $100 million from reduced energy use and related environmental improvements."[16]

To what extent that this thesis will play out in the real world, particularly among non-monolithic companies, is yet to be seen, but this just shows that despite the theories laid out here, there is still much to be learned in this matter. The ultimate result may not be as conclusive as the theory may belie, but that is why we must continue to research the matter ever more fully.

Investors also value management adjusted performance measures (APMs), which enable them to better understand a company's performance success and related risks. Investment professionals suggest the following guidelines for APM reporting:[17]

- Clarity and consistency of definitions of measures and adjustments
- Focus should be on important and relevant APMs

---

15   Reich, 2008.
16   Reich, 2008.
17   PricewaterhouseCoopers, 2014b.

- Explanation of why considered APMs are relevant and what adjustments are made

- Presentation of comparative data and its restatement

- Reconciliation of APMs to GAAP measurements

- Communications of both GAAP and non-GAAP measures

- Presentation of audited GAAP measures and assured non-GAAP measures

2.5 Corporate reporting

Best practices of business sustainability encourage corporations to be responsible and accountable for their multiple bottom line activities and affairs. Corporate citizenships, corporate accountability, corporate social responsibility, corporate sustainability, and corporate responsibility are terms that have been used interchangeably to address corporations' responsibility and accountability to their various constituencies, commonly referred to as stakeholders, and these include shareholders, suppliers, customers, employees, government, and society in general for their economic and social affairs. Definitions of these terms vary, with one emerging theme of focusing on the long-term and sustainable impact of business on a broader set of stakeholders beyond solely shareholders. The two overriding principles of these definitions are long-term impacts (sustainable performance) and stakeholders. Corporations should be accountable and responsible to a variety of stakeholders for their sustainable performance in areas of economic, governance, ethical, environmental, and social activities. Stakeholders are generally defined as shareholders and their representatives (institutional investors), creditors, employees and their representatives (unions), customers, consumer groups, governments, suppliers, trade associations, competitors, non-governmental organizations (NGOs), interest groups, the global community, and society at large.

The ever-increasing broader attention on corporate responsibility demands greater corporate accountability, increased corporate transparency, improved reporting disclosures, and requirements for bottom lines. Proper disclosure, whether voluntary or mandatory, is a theme of corporate accountability. Corporations are currently required to report their financial performance. This is commonly referred to as the "single bottom line" (earnings-based), whereas reporting of nonfinancial matters is known as "multiple bottom line," (economic, governance, social, ethical, and environmental activities) occasionally disclosed on a voluntary basis. Conventional financial reporting is considered to be inadequate and companies should disclose financial and nonfinancial key performance indicators (KPIs) of their multiple bottom line. Multiple bottom line reports reflect the company's KPIs in all activities including economic, governance, social, ethical, and environmental and reflect the interests of all stakeholders.

According to a report by the CGMA, nowadays, and for the past decade, "the value of intangible assets has now grown to over 80% of total market value for S&P 500 companies".[18] Thus, stakeholders who look to the traditional value of a company being its economic output are missing a great deal of information to help better price their targets. To remedy this, companies are issuing more Integrated Reports to ensure that their stakeholders, who may be experts in one or several parts of the company's operations, can utilize as much information as possible to value the company in a true manner. Some principals may abjure this practice, particularly if they make abnormal returns from having discrete knowledge of the company's inner workings, but Integrated Reporting helps the company as a whole create better value for itself, as each stakeholder can see how company operations interact with each other. By being able to spend less time researching the company's operations and having less risk of unanticipated adverse events occurring, stakeholders can better see how the company interacts with its market and suggest/force the company to make changes to better align their interests with the reality of the situation. One consequence of this may be that some stakeholders may bicker more with others, but rational stakeholders should understand that all parts must work together for a sustainable company to thrive.

2.6 Value relevance of conventional financial reports

Conventional financial statements, providing historical financial information concerning an entity's financial condition and results of operations as a proxy for future business performance, may not provide relevant information to investors. Investors demand forward-looking financial and

18   Topazio, 2014a.

nonfinancial information on key performance indicators (KPIs) concerning the entity's governance, economic, ethical, social, and environmental activities. The narrow focus on achieving economic performance has been criticized for ignoring other social, ethical, and environmental responsibilities of corporations. Reliability, transparency, and quality of sustainability EGSEE information are the lifeblood of the capital markets. The efficiency of the markets depends on the reliability of that information which enables the markets to act as signaling mechanisms for proper capital allocation, fulfillment of social responsibilities, and achievement of governance, ethical, and environmental performance. Sustainability reporting is now gaining acceptance and emerging as the best way to communicate sustainability performance information to the interested users of sustainability reports. One way to communicate sustainability information is to integrate it with financial reporting and issue an integrated corporate report on all five dimensions of sustainability EGSEE performance. There is no mandatory guidance at this time for sustainability reporting. However, there are several voluntary guidelines for sustainability reporting including:

- The reporting frameworks released by the Global Reporting Initiatives
- The Connected Reporting Framework
- Reporting publications of Accountability as discussed in previous sections

Although the primary focus of corporate reporting will continue to be an economic issue to create sustainable long-term shareholder value, the issues of social, ethical, and environmental performance will gain momentum as we look ahead. The sustainability and financial health of public companies are essential to keeping investor confidence high. This sustainability requires public trust in the suitability, reliability, and timeliness of corporate reports in disclosing relevant information on financial and nonfinancial KPIs.

Business sustainability promotes the achievement of long-term financial performance that generates enduring future cash flows for investors to maximize their long-term share value and thus, maximizing overall firm value. Building on the theoretical frameworks of Jensen (2001) and others, we argue that there is a positive relation between sustainability performance and firm value. Focusing on EGSEE sustainability performance enables the achievement of long-term firm value maximization by creating value for shareholders and meeting the claims of other stakeholders. Conventional performance measurements often focus on one-dimensional and short-term performance of total return to shareholders (TRS). This measurement of TRS is influenced by many financial attributes (e.g., return on investment, profit, and cash flows) and nonfinancial variables (e.g., market power and firm reputation)

The traditional trend toward having a single bottom line, namely the economic profit-driven bottom line, is washing away as more companies utilize sustainability measures to determine the true value of the company. Those who are eager to disclose more sustainability measures see this as creating more value for their company, for as more highly sought-after employees are attracted, retained, and motivated, the company can save money on externalities previously unseen, and many other such things. In addition, investors who take the long-term perspective with regard to the company will be encouraged by seeing a more sustainable course of action taking place. A report by the Toronto Stock Exchange states, "[Investors] also want to understand if the issuer has business opportunities and competitive advantages related to environmental and social issues."[19] The report goes on to say that these companies need to focus on the principles laid out by various standards-writing groups such as the UN PRI (United Nations Principles of Responsible Investing), the CDP (Carbon Disclosure Project), the EPs (The Equator Principles), the UN Principles for Sustainable Insurance, the UN Global Compact (particularly Human Rights, Labor, Environment, and Anti-Corruption), the UN Guiding Principles on Business and Human Rights, ISO 26000 – Guidance Standard on Social Responsibility, and the OECD Guidelines for Multinational Enterprises. Though these resources are expansive and seemingly overwhelming for companies starting sustainability assurance measures, the reward from gathering all of this information should be a higher net worth for the company and a brighter, more sustainable future.

2.7 Future of corporate reporting

Given the purpose of corporate reporting is disseminating high-quality financial and nonfinancial information regarding all five EGSEE dimensions

19   Toronto Stock Exchange and Chartered Professional Accountants of Canada, 2014.

of sustainability performance to enable all corporate stakeholders to make sound decisions, corporations should integrate all five EGSEE dimensions of sustainability performance in one report. This integrated report can be prepared in compliance with the guidelines of G4 of the GRI, be forward-looking, and presents the following key principles:[20]

- **Encourage innovation and change.** Corporate reporting should promote innovation and respond to changes in the economic and business environment to ensure public trust and investor confidence in financial information.

- **Balance judgment and compliance.** Corporate reporting should ensure compliance with all applicable laws, rules, regulations, and standards while providing flexibility for companies and their directors and officers to use professional judgment in presenting useful and relevant information without compromising accountability.

- **Support company decision-making.** Corporate reporting as a main vehicle to communicate with all stakeholders should focus on the key drivers of sustainable value creations and associated risks in aligning management reporting and external reporting.

- **Make corporate reporting accessible, relevant and timely.** Corporate reports should reflect all material and relevant information about the past, present, and future company's sustainable performance and success stories in a factual, objective, and timely manner.

- **Support shareholder and investor decision-making.** Shareholders are the main corporate constituency that bears the ultimate risk. Thus corporate reports should reflect the company's capabilities in creating shareholder value while protecting the interests of other stakeholders.

- **Recognize the importance of those who have responsibility for the oversight of the system.** Corporate reporting should engage all corporate gatekeepers from the board of directors to management, auditors, legal counsel, and advisors in producing high-quality, reliable and transparent reports, and hold them accountable for their engagement and responsibilities.

20   Toronto Stock Exchange and Chartered Professional Accountants of Canada, 2014.

PwC's 2014 report entitled *Tomorrow's Corporate Reporting* highlights the following challenges that must be addressed to improve the value relevance of corporate reporting in reflecting changes in business environment and sustainable value creation for all stakeholders:[21]

- **A "jigsaw in pieces" with many participants and differing goals.** Corporate reporting should satisfy financial needs of diverse and disparate constituencies.

- **Data, not people.** Current corporate reporting is all about an information system for processing whereas people, institutions, and professionals with disparate agenda, goals, mind-sets, behavior, and culture make up the corporation and its system.

- **Few on the same page.** The overriding view about the primary goal of corporate reporting is to serve the financial and voting agendas of shareholders/investors. However, the interests of other stakeholders should be considered.

- **Systems within a system.** There is a variety of corporate reports from financial statements disseminated to shareholders to internal management information, voluntary earnings guidance, and voluntary sustainability reports on nonfinancial information. There should be an integrated report reflecting both financial and nonfinancial information that can be used by all corporate stakeholders.

- **Quantity, not quality.** There is a need for modernizing and rationalizing corporate reports on both financial and nonfinancial information by focusing on the materiality and quality of information to avoid information overload.

- **Competence and lack of concern.** Complexity and perceived information overload is preventing market participants and corporate stakeholders to digest, comprehend, and utilize voluminous financial and nonfinancial information. Thus, there are many concerns and incentives by users to support reporting changes or innovations that might affect their confidence in and assessed risks of corporate reporting.

- **Looking back, not forward.** Corporate reporting is often viewed as backward-looking rather than forward-looking and is not adjusted

21   PricewaterhouseCoopers, 2014c.

to emerging initiatives and changes in the global economic, social, and environmental situations. Future corporate reporting should be futuristic and capable of anticipating and adapting to emerging changes.

2.8 Value relevance of sustainability information/ conceptual framework

The modern corporate structure necessitates the separation of ownership and control of a company where owners (shareholders) invest financial capital and management provides human capital. This formation allows anyone to invest in companies without having the expertise or devoting the extensive time needed to run a business. This formation functions well where investors (principals) can contribute capital and leave the business decisions to management (agent) and where management runs the company in the best interest of the principals. In reality, a potential conflict of interest exists when decision control is separated from ownership control and management is able to withhold private information from investors. Investors normally want transparency in financial and nonfinancial reports regardless of their attitude toward risk (e.g., risk averse, tolerant of risks, or embraces risk). Overall investors wish to make informed analyses and educated decisions on risk/reward aspects of their investment targets and have access to all available information.

The proper measurement of sustainability performance should address:

- The time-horizon of balancing short-term and long-term performance with a keen focus on long-term performance
- The multi-dimensional nature of sustainability performance in all EGSEE areas

The selection of an appropriate time-horizon (period) to measure sustainability performance is very important and should be linked to the length of factors that drive sustainability performance. The overriding factors that derive sustainability performance are reaching the maturity stage of competitive positioning, efficient utilization of resources, and completing at least one business cycle. Achievement of this level of sustainable performance can take ten or more years.

The multi-dimensional EGSEE sustainability performance is interrelated. The relative importance of the dimensions with respect to each other and their contribution to the overall firm's long-term value maximization is affected by whether these EGSEE dimensions are viewed as being competing, conflicting, or complementing each other. These five EGSEE dimensions of sustainability performance are complementary because a firm that is governed effectively, adheres to ethical principles, and commits to CSR and environmental obligations is also enabled to be sustainable in generating long-term financial performance. Furthermore, firms must do well financially in the long-term to be able to do well in terms of CSR and environmental activities. Firms that engage in business sustainability can develop a long-term focus on sustainable economic performance, as well as establishing other capabilities, resources, and competencies to build up better customer/supplier relationships, employees' workplace, and environmental and CSR initiatives.

The main goal under sustainability is to maximize firm value by improving sustainable economic performance. The debate over the merit of all other nonfinancial dimensions sustainability performance including governance, social, ethical and environmental (GSEE) revolves around whether any investments and managerial efforts on GSEE are viewed by shareholders as value-enhancing or value-destroying activities. Investments in achieving sustainable (GSEE) performance can be considered from a risk management perspective of arguing that management should use sustainability as a tool to manage risk. Business sustainability can enable management to develop better long-term focus, skills, and processes to manage risks associated with financial, compliance, strategic, operating, and reputation risks.

Corporations can survive and produce sustainable performance when they continue to be profitable and generate enduring performance that creates shareholder value. However, EGSEE sustainability performance dimensions are not mutually exclusive: they supplement each other and trade-offs can occur between them. On one hand, corporations that are managed ethically, governed effectively, and are socially and environmentally responsible are expected to produce sustainable performance, create shareholder value, and gain public trust and investor confidence. On the other hand, more economically profitable and viable corporations are in better positions and have more resources to create jobs and wealth and better fulfill their social and environmental responsibilities. Although the primary goal of many corporations will continue to be the enhancement of shareholder value through producing sustainable economic performance, they must also effectively deal with ethical, social, governance, and environmental issues to ensure they are adding value for their shareholders and other stakeholders.

The 2014 PwC report on "Corporate Performance" suggests that:[22]

- High-quality corporate reporting is the reflection of effective management
- Corporate disclosures should be both financial and nonfinancial and linked to strategy
- Nonfinancial disclosures on strategy should reflect priorities, decisions, actions, and progress
- Effective risk assessment, management, and reporting should relate to strategy and represent management views
- KPIs should be defined, measured, and linked to strategy, risks, and compensation
- Users value corporate reports for reliability, quality, and comprehensiveness.

2.9 Ways to improve quality and quantity of sustainability performance and reporting

Sustainability performance and reporting can be significantly improved by focusing on achieving both financial performance and nonfinancial performance in areas of governance, social, and environmental issues. Sustainability reporting can be improved by integrating both financial and nonfinancial information in a stand-alone integrated report reflecting all five EGSEE dimensions of sustainability. Just as financial information reflects profit and growth, nonfinancial information can be used by companies as a tool for strategic growth. However, there is no standard written in stone for the reporting of nonfinancial information. Companies that report sustainability performance may disclose differently in terms of the format, structure, and information.

Currently, there are a few guidelines and regulations in some parts of the world. The Global Reporting Initiative (GRI), in its G4 sustainability

22   PricewaterhouseCoopers, 2014b.

guidelines, promotes an integrated reporting on these five EGSEE dimensions of sustainability performance with the ethical dimension being incorporated into other dimensions.[23] To improve the quality and quantity of sustainability performance reporting, there needs to be a global standard that serves as the guideline, and governments must chip in through by regulation. Perhaps the most important group of actors in writing these new standards for integrated reporting in the upcoming years is the management accountants, which Paul Druckman, CEO of the IIRC, states will make the reports less about the quantity of information released and more about the quality of the information.[24] A high-quality, reliable, and relevant integrated report can be achieved by applying the following principles in corporate reporting to improve its value relevance to investors and other stakeholders:[25]

- **Business model.** The business model should clearly define the company's competitive edge in the industry and market, its main activities and performance, and the flow of cash and capital through the business model.

- **Strategy.** The business strategy should present strategic goals and priorities, ways to achieve these goals, and measures of KPIs in achieving these goals.

- **Risk.** The Company's risk management should be comprehensive in describing all major events, activities, and associated risks in ensuring risk assessment and management to the business model, strategy, and performance.

- **KPIs.** KPIs should be directly linked to the five dimensions of sustainability activities, explicitly identified, be relevant to performance, and explain the link between strategy, key risks, and KPIs.

- **Linkage.** The linkage should depict the information flow from the business model to strategy, risks, KPIs, and financial performance.

- **Annual report.** Corporate reports should be used as a communication channel to provide both financial and nonfinancial information on all five dimensions of sustainability performance to all stakeholders including investors.

23   Global Reporting Initiative, 2013a.
24   Druckman, 2013.
25   PricewaterhouseCoopers, 2014b.

2.10 Integration of financial and nonfinancial information

The common theme for much of the existence of businesses has been that the bottom line, until recently solely financial information, was the sole determinant of a company's success or failure. However, as shown in the above article, the bottom line is not so easily measured as before with the advent of integrated reporting. The integration of financial and nonfinancial information into a single, cohesive report enables the entirety of the company's operations to be viewed together to give stakeholders a more complete picture. Integrated reporting connects financial and nonfinancial information to allow companies' top executives to make business strategies and goals on the fly. Not only will more businesses recognize the importance of sustainability, but nonfinancial data can be retrieved from the report easily. According to a recent report, how well a company integrates its financial and nonfinancial information into an integrated report can affect the bottom line for a company. The PwC report reveals that about 63% of investors believe the quality of a company's reporting could have a direct impact on its cost of capital.[26] Another 80% of investors believe that the quality of a company's reporting reflects the effectiveness of its management.[27] To integrate financial and nonfinancial information, companies need to tie strategic objectives to potential sustainability issues. KPIs are established to measure the actions taken to address those sustainability issues. The progress is tracked and a report is created to compare the lifetime financial savings and the additional cost used for sustainability. Hypothetically, any premium cost paid to implement sustainability should best be offset and topped by lifetime financial savings for going sustainable. An example is opening a new chain store. The lifetime energy savings in financial costs is measured against the investment premium to build an eco-friendly store, with the former outweighing the latter.

In April 2013, the Investment Responsibility Research Center (IRRC) Institute released a report on the current status of integrated reporting and sustainability measures in the U.S.A. The exhaustive report details a great amount of information on the extent to which companies disclose sustainability information, broken down by many metrics, such as industry, size, sustainability topics, and other such trends. The author begins by stating:

26   Amato, 2014.
27   Amato, 2014.

> Integrated reporting, as defined by its present champions, seeks to identify value drivers in companies linked to human, intellectual, natural and social capital, in addition to more traditional financial and manufactured forms of capital, and to present this information to investors in regulatory filings.[28]

This definition shows that financial and nonfinancial information are inexorably linked, even if until recently they have not been fleshed out in so many words. Each output from one company is an input into another, and the reconciliation of these inputs and outputs is the heart of integrated reporting. Whenever, as shown above, a negative externality occurs and benefits one stakeholder at the expense of another without there being a report on such, the injured stakeholder would have to eat the cost of that externality. With integrated reporting, however, along with a market economy that gives value to these externalities, both the benefit to the first stakeholder and the detriment to the latter stakeholder will be reduced, thus leading to a state of more equilibrium in the market.

2.11 Financial and nonfinancial key performance indicators (KPIs)

Corporate success stories can be measured and disclosed through key performance indicators (KPIs). KPIs can be prepared for both financial and nonfinancial activities to present a company's progress toward achieving its goals. KPIs should reflect a company's strategic mission, goals, and how these goals are measured and achieved. KPIs should communicate key activities used by the board of directors and officers in managing an organization, such as achieving desired return on investment for shareholders, maximizing customer satisfaction, or attracting and retaining the best and most talented employees. The extent and type of both financial and nonfinancial KPIs varies among companies, their peers, industries, and countries with one overriding determinant of being relevant to the company and its operations. For example, KPIs most relevant to a petroleum industry are exploration success rate, refinery capacity and utilization, reserve resources, and related replacement costs, whereas in the banking industry the most common KPIs are deposits and assets under management, loans and loan loss provisions, capital adequacy, and asset quality. The number of

28   IRRC Institute, 2013.

KPIs depends on the type and size of the business and its strategy, mission, goals, and activities with at least one KPI for each major activity and up to 15 KPIs for each of the five EGSEE dimensions of sustainability performance.

The guiding principles for the relevant KPIs are their linkages to the corporate strategies, precise definitions and measurements, intended purposes, benchmarks, sources, interpretations, assumptions, and limitations. KPIs should be forward-looking, oriented toward identifying, measuring, and disclosing trends, drivers, and factors relevant to stakeholders, particularly investors' assessment of current and future EGSEE sustainability performance.

2.11.1 Financial KPIs

KPIs are classified into financial KPIs, reflecting financial aspects of business organizations, and nonfinancial KPIs on environmental, ethical, social and governance (EESG) activities. Brockett and Rezaee suggest the following financial KPIs:[29]

- Financial statements (balance sheet, income statement, statement of cash flows, owners' equity)
- Financial note disclosures
- Accounting policies
- Segment information
- Changes in business structure (business combination, discontinued operation)
- Material and unusual items
- Post balance sheet events
- Stock prices
- Risk management
- Codes of conduct and ethics
- Executive compensation
- Stock-based compensation
- Dividend policy
- Budget and performance evaluation

29   Brockett and Rezaee, 2012a.

- Earnings releases

- Non-GAAP financial measures

- Operational information

- Quantitative analysis

- Operating margins

- Free cash flow

- Profitability ratios

- Solvency ratios

- Liquidity ratios

- Cost of equity

- Cost of debt

- Capital expenditures

- Forward-looking data

- Any changes in accounting policies and practices

- Significant financial adjustments suggested by auditors

- Going concern assumptions and any qualifications

2.11.2 Nonfinancial KPIs

The Balanced scorecard as a strategic management system can be used to associate financial KPIs to nonfinancial KPIs and their integrated link to business strategy using a multi-dimensional set of financial and nonfinancial performance metrics. Nonfinancial KPIs are relevant to environmental, ethical, social, and governance (EESG) dimensions of sustainability performance as summarized below:

- Environmental KPIs:
    - Continuous replacement of scarce resources that are nonrenewable
    - Disclosure of ecosystem changes
    - Disclosure of gigajoules of total energy consumed
    - Disclosure of metric tons of total CO_2 emitted

– Disclosure of risk exposure and opportunities of climate changes

– Disclosure of toxic chemical use and disposal

– Efficient utilization of unconventional renewable and nonrenewable natural resources

– Efficient use of recycled materials

– Environmental profitability analysis and assessment

– Maximum effective utilization of scarce natural resources

– Measurement of resource depletion

– Minimizing the use of environmentally harmful materials and products

– Preventing negative impacts on ecosystems

– Production and use of environmentally safe products

– Promoting environmental performance

– The types of emission and respective emission data

– Greenhouse gas emissions in total and intensity

– Total hazardous waste and nonhazardous waste produced in total and intensity

– Policies and practices on efficient and effective use of resources including water, energy, and other raw materials

– Policies and practices on minimizing the operation's significant effects on the environment and utilization of natural resources

• Social KPIs:

– Percentage of employees who consider that their business acts responsibly

– Number of full-time employees (FTE) dedicated to social investment projects

– Funds raised per FTE for nonprofit and humanitarian organizations

– Philanthropy as a percentage of (pretax) profit

– Percentage of operating income dedicated to social contribution

– Percentage of suppliers that affirmed business code of conduct

– Social contributions spent per employee

– Percentage of eligible employees who signed the Code of Conduct and Ethics Policy

- Number of initiatives to promote greater environmental responsibility
- Total investment in the community
- Donations and other social expenses
- Description of social and ethical activities and projects
- Diversity and equal opportunities
- Fair wages, contracts, and benefits for employees
- Training and internal continuing education
- Employee diversity and compositions by age, specialization, minority, and ethnicity
- Number of employees, turnover, and hiring/firing procedures
- Whistle-blowing policies, programs, and procedures
- Employee productivity
- Employee satisfaction, competence, and commitment
- Customer satisfaction, retention, loyalty
- Fair competition
- Truthful advertising
- Policies and practices related to health and safety, advertising, labeling, and privacy matters
- Policies and practices related to community engagements

- Governance KPIs:
  - Number of board committees
  - Percentage of board independence
  - Full independence of board committees
  - Board diversity in terms of ethnicity, sex, expertise, minority
  - Staggered board
  - Separation of the position of the chair of the board and chief executive officer (CEO)
  - Board accountability and liability
  - Number of board meetings
  - Number of members on the board
  - Percentage of insider directors on the board
  - Number of members in the audit committee

  – Number of audit committee meetings
  – Number of audit committee financial experts
  – Value of stock options awarded to the directors.
  – The link between executive compensation and financial performance

- Ethical KPIs:
  – Existence of business codes of conduct
  – Uniform and fair enforcement of business codes of conduct
  – Certification of compliance with business codes of conduct
  – Resolution of conflicts of interest
  – Compliance with applicable laws, rules, regulations, and standards
  – Compliance with best practices and norms
  – Promotion of core values of mutual respect, fairness, openness, honesty, and trust
  – Enforcement of responsibility and accountability
  – Promotion of tolerance, acceptance, caring, and compassion
  – Compliance with all applicable laws, rules, regulations, standards, and moral principles
  – Policies and procedures on anticorruption including bribery, extortion, money laundering, and fraud
  – Whistle-blowing policies and procedures
  – Tone at the top promoting competence and integrity

2.12 Conclusions

Conventional corporate reports do not effectively reflect corporate accountability to all stakeholders. Future corporate reporting should disseminate high-quality financial and nonfinancial information regarding all five EGSEE dimensions of sustainability performance to enable all corporate stakeholders to make sound decisions. All relevant information pertaining to the five EGSEE dimensions of sustainability performance can be incorporated into one report, commonly known as the "integrated report." This integrated report can be prepared in compliance with the guidelines of G4 of the GRI, be forward-looking, and presents both financial and nonfinancial KPIs discussed in this chapter.

2.13 Action points

- Identify your constituencies and stakeholders

- Make sure your corporate reports are comprehensive and relevant in portraying both financial and nonfinancial information on all five EGSEE dimensions of sustainability performance to all stakeholders

- Develop your business model consisting of strategy, KPIs, risks, and compensation

- Establish policies and procedures to achieve strategies and goals

- Establish a clear linkage between your KPIs, business model, strategy, and risk management and disclosures

- Develop a business model to improve governance and Board effectiveness

- Align corporate reporting and communication strategy

- Improve relationships with all key stakeholders

- Effective implementation of all five EGSEE dimensions of sustainability performance is essential in creating sustainability value for all stakeholders

- Sustainability managers have more incentives to focus on financial sustainability performance that can create tangible shareholder value (return on investment) than, for example, social investment with less tangible outcomes

- Sustainability managers should understand that shareholder value can be improved by enhancing value creation for other stakeholders

- Sustainability managers should use the balanced scorecard to link nonfinancial KPIs to financial KPIs and their integrated impacts on achieving the organization's objectives in creating sustainable value for all stakeholders

3
Business sustainability drivers

In the aftermath of the global 2007–2009 financial crisis, business organizations should improve their performance in all five economic, governance, social, ethics, and environmental (EGSEE) dimensions. Corporations should also effectively communicate their EGSEE sustainability performance to all of their stakeholders through sustainability reporting. This chapter discusses drivers of recent moves toward business sustainability, integrated reporting, and sustainability reporting and assurance. Sustainability reporting can be promoted in three ways:

1. Through market forces of the demand for and interests in EGSEE performance reporting by investors and financial markets as the socially responsible investment fund has grown substantially during the past two decades.

2. Through mandatory sustainability reporting by listing standards of stock exchanges (Singapore Exchange, 2011; Hong Kong Stock Exchange, 2015) and regulators (European Commission, 2014).

3. Combination of mandatory and voluntary initiatives as promoted by the Global Reporting Initiative (GRI), International Integrated Reporting Council (IIRC), Sustainability Accounting Standards Board (SASB).

3.1 Introduction

Many public companies now voluntarily manage, measure, recognize, and disclose their commitments and events and transactions relevant to all five economic, governance, social, ethical, and environmental (EGSEE) dimensions of sustainability performance. More than 6,000 companies worldwide currently disclose sustainability on various EGSEE dimensions of their sustainability performance. According to GRI, in the year 2000, fewer than 50 global companies released sustainability information on a voluntary basis. By 2005, this number increased to 300 companies, 1,500 companies in 2009, over 2,000 in 2010, and more than 5,000 in 2014, and the number keeps growing.[1] However, the move toward the issuance of mandatory sustainability reporting has been very slow. There is no mandatory guidance for sustainability performance reporting at this time. However, there are several voluntary guidelines for sustainability reporting, including the reporting frameworks released by GRI, the Connected Reporting Framework, the reporting publications of AccountAbility, and integrated reporting promoted by the International Integrated Reporting Council (IIRC). An alternative to mandatory sustainability reports is to standardize the sustainability performance reporting and assurance by considering accomplishing the following:

- Standardize disparate sustainability reports that are currently issued

- Establish a globally accepted reporting framework for sustainability information

- Create uniformity in objectively reporting all five dimensions of EGSEE performance

- Ensure that a wide range of users, including investors, have access to uniform and comparable sustainability reports

- Facilitate uniform sustainability assurance

These and other suggestions for developing a set of globally accepted best practices for sustainability performance, reporting, and assurance are presented in this chapter. Sustainability theories and standards are also examined in this chapter as the primary drivers of the global move toward sustainability development, performance, reporting, and assurance.

---

1   Global Reporting Initiative (2014).

3.2 Sustainability theories

The effective implementation of business sustainability requires that a firm extend its focus beyond maximizing short-term shareholder profit by considering the impact of its operation on all stakeholders including the community, society, and the environment. Several sustainability theories including agency/shareholder, stakeholder, signaling/disclosure, and legitimacy discussed in this section can explain the interrelated and integrated five EGSEE dimensions of sustainability performance.

3.2.1 Shareholder/agency theory

The shareholder/agency theory addresses risk sharing and agency problems between the principal (owner) and agent (management) and suggests that three agency costs (monitoring, bonding, and residual) are assumed by principals to align their interests with those of the agent.[2] When the interests of the agent are not aligned with those of the principal, the agent has incentives and may not act in the best interest of and/or withhold important information from the principal.[3] The shareholder theory suggests that management can maximize the interests of shareholders by engaging in positive net present value (NPV) projects that create shareholder value. Thus, management may not invest in any social and environmental initiatives that do not generate positive net cash flows. The implications of the shareholder theory for sustainability performance is that management incentives and activities may focus around meeting short-term earnings targets and away from achieving sustainable and long-term financial performance as well as nonfinancial ESG performance for all stakeholders including shareholders.

3.2.2 Stakeholder theory

This theory promotes maximization of sustainable performance and the long-term value of the firm as the criterion for balancing the interests of all stakeholders.[4] Stakeholder welfare maximization can include the interests of employees, customers, and the broader community within which a firm operates. In the context of shareholder wealth maximization and stakeholder welfare maximization, nonfinancial sustainability efforts (e.g., social,

2   Fama and Jensen, 1983.
3   Fama and Jensen, 1983.
4   Jensen, 2001.

environmental) can create both synergies and conflicts. The stakeholder theory suggests sustainability activities and performance enhance the long-term value of the firm by fulfilling the firms' social responsibilities, meeting their environmental obligations, and improving their reputation. However, these sustainability efforts may require considerable resource allocation that could conflict with shareholder wealth maximization objectives, and thus management would invest in sustainability initiatives (social and environmental) that would result in long-term financial sustainability.

Stakeholders are those who have vested interests in a firm through their investments in the form of financial capital (shareholders), human capital (employees), physical capital (customers and suppliers), social capital (society), environmental capital (environment), and regulatory capital (government). Stakeholders have a reciprocal relation and interaction with a firm in the sense that they contribute to the firm value creation and their wellbeing is also affected by the firm. The stakeholder theory promotes stakeholder value creation by considering sustainability including CSR activities as an integral component of a firm's strategic decision and performance. This suggests that interests of all stakeholders including shareholders should be considered and protected. Thus, stakeholder value creation promoted by business sustainability is important because firms have a responsibility to all stakeholders that are affected by (or affect) their activities

3.2.3 Legitimacy theory

The legitimacy theory suggests that firms are facing social, community and political pressure to preserve their legitimacy by fulfilling their social contract and environmental obligations. The legitimacy theory is often used to justify the importance of nonfinancial performance, particularly the social and environmental dimensions of sustainability performance. The legitimacy theory suggests that firms disclose relevant financial and non-financial ESG sustainability performance information to obtain legitimacy and thus fulfill the "social contract" and gain the support of society.[5] The legitimacy theory also suggests that social and environmental sustainability performance is desirable by all stakeholders including customers and that non-compliance with social norms and environmental requirements threatens organizational legitimacy and its financial sustainability.[6]

---

5   Guthriea and Parkerb, 1989.
6   Tilling, 2004.

3.2.4 Signaling theory

The signaling theory suggests that firms attempt to signal "good news" pertaining to their financial and nonfinancial ESG sustainability performance. However, the perceived link between a firm's voluntary nonfinancial sustainability performance (e.g., social, governance, and environmental) reporting and financial sustainability performance information and thus the use of these signals in creating legitimacy and reputation for the firm is ambiguous. The signaling theory suggests firms with good EGSEE sustainability performance differentiate themselves from firms with bad EGSEE sustainability performance and thus through sustainability reporting firms signal their good sustainability performance that cannot be easily mimicked by non-sustainable firms.[7]

Sustainability theories discussed above suggests that a firm must extend its focus beyond maximizing short-term shareholder profit under the shareholder theory by considering the impact of its operation on all stakeholders including the community, society, and the environment. Disclosure of EGSEE dimensions of sustainability performance while signaling the company's commitment to all stakeholders including the environment and society. For example, any environmental initiatives pertaining to reducing pollution levels or saving energy costs may require huge upfront capital expenditures but in the long run will also reduce contingent and actual environmental liabilities. Another example: tobacco companies may increase their shareholder wealth (promoted by the shareholder theory) by selling their products at the risk of being detrimental to the health of customers. Sustainability is an integral component of corporate culture and infrastructure, business model and management strategies, decisions and actions, particularly when there is a conflict between the corporate goals of maximizing profits and social goals.

3.3 Sustainability standards

The effective achievement of EGSEE sustainability performance requires compliance with a set of globally accepted standards in certifying the accuracy, completeness, and reliability of sustainability reports. A set of standards published by the International Organization for Standardization

---

7   Grinblatt and Hwang, 1989.

(ISO) is relevant to all five EGSEE dimensions of sustainability performance in providing assurance on sustainability performance reports. The ISO certifications can ensure high-quality products and promote compliance with environmental regulations and social standards. A comprehensive set of ISO standards and their integrated link to sustainability theories and all five dimensions of sustainability performance are presented in this section. Specifically, ISO 9000 on quality control, ISO 14000 on environmental programs, ISO 20121 on sustainability events, ISO 26000 on corporate social responsibility, ISO 27001 on information security, and ISO 31000 on risk assessment are relevant to sustainability performance.

3.3.1 ISO 9000

ISO 9000 is the standard that provides a set of standardized requirements for a quality management system, regardless of what the user organization does, its size, or whether it is in the private or public sector.[8] It is the only standard in the family against which organizations can be certified – although certification is not a compulsory requirement of the standard. The other standards in the family cover specific aspects such as fundamentals and vocabulary, performance improvements, documentation, training, and financial and economic aspects. ISO 9000 standards are intended to improve the quality of products and services and thus directly related to enhancing economic sustainability performance and the achievement of financial sustainability.

3.3.2 ISO 14000

The ISO 14000 family addresses various aspects of environmental management (ISO 14000). The first two standards, ISO 14001:2004 and ISO 14004:2004, deal with environmental management systems (EMS).[9] ISO 14001:2004 provides the requirements for an EMS and ISO 14004:2004 gives general EMS guidelines. The other standards and guidelines in the family address specific environmental aspects, including: labeling, performance evaluation, life-cycle analysis, communication, and auditing. Guidelines provided in ISO 14000 regarding environmental performance, reporting, and auditing are relevant to the environmental dimension of sustainability

---

8   International Organization for Standardization (ISO), 2015a.
9   International Organization for Standardization (ISO), 2015b.

performance and thus the achievement of environmental goals and fulfill-ment of commitments to the environment.

3.3.3 ISO 20121

ISO 20121 (entitled "Sustainable Events") addresses events that can gener-ate significant waste, affecting resources, society, and the environment.[10] This standard puts a constraint on local resources such as water or energy and offers guidelines and best practices to help manage events and control their social, economic, and environmental impact. It recognizes the harm-ful impacts of events on social, economic, and environmental constituen-cies and suggests ways to minimize their negative effects, and to capitalize on positive effects through improved planning and procedures. ISO 20121 offers benefits for integrating its guidelines in all stages of management processes, including supply chain management, which promotes best busi-ness practices and reputational advantages. The monitoring and measuring required by ISO 20121 provides opportunities and enables organizations to reduce their use of resources and cut costs. It also empowers leaders in event management sustainability to establish their actions in a credible and transparent way and to communicate their commitment to sustainability in a globally recognized manner.

3.3.4 ISO 26000

ISO 26000 covers a broad range of an organization's activities from economic to social, governance, ethics, and environmental issues.[11] ISO 26000 is a globally accepted guidance document for social responsibility that assists organizations worldwide in fulfilling their CSR goals. The social responsi-bility performance promoted in ISO 26000 is conceptually and practically associated with the development of achieving sustainable performance because the fulfillment of social responsibility necessitates and ensures sustainability development. ISO 26000 goes beyond profit maximization by presenting a framework for organizations to contribute to sustainable development and the welfare of society. The core subject areas of ISO 26000 take into account all aspects of the triple bottom line's (TBL) key financial and nonfinancial performance relevant to people, planet, and profit:

---

10   International Organization for Standardization (ISO), 2012, 2015c.
11   International Organization for Standardization (ISO), 2010a.

- **People.** ISO 26000 encourages companies to recognize human rights as a critical aspect of social responsibility by ensuring that countries in which they operate respect the political, civil, social, and cultural rights of the citizens.

- **Planet.** ISO 26000 promotes sustainable resource management to ensure that business organizations are not exploiting the environment in which they are operating.

- **Profit.** The primary goal of business organizations has been and will continue to be generating profits in a socially responsible way to ensure shareholder value creation and the achievement of the desired rate of return on investment.

3.3.5 ISO 27001

The purpose of ISO 27001 is to offer organizations guidance on keeping information assets secure by providing guidelines and suggesting requirements for an information security management system (ISMS).[12] Using this family of standards enables organizations to manage the security of assets such as financial information, intellectual property, employee details, or information entrusted to them by third parties. The ISMS is a systematic approach to managing sensitive information and protecting its integrity. Furthermore, it helps identify the risks associated with important information and control activities designed and implemented to manage the risk. It suggests application of risk assessment and management to people, processes, and IT systems for organizations of all sizes and types.

3.3.6 ISO 31000

ISO 31000 standards set out principles, frameworks, and processes for risk assessment and management and are applicable to any type of organization in the public or private sector.[13] These standards do not mandate a "one size fits all" approach, but rather emphasize the fact that risk assessment and management must be tailored to the specific needs and structure of the particular organization. Guidelines provided in ISO 31000 are applicable in the assessment and management of risks associated with all five EGSEE

---

12   International Organization for Standardization (ISO), 2015d.
13   International Organization for Standardization (ISO), 2015e.

dimensions of sustainability performance. These risks include strategic, financial, compliance, operational, supply chain, and reputational risks.

Implementing these ISO standards to various dimensions of sustainability performance and certifications of compliance with these standards promote improvements in the quality of products and services that directly affect earnings, ensure compliance with environmental regulations and social standards, strengthen governance measures and ethical value, and improve the effectiveness of sustainability programs. These standards also establish practical foundations that can be the build-up based on the sustainability theoretical framework. Sustainability reports reflecting all five EGSEE dimensions of sustainability performance are deemed to be useful when they are complete, accurate and their reliability, objectivity, and credibility are ascertained by ISO certifications. These ISO certifications of sustainability performance provide external assurance about the credibility and legitimacy of the sustainability programs, sustaining sustainability and communication of sustainability performance information to all stakeholders.

3.4 Regulatory-led sustainability initiatives

Sustainability reporting – fueled by investor interest – can be promoted through compulsory sustainability reporting, listing standards of stock exchanges,[14] or a combination of mandatory and voluntary initiatives. The emerging global move toward sustainability reporting requires management to develop a proper balance of managing all five EGSEE sustainability performance activities in creating sustainable shareholder value while protecting the interests of other stakeholders, including creditors, employees, suppliers, customers, the government, the environment, and society. Many public companies voluntarily manage, measure, recognize, and disclose their commitment to EGSEE and relevant events and transactions. This expansion into determining sustainable performance and long-term value-adding strategies has driven a need for new accountability structures, which extend beyond financial statements into nonfinancial KPIs based on environmental impact and social responsibility.

---

14   For example, Singapore Exchange, 2011.

The evolution of business sustainability begins with the creation of the U.S. Environmental Protection Agency (EPA), the passage of the Endangered Species Act, and the Clean Water Act in the early 1980s. The legislation was instrumental in the development of the environmental aspect of sustainability reporting.[15] Then, in the aftermath of the 1989 *Exxon Valdez* disaster, the U.S.-based Coalition for Environmentally Responsible Economies (CERES), established the "CERES/Valdez Principles."[16] These principles defined a set of environmental reporting guidelines on behalf of the Social Investment Forum (SIF). While sustainability reporting has gained momentum since the mid-1980s, the standardization of sustainability reporting is a recent development:

- The International Integrated Reporting Council recently published a framework known as the G4 Guidelines, expressing therein how companies should communicate with their shareholders. An "integrated report" is to promote transparency and address how an organization's performance will benefit both shareholders and stakeholders. The purpose of the report is to be a further extension of a company's external financial reports and is aimed to a specialist audience such as regulators and lawyers.

- The framework was published in May 2013, yet improvements are still being made every day. The challenges presented include figuring out how the design of the integrated report will evolve and how responsive it must be to the needs of companies creating them and to people reading them. Cultural differences worldwide present a challenge for the adoption of the integrated report.

- An issue currently at hand is whether or not a company will need new reporting tools to conform to the framework. According to Ventana Research, the IIRC will probably not require new tools. Organizations tend to use spreadsheets and will probably continue to use them.[17]

- The IIRC released a prototype to aid in compilations of nonfinancial information with financial information. A "worldwide invitation" has been issued and the IIRC is holding 15 events to launch the consultation framework.

15   Brockett and Rezaee, 2012a.
16   Brockett and Rezaee, 2012a.
17   Kugel, 2013.

- The framework is the product of business and investor input and testing involving over 300 individuals and organizations. The IIRC has recruited businesses and investors to its pilot program.

- Many companies already acknowledge the need to provide more social and environmental information, as they are currently facing constraints.[18]

In 2009, the Social Investment Forum (SIF) requested that the Obama Administration take initiative to restore investor confidence by strengthening mandatory reporting on corporate environmental, social, and governance (ESG) practices.[19] To provide more accountability, the SIF has developed a proposal requesting that the SEC require public companies to:[20]

- Report annually their sustainability information in compliance with the GRI guidelines

- Disclose their short-term and long-term sustainability risks in the Management Discussion and Analysis (MD&A) section of their 10-K forms

Furthermore, in March 2013, the U.S. Sustainability Accounting Standards Board (SASB) released its proposed sustainability accounting standards for the healthcare sector.[21] A 2013 Joint study by the Investor Responsibility Research Center Institute (IRRCI) and the Sustainable Investments Institute (Si2) reports that only 1.4% of S&P 500 companies (seven firms) issued a stand-alone sustainability report by mentioning sustainability reporting in their regulatory filing of 10-K reports, whereas almost all S&P 500 companies disclosed at least one piece of sustainability information, 74% placed monetary value on their sustainability-related disclosures, and about 44% of the companies linked their executive compensation to some type of sustainability criteria.[22]

The Carbon Disclosure Project (CDP) is an international, not-for-profit organization that includes 655 institutional investors and collects information from companies on their greenhouse gas emissions and assessment of climate change and water risk and opportunity. The Climate Disclosure

18   Singh, 2013.
19   Singh, 2013.
20   Singh, 2013.
21   Deloitte, 2013.
22   IRRC Institute and Sustainable Investments Institute, 2013.

Standards Board released a framework for climate change reporting in 2010. On November 6, 2012, the CDP and the Climate Disclosure Standards Board (CDSB) released the XBRL climate change reporting taxonomy.[23] This taxonomy streamlines the process for reporting climate change information so that the information can be more easily promulgated into financial reports and dispersed to the interested parties.

3.5 Global best practices of sustainability development, performance and reporting

Business sustainability enables companies to design and implement strategies that contribute to enduring performance in all EGSEE areas and thus ensures achievement of long-term earnings targets while protecting the wellbeing of the society, the planet, and people. The idea is that a company must extend its focus beyond making profit by considering the impact of its operation on the community, society, and the environment. This expansion in determining an organization's sustainable performance and long-term value-adding strategies has created a need for new reporting and accountability structures which extend beyond financial statements into nonfinancial key performance indicators based on environmental impact and social responsibility. The most important and commonly accepted dimension of sustainability is the "economic viability and performance" which is the cornerstone of business sustainability. Companies can survive and produce sustainable performance when they continue to be profitable and produce enduring performance that creates shareholder value. However, these dimensions are not mutually exclusive; they supplement each other. On one hand, companies that are run ethically, governed effectively, and are socially and environmentally responsible are expected to produce sustainable performance, create shareholder value, and gain public trust and investor confidence. On the other hand, more economically profitable and viable companies are in better positions and have more resources to create jobs and wealth and better fulfill their social and environmental responsibilities. Although the primary goal of many business entities will continue to be creating shareholder value through pursuit of a commercial imperative and production of sustainable economic performance, they must also

23   Climate Disclosure Standards Board, 2012.

effectively deal with ethical, social, and environmental issues to ensure they add value for their shareholders and other stakeholders.

Best practices for sustainability development, performance, and reporting are still being developed as more professional organizations and Key Opinion Leaders (KOLs) decide what is best for the sustainability standards. To wit, there are several organizations striving to collate these best practices into standards.[24] Table 3.1 presents many organizations currently initiating and collaborating on the development of guidelines and best practices for sustainability performance, reporting, and assurance.

Despite the various proposals for best practices, some best practices do stand out as being standard. In general, companies are starting to look to outside assurance providers to gauge their sustainability practices and to ensure that they follow proper regulatory and corporate procedures, as these outside assurance providers are more knowledgeable and skilled in matters affecting sustainability. A recent report by Grant Thornton suggests that while early sustainability practices have focused on providing internal assurance, stakeholders are more inclined to tell companies, "I trust you, but show me anyway."[25] In addition, having an organization that specializes in these matters will enable the companies not only to see matters with fresh (and objective) eyes, but will also empower them to incorporate those changes into their everyday practices. This report also shows that companies' use of sustainability practices grows with the size of the company, as those companies which have the most free capital to utilize on sustainability projects tend to be those which spend the most time and money on sustainability disclosures. Perhaps most important is that executives need to pay greater attention to the concerns of their markets and their companies' practices to ensure that they utilize every resource to its greatest extent. It is insufficient to simply issue reports and expect others to fall in line with determining the value of the company through its financial and nonfinancial assets; executives of all stripes should know at least the basics of their companies' sustainability practices and be able to answer questions from and lead employees to enact them and stakeholders to value them. They must not simply "go on with what they know," but rather must "know what is going on" at all times. In order to achieve this, executives must learn how to communicate these practices to their stakeholders in a cogent manner.

24   Grant Thornton, 2014.
25   Grant Thornton, 2014.

Guidelines/framework	Intent/purpose	Description/coverage
European Commission	European Directive requiring public companies to disclose their social, environmental, governance, and diversity performance activities	About 6,000 large European companies starting 2017
Global Reporting Initiative (GRI)	Guidelines, G4 which provide framework for disclosure of economic, governance, environmental, and social performance.	Global; all corporations any types and sizes.
Sustainability Accounting Standards Board (SASB)	Provides guidelines for reporting nonfinancial information on material and related appropriate KPI metrics on EGSEE performance that can be reported in Form 10-Ks.	Publicly listed U.S. corporations; foreign companies that are traded on a U.S. exchange. Guidance by industry.
United Nations Global Compact (UNGC)	A platform for business and nonbusiness entities to develop a sustainable and inclusive global economy and report on nonfinancial performance in areas of human rights, labor, environment, and anticorruption.	Business and nonbusiness entities worldwide
Accountability AA1000 standards	Principles-based standards to assist organizations worldwide in becoming more sustainable, socially responsible and economically accountable.	Global; corporations, not-for-profit organizations, and government entities.
ISO 26000	Guidelines on the triple bottom line of focusing on planet, people, and profit to assist organizations in effectively fulfilling their social responsibilities.	All business and nonbusiness organizations worldwide regardless of types and sizes.
Stock exchanges	Guidelines requiring companies traded on a stock exchange to report their environmental, social, and governance performance	Listed companies on their stock exchanges
International Integrated Reporting Council (IIRC)	Promotes integrated reporting by providing the International <IR> Framework for organizations to communicate ESG performance with their stakeholders.	All business and nonbusiness organizations worldwide regardless of types and sizes.

TABLE 3.1 Organizations engaged in sustainability

Mark O'Sullivan, Director of Corporate Reporting at PwC, writes that these challenges can be summarized as follows:[26]

- **Conciseness paradox.** How do you communicate in a concise and believable way without it coming across as marketing and spin?

- **Create connections.** How do you present an integrated picture of the business that clearly links key elements such as the business model, strategy, risks, and KPIs?

- **Broaden horizons.** How can you consider, manage, and communicate your organization's dependence on key resources and relationships and its wider impact on society?

- **Rethink performance.** How can you communicate operational progress, your wider impact, and its effect on the bottom line?

- **Tell an authentic story.** How can you communicate your story while looking to comply with the <IR> framework?

Once executives can synthesize the above challenges into a clear picture of how the company intends to grow and develop itself, they can bring that to their stakeholders, who should be able to use that information to more accurately value the company and in turn increase its viability. Around the world, multinational companies and global brands are trendsetters, kick-starting the business industry into sustainability development. This portion will depict a few examples of early birds in the sustainability business, as well as their goals and successes.

Ben & Jerry's is a world-famous ice cream company that began in 1977 in Burlington, Vermont with a unique business proposition. Its founders, Ben Cohen and Jerry Greenfield, wished to have a company that could sell premium ice cream in many unorthodox flavors and enact sustainability throughout its sourcing of product and labor and its engagement with the local community and their social beliefs. This practice is not uncommon these days, but it was unusual at the time. Instead of settling for a profitable business, the company and its founders were able to ensure that the stakeholders were all treated with care, even if they were not attended to as much as each would hope for individually. Prior to its acquisition by Unilever in 2000, Ben & Jerry's was able not only to divert a significant portion of its revenues to sustainable development, but also to enact its corporate structure so as to ensure that its principals could pursue their sustainability measures without interference from common shareholders.[27]

SABMiller is a multinational brewery and beverage company located in London, England. The company is the world's second-largest brewer by revenue and a major bottler for Coca-Cola. In their 2014 sustainability report, they set a series of targets to reduce their carbon footprint by 25% per liter of beer and by an average of 50% across all breweries by the end of the decade. The report also stated they have already achieved a 29% reduction in carbon emissions since 2008.

McDonald's, the world's largest hamburger chain and second-largest fast-food chain, is pledging to buy and serve sustainable beef based on region-specific standards. In the report, they vow to start verifying purchased beef by 2016 with the goal of 100% sustainable beef purchase. In addition, McDonald's has set a target of a 20% improvement in energy efficiency for restaurants in top markets by 2020.

As mentioned briefly in Chapter 1, UPS is the largest shipment and logistics company in the world, delivering to more than 6.1 million customers in more than 220 countries. From using "eco-packaging" to efficient transportation, UPS has been recognized as a company with one of the most robust and detailed sustainability programs around. UPS is verified by Deloitte & Touche, Société Générale de Surveillance (SGS), and The CarbonNeutral Company.

Chipotle is a prime example of how a company can focus on sustainable practices and achieve great economic profit. Founded in 1993 in Denver, Colorado, Chipotle introduced not only a new style of food – the Mexican grill concept – that has become very popular in recent years, but also did so while constantly improving its sustainability standards and practices. In the brief 20 years that the company has been in operation, they have managed to source all of their meat from naturally grown pigs, chicken, and cows[28] while still maintaining an enviable growth rate. Despite the higher prices paid by Chipotle for their materials, their customers are more than willing to absorb these costs in order to get a better, more sustainable product.

The CalSTRS, or the California State Teachers' Retirement System, is the nation's largest teachers' pension fund, and in their first corporate governance report state, "The successful public company must monitor a variety of issues in order to remain successful, among them: sales and marketing,

27   Bruner *et al.*, 2013, Case 3: Ben & Jerry's Homemade.
28   Chipotle, 2014.

personnel, pricing, product development, suppliers, and last but not least, staying a step ahead of the competition. Less obvious, but no less important for a company to monitor, is its corporate governance."[29] Having been around for more than 100 years, the fund knows its fair share of sustainability practices. As part of its corporate governance, the fund deals with many players in the business world in order to extract rent to increase the fund's overall wealth for its participants. In addition, the CalSTRS fund advocates ESG changes in the companies in which it has voting rights and performs research about and educates on the matters of interest to its stakeholders in order to increase the efficacy of its goals. Thus, this multipronged approach can be applied to the market at large as a way in which companies can, in their small (or big) ways change the environment in which they operate.

Though the example of CalSTRS is a fairly small example in the world of financial transactions, it does show that good corporate governance need not come at the price of profits. The alignment of the goals of myriad companies into a standard set of best practices has proven to be an effective strategy in increasing the ability to affect change in the corporate world.

Many global professional organizations, including the GRI, the IIRC, and the International Federation of Accountants (IFAC) are working to develop a set of globally accepted, uniform, and standardized sustainability reporting guidelines. These professional organizations call for uniform integrated reporting as the means by which companies should communicate with all of their stakeholders, including investors, about their strategy, governance, actions, performance, and processes that add value in the short, medium, and long term.[30] The GRI initially focused on a triple bottom line of economic, social, and environmental performance with version 3.1 (G3) of its sustainability framework. However, in 2011 the GRI started to develop version 4.1, or the fourth generation (G4) of guidelines, which covers economic, governance, social, and environmental performance.

The Global Reporting Initiative (GRI) was launched in 1997 to bring consistency and global standardization to sustainability reporting.[31] The evolution of GRI guidelines began with the initial focus on incorporating environmental performance into corporate reporting with its first publication *Sustainability Reporting Guidelines* in 2000. In its G4 guidelines released in May 2013, the GRI promotes sustainability reporting as a standard

29   California State Teachers' Retirement System, 2013.
30   International Integrated Reporting Council, 2013b.
31   Global Reporting Initiative, 2011.

practice of disclosing sustainability-related issues relevant to companies and their stakeholders.[32] The G4 Guidelines present Reporting Principles, Standard Disclosures, and an Implementation Manual for sustainability reporting on economic, environmental, social, and governance performance (EESG) by all organizations regardless of their type, size, sector, or location.[33] The GRI reporting process enables organizations to disclose sustainability information based on one of the three application levels (A, B, or C) depending on the extent of information provided. GRI also recommends that assurance be provided on sustainability reports by external assurance providers, which can be designated with a "+" added to the application level declared. However, GRI guidelines do not provide assessments on the quality or reliability of disclosed sustainability information. In response to the lack of accountability for the quality, many countries (e.g., France, Malaysia, Sweden, and the U.K.) have modernized their corporate reporting systems to include environmental, social, and governance (ESG) factors in compliance with GRI guidelines.[34] The European Commission (EC) has recently started to consider whether to require disclosure of nonfinancial ESG information. The EC is considering determining what types of organization would be required to disclose ESG information, which international framework (e.g., GRI) would serve as a standard reporting guideline, and if and to what extent ESG disclosure would be integrated with financial information in one annual report.

The EC previously defined Corporate Social Responsibility (CSR) as "a concept whereby companies integrate social and environmental concerns in their business operations and in their interactions with their stakeholders on a voluntary basis," but now defines CSR as "the responsibility of enterprises for their impacts on society."[35] The motivation for the new definition comes from the effects of the 2007–2009 financial crisis, which impacted consumer confidence and trust in businesses, and aims to ensure that businesses will better society through their actions rather than just align their current actions with the betterment of society. In other words, this new definition means that businesses should put society at large at the forefront of their decision-making processes, not on the back burner. To that end, the EC considers the following measures necessary to fully comprise the issues to be covered by CSR:

32   Global Reporting Initiative, 2013b.
33   Global Reporting Initiative, 2013b.
34   PricewaterhouseCoopers, 2014a.
35   European Commission, 2011.

- Human rights, labor, and employment practices

- Environmental issues

- Combating bribery and corruption

Of lesser importance, but still vital to the CSR process, are the following issues:

- Community involvement and development

- Integration of disabled persons

- Consumer interests, including privacy

- Promotion of social and environmental responsibility through the supply chain

- Disclosure of nonfinancial information

- Good tax governance in relations between countries:
  - Transparency
  - Exchange of information
  - Fair tax competition

The EC considers that this can best be performed through joint ventures by trade unions and civil society organizations, as they are more tightly linked than the same in America. Together, these trade unions and civil society organizations can affect greater change in companies' behaviors by focusing their attention toward cohesion in both their reporting and inter-actions with their stakeholders. The aim of this initiative is that outside of simply following regulations and codes, having companies and their stake-holders join together for impactful actions in their day-to-day interactions will allow them to progress more quickly toward a common goal.

G4 introduces 27 new disclosures and a new structure for the guidance documents. G4 provides guidance on how to select material topics and illustrates the boundaries of where these occur. In G4 there are two options, namely core and comprehensive, which concentrate on the process for defining material aspects and boundaries. The revised guidelines empha-size materiality in sustainability reporting and include new and updated disclosures in various areas, including governance (G4.34-55), ethics and integrity (G4.56-58), supply chain (G4-12 and G4-EC9), anticorruption (G4 SO3-SO6), greenhouse gas (GHG) emissions, Energy G4 (EN3-EN7), and G4 (EN15-21).

An implementation manual was created in order to apply the reporting principles and prepare the standard disclosures.[36] There are five key
changes for G4 compared with G3.1:[37]

1. **Materiality takes center stage.** The G4 Guidelines could lead to
   explaining the process that companies use to identify their Material Aspects.

2. **Reporting boundaries redefined.** According to the G4 Guidelines,
   companies need to report on the process they use to define the
   boundary of impact for each Material Aspect.

3. **"In accordance" levels replace A, B, C.** Organizations need to
   meet more criteria to achieve the Core and Comprehensive "In
   Accordance" levels and simply use the G4 Guidelines more as a
   broad guide to reporting than they did to achieve the previous A,
   B, or C application levels.

4. **New governance disclosure requirements.** The G4 Guidelines
   contain ten new standard disclosures on governance. In order to
   achieve the "Comprehensive" level of reporting, organizations will
   need to disclose more complex governance indicators.

5. **New supply chain requirements.** Compared with G3, G4 requires
   companies to disclose significantly more information on supply
   chain impacts, including details of supply chain assessments,
   risks identified, the organization's performance in managing these
   risks, and the management processes put into place.

In the post-financial crisis and new regulatory framework era, corporations are searching for more effective, efficient, and feasible ways to improve
the quality of their financial reporting, all while ensuring compliance with
all applicable rules, laws, regulations, and standards. Sustainability reporting can offer solutions to emerging and widening corporate reporting
challenges facing business firms. Many factors have caused more interest in business sustainability, including pressure on the effective use of
natural and scarce raw materials, consumer awareness of corporate social
responsibility, energy prices, and regulatory reforms. Business sustainability is a process of enabling organizations to design and implement strategies that contribute to enduring performance in all EGSEE areas. Business

36   KPMG, 2013b.
37   KPMG, 2013b.

sustainability not only ensures long-term profitability and competitive advantage, but also helps in maintaining the well-being of the society, the planet, and people.[38] This expansion of determining sustainable performance and long-term value-adding strategies drives a need for new reporting and accountability structures which extend beyond financial statements into nonfinancial KPIs based on environmental impact and social responsibility. Traditionally, firms have focused on earnings as the "bottom line" and the major KPIs for measuring sustainable performance. As businesses have evolved, their role in society as good citizens has developed, and their impacts and possible external costs have become more noticeable, making a focus on the multiple bottom line inevitable. The "multiple bottom line" does not replace, but rather supplements, the conventional economic bottom line by measuring performance in all areas of EGSEE. Thus, the true measure of success for corporations is determined not only by reported earnings, but also by their corporate governance effectiveness, fulfillment of social responsibility, ethical behavior, and environmental initiatives.

The long-term objective of sustainability lies not only in the sustainability of the companies themselves, but also of the entire business environment which they make up. Though increased sustainability reporting may prove to be less profitable for any one particular company that has new negative externalities (particularly in the short term), the increased information will bring in more investors as they feel more sure about their investments. The most basic manner in which investment in sustainability measures can improve investor confidence is through infrastructure investment; with fewer barriers to entering into a market comes less systematic risk (i.e., market risk) given a mature environment, and therefore investors will park more money in the system that gives them higher returns. A recent report by the B20 Coalition discusses this need for increased infrastructure investment through a panel discussion of the top six global accounting networks (BDO, Deloitte, EY, Grant Thornton, KPMG, and PwC). Their conclusions can be summarized as follows:[39]

- Increased outlooks on the long-term value of the firm and removing practical, legal, or regulatory barriers to improved corporate reporting should make the environment for infrastructure investment more conducive to doing business.

---

38   International Organization for Standardization (ISO), 2011.
39   B20 Panel of Six International Accounting Networks, 2014.

- Since accounting practices vary worldwide and incentivize short-termism, they are not good vehicles for intervention in long-term infrastructure investments. Instead, the IASB should work to create standards to avoid accounting mismatches in insurance contracts as a way to encourage infrastructure development.

- Regulators should assess to what extent the market risk for various environments correlates with the risk patterns of the same areas, and if not, then make the proper adjustments to align them.

Based on estimates by S&P and McKinsey,[40] there could be a sizable gap in the amount of funding available for infrastructure spending versus the needs for the public sector over the next 15 years. As such, there are two avenues for combating this gap:

- Increase government efforts at reaching investors by being more transparent about how the projects are thought out.

- Create more public–private partnerships that will increase competition, thus lowering costs, and be more efficient at providing the ultimate product.

In both situations, increased information will be needed; in the first situation, stakeholders, particularly the citizens of the governments, will need more information to ensure that their money is invested well, and in the second situation, the increased information from the private companies will ensure the public and their representatives that their work will be on par with that from the public sector. In other words, governments need to be trusted that they will create good value from their constituents' investments (e.g., taxes, bond purchases, public utilities, etc.) and private companies must show that they are not seeking undue and abnormal rent through their public partnerships. As quoted in the CoST *Factsheet*:

> Strengthening transparency and accountability in public construction yields benefits both domestic and international. It curbs mismanagement, waste, and corruption and reduces risks to public safety from poor building practices. It improves fairness in competition for contracts and can also increase the flow of foreign direct investment and development finance into a country's construction sector.[41]

40   Boston Consulting Group, 2013; World Economic Forum, 2013.
41   Construction Sector Transparency Initiative, 2013.

The most important matter in all of this is that while there need be standards for corporate reporting, they must be flexible to meet the demands of the industries involved, the countries or localities in which they do business, the investors they wish to seek (particularly at various and discrete stages of the business process), and public and market insecurity about investments. Being too strict in these matters will lead to companies not investing as much time and effort into reporting and may lead to information overload for stakeholders if not properly condensed, thus diminishing the returns that could be gained from proper reporting.

3.6 Business sustainability disclosures

Business sustainability disclosure is the act of communicating organizational performance on material matters relating to financial, environmental, social, and governance activities. The terms "environmental, social, and governance (ESG) reporting," "risk compliance, and governance (RCG) reporting," "CSR reporting," "integrated reporting," and "sustainability reporting," have been used interchangeably to describe the disclosure of sustainability performance. Moreover, these terms have a wide range of coverage of financial and nonfinancial KPIs pertaining to economic, risk, compliance, environmental, social, and governance issues. Business organizations and their stakeholders can benefit from sustainability disclosures on all five EGSEE sustainability performance dimensions. Sustainability topics or KPIs that are material or significant should be included in sustainability disclosures. Information regarding an organization's sustainability has been disclosed through various channels, including external websites, social media channels, intranet sites, marketing materials, internal signage and postings, presentations, and newsletters. There are generally two forms of disclosures: voluntary and mandatory.

3.6.1 Mandatory sustainability disclosures

Corporate mandatory disclosures are designed to provide investors with relevant, useful, and reliable information in making sound investment decisions and are thus vital to the financial market. In the context of the agency theory, a moral hazard occurs in the presence of information asymmetry where the agent (management) acting on behalf of the principal (shareholders) knows more about its actions and/or intentions than the principal does because of lack of proper monitoring of the agent. When the interests of the agent are not aligned with those of the principal, the agent has incentives and may not act in the best interest of and/or withhold important information from the principal. In the case of mandatory disclosures, there is less opportunity for the existence of information asymmetry. As of now, there is no mandatory disclosure of sustainability performance information. Corporate disclosure (either mandatory or voluntary) is the backbone of financial markets worldwide. Public companies are required to disclose a set of financial information as long as their securities are held by the public. The primary purpose of corporate disclosure is to provide economic agents (e.g., shareholders, creditors) with adequate information to make appropriate decisions. The primary goals of mandatory disclosures are to provide adequate financial information to investors in making appropriate decisions that protect their interests and enhance their confidence in the financial reports and markets, to mitigate the information asymmetry associated with the agency problems, and to ensure that stock prices fully reflect all value-relevant information in an efficient capital market.

The 2012 survey conducted by the *MIT Sloan Management Review*-Boston Consulting Group indicates that 31% of surveyed companies report that sustainability contributes to their profits, whereas 70% consider sustainability permanently on their management agenda.[42] Meanwhile, investors are also concerned about the value relevance and quality of corporate reports and thus demand more accurate, reliable, and relevant financial and nonfinancial information on KPIs. Furthermore, stock exchanges worldwide continue to require sustainability reporting.[43] Business sustainability encourages management to manage earnings in different ways to meet the needs of a variety of stakeholders. A shareholder, for example, may believe that the purpose of the company is to create value in order to generate a desired return on investment. Customers, on the other hand, may expect that the company provides not only the product or service advertised, but also gives back to society in a meaningful way. Customer satisfaction, business reputation, brand value, environmental initiatives, and social responsibility are often considered as intangible business assets which cannot be described adequately in purely economic terms. Likewise, these assets and their value should be linked to their related economic value over the long

42   Boston Consulting Group, 2012.
43   For example, Singapore Exchange, 2011.

term.[44] Shareholders are better off in the long-term by recognizing the various financial benefits derived from the intangible business assets generated through sustainability efforts and development. Thus, management should be motivated to achieve sustainable economic performance for shareholders while protecting the interests of other stakeholders. Mandatory disclosures are disclosures of information required by law or regulation. This sustainability information can occur within financial filings such as 10-Qs, annual reports, and management disclosure and analysis, or nonfinancial reports such as health and safety reports or pollutant release/emissions reports.

Arguments about the detrimental effects of conventional financial reporting focusing only on economic performance are mounting. While financial information may have a short-term impact on market efficiency and thus require interim trading updates, in the long-term it leads to substantial pressures on management from the market to meet short-term targets.[45] There are basically two detrimental effects of conventional financial reporting:

1. It encourages short-termism

2. It compromises the quality of financial reporting

Short-termism is defined as a phenomenon that leads managerial decisions and actions disproportionally toward achieving short-term earnings targets at the expense of sustainable performance. Conventional financial reporting encourages management to focus on short-term performance and the goal of meeting or exceeding short-term targets or analysts' forecast estimates. Such an impact on management behavior prevents management from directing its resources toward sustainable and enduring plans, activities, and EGSEE sustainability performance. Uncertainty about the future, including government policies, regulations, markets, and other unforeseeable factors drive managerial planning to short-term considerations rather than long-term sustainable performance.

Consequences of short-term considerations (short-termism) are a divergence of resources from contributing to economic growth and ineffective misallocation of resources in several ways, including:[46]

44   Wheeler *et al.*, 2003.
45   Committee for Economic Development, 2007.
46   Committee for Economic Development, 2007.

- Sacrificing, delaying, or decreasing discretionary spending on long-term investments or projects to achieve short-term financial targets that meet financial market expectations

- Gearing management's time and efforts toward meeting expectations of short-term results rather than focusing on activities that add sustainable value to the company

- Encouraging earnings management by either deferring costs or shifting revenues

- Tying excessive executive compensation to the achievement of short-term financial targets at the expense of sustainable economic value creation

- Higher-risk premiums resulting from frequent trading done by speculators who target short-term movement in stock prices

- Incurring expenses by mutual funds because of overactive trading caused by focus on short-term considerations

This short-termism practice undermines the sustainable economic performance of many companies by encouraging management to emphasize short-term financial performance with little or no focus on the sustainability of economic performance and its impacts on people, planet, and society. Sustainability reporting, on the other hand, reduces pressures on management from the market to meet short-term targets and thus has potential to affect earnings management.

The European Commission has long promoted CSR and its integration into corporate strategic decisions by defining CSR as "a concept whereby companies integrate social and environmental concerns in their business".[47] This definition of CSR suggests companies take social actions above and beyond their mandatory requirements toward society and environment. Business sustainability with a keen focus on CSR can "bring benefits in terms of risk management, cost savings, access to capital, customer relationships, human resource management, and innovation capacity".[48] Thus, disclosure of such information promotes interaction with all stakeholders on important nonfinancial ESG sustainability performance. Disclosure of nonfinancial ESG sustainability performance demonstrates companies' commitment and move toward achieving the European Union's treaty

---

47   European Commission, 2011.
48   European Commission, 2011.

objectives of "the Europe 2020 strategy for smart, sustainable, and inclusive growth, including the 75% employment target".[49] It also facilitates engagement with stakeholders regarding sustainable growth and risks in building trust in the company and shareholders regarding allocation capital and achievement of long-term investment goals.

The European Commission, on September 29, 2014, endorsed the adoption by the Council of the Directive on disclosure of nonfinancial sustainability information for more than 6,000 companies for their financial year 2017.[50] The Directive provides nonbinding guidelines in facilitating the disclosure of nonfinancial information by large public companies and their stakeholders, including investors and society at large, are intended to benefit from this increased transparency of nonfinancial sustainability information. The Directive also provides large companies with significant flexibility to disclose nonfinancial information either as a separate report or an integrated report along with financial information. It is expected that other countries will follow the European suite in requiring disclosure of sustainability information on all or some five EGSEE dimensions of sustainability performance.

3.6.2 Voluntary sustainability disclosures

Voluntary disclosure often takes the form of corporate responsibility reports and responses to surveys or data requests. The fourth generation (G4) of GRI's Guidelines covers economic, governance, social, and environmental performance.[51] The GRI reporting process enables organizations to self-declare sustainability information based on one of three application levels (A, B, or C), depending on the extent of the information provided. The GRI initially focused on a triple bottom line of economic, social, and environmental performance with version 3.1 (G3) of its sustainability framework. However, in 2011 the GRI developed version 4.1 or the fourth generation (G4) of guidelines, which covers economic, governance, social, and environmental performance. Unlike audit reports on financial statements, assurance reports on sustainability information are neither standardized, regulated, nor licensed.

The SASB, in its 2013 Conceptual Framework for Sustainability, suggests that sustainability performance disclosures be made as a complete set in the Management's Discussion and Analysis of Financial Condition and

49   European Commission, 2011.
50   European Commission, 2014.
51   Global Reporting Initiative, 2013a.

Results of Operations (MD&A) section of Form 10-K, in a sub-section titled "Sustainability Accounting Standard Disclosures filed with the SEC and disseminated to shareholders."[52] The IFAC released its revised "International Standard on Assurance Engagements Other Than Audits or Reviews of Historical Financial Information," 3000 (ISAE 3000).[53] Specifically, ISAE 3410 deals with assurance engagements for an organization reporting greenhouse gas (GHG) statements. Alternatively, GRI can examine the content of detailed sustainability reports and express an opinion on the extent of compliance with GRI guidelines, but not the quality and/or reliability of disclosed sustainability information.[54]

3.7 Academic research on sustainability disclosures

Looking from a macroscopic perspective at the issue of affecting widespread business sustainability practices through mandatory or voluntary schemes may give insight into how best to obtain clear, concise, and valuable sustainability reporting for different environments. A recent paper by Ioannou and Serafeim[55] seeks to ascertain how these interactions between, in this case, various countries' overall outlooks and personalities influence their leaning toward one pillar of sustainability or another. For example, the researchers found that firms in countries that encourage them to compete tend to focus less on environmental and social concerns, while the same detriments are found in those countries with a majority/plurality of leftist governance. The reasons for the similarity between those two groups, disparate as the two groups may seem to be, lie in the conflicting motivations of the stakeholders in question. The paper suggests that in the first case, the decreased performance in environmental and social matters is due in large part to the increase in competitive efficiencies, while the latter group's actions may be explained by the higher corporate taxes and the subsequent fiscal inability to take on more CSR matters. Thus, there must be an active balancing of the various issues surrounding CSR by a dynamic set of regulations, guidelines, initiatives, and best practices. To that end, there is a great need for research

---

52   Sustainability Accounting Standards Board, 2013.
53   International Federation of Accountants, 2011.
54   Global Reporting Initiative, 2013a.
55   Ioannou and Serafeim, 2010.

in this area from the various perspectives of accounting, finance, economics, psychology, sociology, political science, and other disciplines.

A recent survey sponsored by the Investor Responsibility Research Center (IRRC) Institute in conjunction with the National Association for Environmental Management (NAEM) finds the following:[56]

- Investors, companies, and regulators are increasingly interested in the various dimensions of sustainability performance and their potential impacts on firm value

- Investors often complain about difficulties in obtaining meaningful sustainability information on EESG performance

- Companies are concerned about "survey fatigue" and the potential cost of providing sustainability information

The survey also documents that:

- There is no consistency among companies in capturing, storing, and disclosing sustainability information, which is tracked at widely varying levels and amounts of detail

- There is a need for more improvements in communicating sustainability information to all stakeholders

- Sustainability reporting and assurance guidelines and practices should be advanced and promoted to create consistency of sustainability information

The 2012 survey conducted by the *MIT Sloan Management Review*-Boston Consulting Group indicates that 31% of surveyed companies report that sustainability contributes to their profits, whereas 70% consider sustainability permanently on their management agenda.[57]

According to GreenBiz and sustainability development at UPS, there are five ways to convince senior executives about the vital importance of sustainability:[58]

1. Sustainability enables cost reduction and efficiency improvement

2. Sustainability incentivizes organizations to focus on risk assessment, management, and mitigations (financial, operational, compliance, strategic, and reputation risks)

---

56   Soyka and Bateman, 2012.
57   Boston Consulting Group, 2012.
58   Kuehn, 2010.

3. Sustainability creates new competitive and revenue opportunities

4. Sustainability encourages innovation

5. Sustainability promotes talented employee recruiting development and retention

Recent studies also find a positive association between the disclosure of CSR (one dimension of business sustainability) and both cost of equity and debt capital.[59]

Other studies, using sustainability data in 58 countries, find that the mandatory adoption of sustainability reporting was associated with increased social responsibility of business leaders, improved sustainable development, employee training and corporate governance, enhanced managerial credibility and ethical practices, and reduced bribery and corruption.[60]

Another academic study investigates whether firms that disclose CSR information also produce more transparent and reliable financial information and find that socially responsible firms are less likely to engage in either AEM or REM and be the subject of SEC investigations.[61] It appears that prior research in business sustainability is fragmented with a lack of an integrated approach covering all EGSEE dimensions, with different authors addressing one or more components of business sustainability without a comprehensive framework for interdisciplinary integration.

Another study examines how business sustainability disclosures affect earnings informativeness and quality by investigating accrual quality and earnings response coefficients (ERCs) of companies that disclose sustainability information and those that do not disclose such information. We find some evidence that sustainability reporting improves both earnings informativeness and quality, and the relationship between business sustainability disclosures and earnings quality is mediated by both accrual-based (AEM) and real earnings (REM) management. They find that:

- Both cost of debt and cost of equity are lower for firms that disclose sustainability performance information

- The effect of business sustainability performance information is stronger for cost of equity than for cost of debt

59   Dhaliwal *et al.*, 2011, 2012.
60   Ioannou and Serafeim, 2011b.
61   Kim *et al.*, 2012.

- Sustainability disclosures pertaining to economic, ethics, and environment performance unambiguously lower both cost of debt and equity

- Disclosures regarding social and governance performance only lower cost of debt, not cost of equity[62]

Voluntary ESG sustainability disclosures are expected to be value-relevant to both external and internal users of such disclosures. Investors and other stakeholders, including suppliers, customers, governments, and society, can access more transparent information about environmental, social, and governance performance, which enables them to make more informed decisions. ESG sustainability disclosures can also improve internal management practices by enabling companies to establish better relationships with investors, customers, suppliers, employees, regulators, and society.

Anecdotal evidence suggests that business sustainability is paying off and that companies continue to gain from their sustainability development as profit from sustainability in 2013 is up to 37% compared with 23% in 2010.[63] Furthermore, focusing on a multiple bottom line should enable management to achieve sustainable performance, which provides more incentives for management to engage in AEM and REM that improve earnings informativeness and quality. Companies that focus on sustainable development and disclose their sustainability performance manage their long-term performance more effectively. We posit that sustainability reporting firms invest more in R&D and therefore have positive discretionary expenses. Those firms may have higher-quality products and charge more; therefore, the firms have higher future cash flows. While attention to short-term considerations and quarterly profit-making is unavoidable and in some cases even desirable, the long-term orientation of emphasizing sustainable and enduring shareholder value creation should be the main goal and benchmark of success for companies.

3.8 Conclusions

Business sustainability is an important corporate decision and its economic consequences are of considerable interest to all stakeholders including

---

62   Rezaee and Ng, 2014.
63   Kiron *et al.*, 2013a.

investors and regulators. Recent developments on sustainability mandatory or voluntary disclosures enable management to exercise judgment in
disclosing sustainability information. Anecdotal and academic evidence
presented in this chapter suggests that more mandatory or voluntary disclosures of sustainability performance information are good practices.
The move toward modernizing and integrating sustainability performance
information is the first right step in incorporating sustainability performance information into corporate reporting. The optimal level of sustainability disclosure can vary across firms and across countries as investor
protection provided by firms and country legal systems can vary. Nonfinancial ESG information may be viewed by policy-makers and regulators as
more conjectural, qualitative, and forward-looking compared with financial
information that is more factual, more quantitative, and backward-looking.

3.9 Action points

- Business organizations should increase the quality and quantity of
  all stakeholder engagements with sustainability reports

- Appropriate sustainability performance metrics are essential in
  promoting business sustainability development

- All five EGSEE dimensions of sustainability performance should be
  supported by and associated with specific key performance indicators (KPIs)

- Multiple measures of KPIs can be both financial and nonfinancial
  and collectively affect the success of sustainability performance

- Some nonfinancial sustainability performance (governance, ethics,
  social, and environmental) may appear to have no financial market
  consequences, however, it is essential to the long-term and enduring success of business organizations

- Risks and rewards of financial sustainability performance should
  be quantified and monetized

- Risks and rewards of nonfinancial sustainability performance
  should be quantified and monetized

4
Financial dimensions of sustainability performance and reporting

Previous chapters presented and synthesized the economic, governance, social, ethical, and environmental (EGSEE) dimensions of sustainability performance. Global investors demand and regulators mandate that business organizations disclose financial and nonfinancial information on their key performance indicators (KPIs) relevant to EGSEE activities. The fast-growing move toward business sustainability has created unprecedented challenges for business organizations worldwide to present reliable and useful financial and nonfinancial information on their KPIs pertaining to all five EGSEE dimensions of sustainability performance. This chapter describes in detail the financial dimension, its importance and relevance in ensuring a sustainable organization, and its value-relevant disclosures, reporting, and assurance. Nonfinancial dimensions of sustainability performance and reporting are presented in the next chapter.

4.1 Introduction

Business sustainability and sustainability performance are gaining global attention because corporations' goals have refocused from maximizing profit to creating shareholder value while protecting the interests of all stakeholders and still fulfilling their social responsibilities. In particular, economic sustainability performance (with a keen focus on long-term financial performance) is gaining more attention from investors. In the context of the agency theory, a moral hazard occurs in the presence of financial short-termism where the agent (management) acting on behalf of the principal (shareholders) has incentives to achieve short-term financial performance and knows more about its actions and/or intentions than the principal does because of a lack of proper monitoring of the agent. When the interests of the agent are not aligned with those of the principal, the agent has incentives and may not act in the best interest of long-term financial sustainability performance and/or withhold important sustainability financial information from the principal. Disclosure of economic sustainability performance information suggests that management has more incentives to focus on short-term performance than sustainable and long-term economic performance and thus fewer incentives to disclose value-relevant sustainable information, which is viewed by investors, asset managers, and equity analysts as a means of focusing on short-term performance. Short-termism is referred to as an excessive focus on a company's quarterly reported financial results rather than on sustainable, enduring and long-term economic performance. This short-termism practice undermines the sustainable economic performance of many companies by encouraging management to emphasize short-term performance of meeting analysts' quarterly earnings forecasts. This chapter examines long-term sustainable economic performance in achieving shareholder value creation.

4.2 Economic versus market value

The two measures of firm value (namely, the economic value and market value) may diverge.[1] The economic value of a business is determined by the discounted net present value of its cash flow generated by selling products or services. The market value of a business, nonetheless, is determined by the supply and demand for its stock. Theoretically, the two measures of value would be the same whereas in reality the economic value and market value can diverge. This divergence can be caused by many factors, including

---

[1]   Committee for Economic Development, 2007.

the quality and quantity of earnings and other financial and nonfinancial information disseminated to the market. Investors may trade shares based on expectations about the company's future growth and performance and to a great extent based on short-term considerations of quarterly earnings guidance that may cause changes in stock prices independent of changes in the company's true condition and long-term sustainable economic performance.

Corporate management, asset managers, equity analysts, and even share-holders are motivated and thus their behaviors are biased toward short-term performance for a variety of reasons.[2] First, management has incentives to focus on short-term considerations because their compensation is linked to the achievement of short-term financial targets and stock price movements. Second, equity analysts often value companies more when they exceed analyst forecasts, and these companies often receive better analyst coverage. Third, technological advances and resolutions have reduced the cost of trading securities, which encourages investors to trade frequently in response to additional disclosures and focus on short-term opportunities and challenges rather than long-term growth and sustainable performance. Fourth, asset managers and hedge funds are motivated to trade large blocks of equities for short-term profits. This in turn encourages management to emphasize short-term tactics at the expense of long-term, sustainable strategies. These market participants thus benefit from reported quarterly earnings guidance and often cause management to sacrifice sustainable long-term performance to boost short-term earnings. Uncertainty about the future including governmental policies, regulations, markets, and other unforeseeable factors drive managerial planning to short-term considerations rather than long-term sustainable economic performance. Fifth, executive compensation packages are often linked to the achievement of short-term financial targets. Finally, significant executive turnovers have caused shortened tenures for chief executive officers (CEOs) who are motivated to focus on short-term results.

The consequences of short-term considerations are a divergence of resources intended to contribute to sustainable economic growth and ineffective misallocation of resources in several ways including:[3]

2　Committee for Economic Development, 2007.
3　Committee for Economic Development, 2007.

- Sacrificing, delaying, or decreasing discretionary spending on long-term investments or projects to achieve short-term financial targets that meet financial market expectations

- Gearing management time and efforts toward meeting expectations of short-term results rather than focusing on activities that add sustainable value to the company

- Encouraging earnings management by either deferring costs or shifting revenues

- Tying oversized executive compensation to the achievement of short-term financial targets at the expense of sustainable economic value creation

- Higher-risk premiums resulting from frequent trading done by speculators who target short-term movement in stock prices

- Incurring expenses by mutual funds because of overactive trading caused by focus on short-term considerations

This short-termism phenomenon also affects asset managers' practices through:[4]

- Frequent trading of shares

- Shorter holding periods of asset funds

- Pressures from market traders and speculators to encourage corporate managers to produce short-term results

- Reduction of sustainable, long-term return on investments

Taken together, short-termism practices of maximizing short-term reported performance are detrimental to long-term investment, research and development, training, and other sustainable value-enhancing corporate activities.

4.3 Sustainable shareholder value creation

Sustainable shareholder value creation, the primary objective for many business organizations, can be achieved by focusing on the economic

4   Committee for Economic Development, 2007.

dimension of sustainability performance examined in detail in the next section. The focus on short-term considerations has an adverse impact on long-term and sustainable shareholder value creation and reduces the expected value of future returns and thus current share prices. Stocks can be priced lower than their potential value through overemphasizing short-term considerations and encouraging asset managers to trade more frequently, forcing long-term investors to get short-changed. This fixation on short-term considerations contributed to the financial scandals of Enron, WorldCom, and other companies. Long-term and sustainable shareholder value creation can be promoted by developing strategic plans and investments with sound, long-term objectives and linking executive compensation to long-term performance.

The short-termism behavior of many corporate managers is in contrast with the long-term view of sustainable economic performance. The main objective of any business organizations is to create shareholder value and thus maximize firm value by establishing a proper balance between financial (economic) sustainability performance and other non-financial dimensions of sustainability performance discussed in Chapter 1. The enlightened value maximization concept of sustainability performance is supported by recent anecdotal evidence which suggests that companies that "see sustainability as both a necessity and opportunity, and change their business models in response, are finding success."[5] Further sustainability information can lead to a better understanding of the link between management actions and sustainable performance and thus could possibly reduce noise in the corporate reporting process as well as short-termism attributes.

Two reports by the Aspen Institute (AI)[6] and the Committee for Economic Development (CED)[7] state that U.S. economic competitiveness is being harmed by companies focusing on short-term performance. The Aspen Institute established a set of guiding principles that encourages companies to focus on long-term shareholder value creation and increased executive compensation accountability.[8] Specifically the principles call for:

- Companies to discontinue issuing quarterly earnings guidance and not to respond to analyst estimates

---

5   Kiron *et al.*, 2013b.
6   Aspen Institute, 2007.
7   Committee for Economic Development, 2007.
8   Aspen Institute, 2007.

- Boards of directors to communicate with "long-term–oriented investors" on executive compensation
- Senior executives to hold their companies' stock for some period beyond their tenure with the company
- Senior executives to refrain from hedging the risk of stock options
- Drawbacks involving recouping senior executive compensation linked to the achievement of performance targets that subsequently vanished from corporate financial restatements.

The issue of whether quarterly reporting in general and earnings guidance in particular encourage short-termism and thus compromise financial reporting quality or improve market efficiency has recently been debated within the business community and among policy-makers, regulators, and standard-setters. While ending earnings guidance may have a short-term impact on market efficiency and thus require interim trading updates, in the long-term it will lead to substantial reduced pressures on management from the market to meet short-term targets. Quarterly earnings guidance can have four detrimental effects of:[9]

1. Encouraging short-termism
2. Adversely affecting the behavior of market participants
3. Compromising the quality of financial reporting
4. Discouraging proper CFO succession planning

4.3.1 Short-termism effects

The issuance of earnings guidance encourages management to focus on short-term performance and the goal of meeting or exceeding short-term targets or analysts' forecast estimates. Such an impact on management behavior prevents management from directing its resources toward sustainable and enduring plans, activities, and performance that create sustainable shareholder value. Discontinuation of earnings guidance, on the other hand, reduces pressures on management from the market to meet short-term targets and thus management has more incentives and opportunities to focus on sustainable economic performance. Short-term companies focus more on their quarterly reported financial results than on their

---

9   Committee for Economic Development, 2007.

sustainable, long-term shareholder value creation. Long-term companies focus on strategic objectives and sustainable value-driver factors, the risks to those factors, and dynamic responses to changes affecting the company's markets. While attention to short-term considerations and quarterly profit-making is unavoidable and in some cases even desirable, the long-term orientation of emphasizing sustainable and enduring shareholder value creation should be the main goal and benchmark of success for companies.

4.3.2 Market participant effect

Market participants always demand relevant and reliable financial and nonfinancial information. The issuance of earnings guidance and the frequency of such reporting may have adversarial effects on the behavior of market participants in terms of preventing them from seeking financial and nonfinancial information on sustainable key performance indicators (KPIs) from multiple sources.

4.3.3 Reporting quality effect

Issuance of earnings guidance in response to earnings forecast by analysts may not give management enough time to prepare, check, and use proper judgment earnings figures. Thus, inappropriate efforts in verifying earnings numbers and a lack of focus on long-term sustainable economic performance may lead to a reduction in the quality of the financial reports.

4.3.4 CFO succession planning

The long-term achievement of sustainable economic performance depends on the continuity and tenure of corporate executives. The shortened tenure of executives (particularly CEOs) encourages them to focus on short-term performance and to link their compensation to short-term results to maximize their short-tenured wealth. Short-tenured CEOs have less or no incentive to invest in sustainable long-term investments when the return on these investments will materialize after the end of a contract period of his or her likely term in office. These CEOs also attempt to maximize their short-term compensation package by accepting a contract with generous bonuses and severance agreements, which drives up executive compensation.

4.4 Economic sustainability performance

The economic performance dimension of EGSEE is the most important component of sustainability, as the primary purpose of business organizations is to maximize economic performance in creating shareholder value. This section discusses the importance of economic performance and its measurement, recognition, and reporting in the context of financial statements and its assurance through audit reports on financial statements and internal control over financial reporting (ICFR). Under the conventional reporting model, businesses have reported financial information to their shareholders on the financial bottom line. Business sustainability covers a broad range of corporate stakeholders and reflects a broader range of multiple-bottom-line performance. Economic performance is related mainly to the profitability of the company. At the same time, future growth is also classified as economic performance.

The economic performance dimension is the cornerstone of business sustainability and its disclosure is mainly the release of information related to the profitability of the company. Information released in such a category could be related to long-term corporate profitability rather than to myopically focused issues. The economic dimension of sustainability performance includes increased focus on long-term sustainability, effectiveness, efficiency, and productivity; cost savings in energy, water, and supplies; attracting new business and building greater customer loyalty and reputation; improved risk management and safety and fostering collaboration with other innovative companies.

Economic sustainability performance is typically reflected in the reported and audited financial statements in terms of earnings, return on assets, and return on equity. However, the annual reports of public companies often contain more information regarding the sustainable economic performance as follows:

- Audited financial statements, including their notes

- Management's discussion and analysis (MD&A) of financial condition and results of operations

- Management certifications of financial statements

- Management certification of the assessments of the effectiveness of internal control over financial reporting

- Audit committee report

- Independent auditor's report on financial statements
- Independent auditor's report on internal control over financial reporting
- Five-year summary of selected financial data
- Summary of selected quarterly financial data for the past two years

Traditional financial statements, providing historical financial information concerning an entity's financial condition and the results of operations as a proxy for future business performance, may not provide relevant information to investors and other stakeholders. Investors demand forward-looking financial and nonfinancial information on key performance indicators (KPIs) concerning the entity's EGSEE activities. Long-term shareholder value is often used as a proxy for long-term economic performance as measured by stock price, which reflects the cash flow generated over time and is available to shareholders, given no share repurchase or equity issuances. High-quality financial information reflecting the economic dimension of sustainability performance enables investors to better assess the risk and return associated with their investments through more accurate and complete financial information. The economic dimension of sustainability should affect cost of both debt and equity in an unambiguous way. When a company discloses more information with respect to economic sustainability, both stock and bond investors have better access to information with respect to corporate profitability. Since investors can make better investment decisions when they have more relevant information about corporate profitability, cost of debt and equity should therefore be lower.

The issue of mandatory internal control reporting for public companies has been debated during the past three decades by policy-makers, regulators, standard-setters, and the business community and accounting profession. Legislators, regulators, and the accounting profession traditionally have advocated for the establishment and maintenance of internal control systems by public companies and reporting on internal control systems by managers and auditors. The passage of SOX and the Dodd-Frank Act of 2010 requires management to step up efforts in achieving sustainable shareholder value creation and enhancement, improving the reliability of financial reports through executive certification of internal controls, and improving financial statements.

Section 301 requires that the audit committee oversee the work of management and the independent auditor as related to ICFR. The audit committee's oversight of Section 404 is essential, as mandatory ICFR is becoming an integral part of financial reporting. Section 404 requires that management state its responsibility for designing and maintaining effective ICFR and its assessment of the effectiveness of such controls as of the end of the company's most recent fiscal year. Executive certification of ICFR requires management to document the effectiveness of internal controls through testing-related control activities and to specify inherent limitations. This suggests that when internal controls are effective, there is only a remote possibility that material misstatements will not be prevented, detected, or corrected on a timely basis. Any detected material weaknesses in internal control (or deficiencies that, taken together, result in a material weakness) must be disclosed in management's report along with actions taken to correct those material weaknesses.

Section 404 of SOX requires that the independent auditor attest to and report on management's assessment of the company's ICFR and directs the PCAOB to issue guidance on the auditor report on internal control. This guidance is contained in PCAOB Auditing Standard (AS) No. 2, *An Audit of Internal Control over Financial Reporting Performed in Conjunction with an Audit of Financial Statements.*[10] Based on AS No. 2, in expressing an opinion on ICFR, the independent auditor must perform tests of controls to evaluate:

- Management's assessment of the effectiveness of ICFR by gathering sufficient competent evidence about both the process used and the conclusion reached by management
- The effectiveness of both the design and operation of ICFR.

Any deficiencies found in ICFR must be evaluated in terms of their possible effects on misstatements of an account balance or disclosure. PCAOB AS No. 2 is superseded by AS No. 5, which makes the audit of ICFR more effective and efficient. PCAOB AS No.5 requires auditors to use a risk-based approach in the audit of ICFR.

The independent auditor's report on ICFR can either be issued separately or be combined with an opinion on the financial statements. The auditor should also render an opinion on the effectiveness of ICFR. The three possible types of audit opinion on internal control are:

10   Public Company Accounting Oversight Board, 2004.

1. An unqualified opinion when there is no material weakness in internal control

2. An adverse opinion when there is at least one material weakness or when there are deficiencies in the internal control system that together can result in a material weakness

3. A disclaimer of opinion when the auditor cannot express an opinion due to scope limitation

There are some circumstances where management may conclude that the company's ICFR is ineffective, so the auditor may issue an unqualified opinion on management's assessment, but render an adverse opinion on the effectiveness of ICFR. There may also be situations where management reports that the company's internal control is effective, but the independent auditor discovers material weaknesses and issues an adverse opinion on the effectiveness of the company's ICFR.

Integrated internal control and financial reporting is financial information contained in published financial statements and reports on internal control over financial reporting (ICFR). Reporting of financial statements and ICFR is vital as it assists shareholders in making appropriate investment and voting decisions, enables them to exercise their ownership rights on an informed basis, and protects them from receiving misleading financial information. Public companies in the U.S.A. are required to publish audited annual financial statements along with reviewed quarterly financial reports. These two disclosure requirements, collectively referred to as IFICR, are intended to facilitate companies' attracting investors, strengthen their competitive edge, and maintain confidence in capital markets.

In preparing mandatory financial statements that reflect the economic dimension of sustainability performance, business organizations have to comply with regulatory reforms. Regulatory reforms require compliance with applicable laws, rules, standards, and specifications that govern financial reporting. Regulations vary significantly throughout the world with an emerging trend toward a demand by global investors for more transparent and reliable financial reports. Executives of global companies are being held more accountable for the effectiveness of internal controls and the integrity of financial statements through regulations such as SOX (e.g., executive certifications) and the European Union's Company Law Directives. Directors, particularly audit committees, are being held more responsible for overseeing their companies' internal controls, financial reporting, risk management, and audit activities. Global investors are provided with integrated financial and internal control reports (IFICR) from management and independent auditors on ICFR and financial statements. These integrated reports should be useful to investors because effective ICFR is vital in preventing and detecting financial misstatements, including fraud.

4.5 Integrated financial and internal control reporting

Integrated financial and internal control reporting (IFICR), as defined in this section, includes:

- Management reporting on and certification of financial statements

- Management reporting on and certification of ICFR

- The independent auditor's opinion on fair and true presentation of financial statements

- Independent auditor opinion on the effectiveness of ICFR

- The audit committee's review of audited financial statements and both management and auditor reports on ICFR

The effectiveness of IFICR depends on a vigilant oversight function by the board of directors (particularly the audit committee), a responsible and accountable managerial function by senior executives, a credible external audit function by the independent auditor, and an objective internal audit function by internal auditors. IFICR adds value by lending credibility to both financial statements and internal controls, which promotes investor confidence and reinforces public trust in public financial information. IFICR reports are expected to reduce the information risks of financial information being misleading, biased, incomplete, inaccurate, or fraudulent. In this context, audits reduce financial information asymmetries between management and shareholders and thus help investors make more informed decisions that in turn make the capital markets more efficient and add to the nation's economic prosperity. The need for IFICR can be attributed to the principal–agent conflict suggested in agency theory where principals (owners) lack reasons to trust their agents (management) primarily because of differing motives and information asymmetries.

4.5.1 Internal control reporting

Legislators, regulators, and the accounting profession have traditionally addressed the establishment and maintenance of internal control systems by public companies, management, and auditors' public reports on internal control systems. The SEC has long been an advocate of internal control reporting but stopped short of making it a requirement for public companies.[11] The SEC:

- Initially in its Release No. 13185, in January 1977, proposed a requirement that management maintain an effective internal control system and expressed interest in mandatory internal control reporting to shareholders

- Advised public companies in February 1978 to make necessary changes in their internal controls and business practices to comply with provisions of the Foreign Corrupt Practices Act (FCPA of 1977) in its Accounting Series Release No. 242[12]

- Proposed rules in April 1979 that would have required SEC registrants to issue a management report and auditor opinion on internal accounting controls, and subsequently in June 1980 withdrew these proposed rules[13]

The American Institute of Certified Public Accountants:

- In its 1978 report to the Commission on Auditor's Responsibilities, recommended auditors report material weakness in internal controls to management or the audit committee as well as management's response to auditors' suggestions for correction of weaknesses

- Issued the Statement on Auditing Standards (SAS) No. 20 in 1977 that required communication of material weaknesses in internal accounting controls to management

- Issued an exposure draft in December 1979 that provided guidance on auditors reports on internal accounting controls based on the review of internal controls

---

11   Securities and Exchange Commission, 1977.
12   Securities and Exchange Commission, 1978.
13   Securities and Exchange Commission, 1979.

- Issued SAS No. 55 in April 1988 and subsequently SAS No. 78, in 1995, which provides guidance for auditors in evaluating the internal control structure as part of the audit of financial statements[14]

The Committee of Sponsoring Organizations of Treadway (COSO) in its first report in 1987 underscored the importance of internal controls in preventing and detecting fraudulent financial activities. The COSO, in its second report in 1992, titled "Internal Control: Integrated Framework," recommended voluntary internal control reporting by both management and independent auditors of public companies.[15] The COSO provided detailed guidance as to what should be the content of internal control reporting including the nature, objectives, components, the role of management, the audit committee, the independent auditor, and the limitation of internal controls. In 2013 the COSO updated its framework on internal control reporting to make more relevant for companies to report on their ICFR and more useful to investors to obtain more information on the integrity and reliability of both internal controls and financial reporting systems. The Framework is very strong on design, analysis, assessments, and reporting. The increased focus on operations, compliance, and nonfinancial reporting objectives is also a major improvement.

Section 404 SOX is intended to improve the effectiveness of design and operation of internal control over financial reporting and compliance with Section 404 is now required for a majority of public companies (accelerated filers) for fiscal years ending on or after November 15, 2004.[16] Section 404 requires that management state its responsibility for designing and maintaining adequate internal controls over financial reporting and its assessment of the effectiveness of such controls as of the end of the company's most recent fiscal year. Executive certification of internal control over financial reporting requires management to document the adequacy and effectiveness of the internal control through testing-related control activities and specify inherent limitations. This suggests that when internal controls are effective, there is only a remote possibility that material misstatements will not be prevented, detected, and corrected on a timely basis. Any detected material weakness in internal controls must be disclosed in the management report, along with actions taken to correct those significant deficiencies and material weaknesses.

---

14   American Institute of Certified Public Accountants, 1977, 1979.
15   Committee of Sponsoring Organizations of the Treadway Commission, 1992.
16   Sarbanes-Oxley Act, 2002.

Section 404 of the Act requires the independent auditor to attest to and report on management's assessment of the company's internal control over financial reporting and directs the PCAOB to issue guidance on the auditor report on internal control. The PCAOB issued its Auditing Standard (AS) No. 2, *An Audit of Internal Control over Financial Reporting Performance in Conjunctions with an Audit of Financial Statements.*[17] PCAOB AS No. 2 establishes guidance for the audit of internal control over financial reporting. In expressing an opinion on internal control over financial reporting, the independent auditor must perform tests of controls to evaluate:

- Management's assessment of the effectiveness of internal control over financial reporting by gathering sufficient competent evidence about both the process used and the conclusion reached by management
- The effectiveness of both the design and operation of internal control over financial reporting

Any deficiencies found in internal control over financial reporting must be evaluated in terms of their possible effects on misstatements of an account balance or disclosure. The PCAOB in 2007 revised and superseded AS No.2 by issuing AS No.5 by making internal control reporting and auditing more cost-effective, efficient, and scalable.[18] PCAOB AS No. 5 is intended to improve the audit by:

- Focusing the audit on the matters most important to internal control
- Eliminating unnecessary audit procedures
- Simplifying the auditor requirements
- Scaling the integrated audit for smaller companies

The independent auditor should issue an opinion on management's assessment of internal control over financial reporting either as a separate report or as a combined report with an opinion on the financial statements. The three possible types of audit opinion on internal control are:

1. Unqualified opinion when there is no material weakness in internal controls

17   Public Company Accounting Oversight Board, 2004.
18   Public Company Accounting Oversight Board, 2007.

2. Adverse opinion when significant deficiencies in internal controls can result in one or more material weaknesses

3. Disclaimer of opinion when the auditor cannot express an opinion due to scope and limitation

PCAOB AS No. 2 mentions some circumstances where management may conclude that the company's internal control over financial reporting is ineffective, and if the auditor concurs with management's assessment, may issue an unqualified opinion on management's assessment and render an adverse opinion on the effectiveness of internal control over financial reporting. There may be situations where management reports that the company's internal controls are effective, but the independent auditor discovers material weaknesses that were not corrected and they issue an adverse opinion on the effectiveness of the company's internal control over financial reporting.

Management certifications of financial statements and ICFR of public companies in the U.S.A., in compliance with Sections 302 and 404 of SOX, can contribute to sustainable financial reporting and internal control reporting in the following ways:

- Creation of a more engaged control environment resulting from active participation and commitment by the board of directors, the audit committee, and management

- Recognition of continuous monitoring as an integral component of the control process with more thoughtful analysis of monitoring controls

- More structure for the year-end closing process and recording of journal entries

- Implementation of antifraud programs and activities to prevent, detect, and correct errors, irregularities, and fraud, including responsibility for follow up to resolve the issues

- Better understanding of risks associated with electronics processing and related computer controls and the need to improve both controls and audit procedures to provide assurance that risks associated with the electronic reporting process and information technology (IT) are properly managed

- Documentation of controls and control process that can serve as a basis for continuous monitoring, training, and best practice guidance

- Improvements in the concept and definition of internal controls and their relation to the organization with risk management

- Better understanding of the internal controls concept throughout the organization at every operational level and reporting unit

- Improvements in the sufficiency and competence of the audit trail as a basis to support operations and the assessment of the effectiveness of ICFR

- Implementation of fundamental controls including segregation of duties, authorization processes, and periodic reconciliation of accounts

- Production of more reliable, credible, and transparent financial reports

- Public report on the soundness of accounting and internal control systems in reflecting economic sustainability performance

4.6 Management role in financial sustainability performance reporting

Preparation and dissemination of reliable, useful, and relevant financial information on the economic dimension of sustainability performance is a key responsibility of management. In addition, the ability to effectively manage the company's business in creating sustainable value requires access to timely, accurate, and transparent information. All stakeholders, particularly shareholders, must be able to place confidence in corporate reports including financial statements if the company wants to be sustainable in the long-term. Management's ability to fulfill its financial and internal control reporting responsibilities in compliance with the provisions of SOX depends in part on the design and effectiveness of the accounting and internal control processes. Sound accounting systems, in compliance with a set of globally accepted accounting standards and effective internal control processes, enable management to prepare timely and reliable financial reports that properly reflect economic sustainability performance in creating shareholder value. While no accounting and internal control systems can absolutely assure that financial reports will never contain material errors or misstatements, it is management's responsibility to assess, manage, and effectively reduce the risk of material misstatements in financial reports. Management can substantially reduce the risk of material misstatements, whether caused by errors or fraud, by effectively implementing the following risk assessment and management processes:

- **Identifying risks.** Management must identify financial reporting areas that are both material and pose a risk to the quality and reliability of financial statements.

- **Assessing risks.** Management must assess whether the identified risks pose a "reasonable possibility" that a material misstatement in the financial statements would not be prevented or detected.

- **Designing adequate controls.** Management must evaluate the adequacy of the existing controls and design appropriate controls to address the identified risks.

- **Evaluating operating effectiveness.** Management should decide which controls need periodic evaluation and which controls warrant continuous and routine evaluation.

- **Assessing control deficiencies.** Management must identify and assess control deficiencies that may trigger financial misstatements.

- **Designing and maintain control activities.** Management must design, implement, and maintain effective control activities to minimize the effects of control deficiencies.

- **Documenting management assessment.** Management assessment of the effectiveness of ICFR should be supported by documented evidence that provides "reasonable support" for its assessment.

- **Reporting significant deficiencies.** Management must report significant deficiencies in the design and operation of ICFR to the audit committee and the external auditor for them to carry out their respective oversight and monitoring responsibilities pertaining to financial reporting.

- **Obtaining audit report on ICFR.** Management must co-operate with auditors in obtaining an audit report on ICFR.

- **Management reporting on ICFR.** Management should evaluate the identified deficiencies in ICFR by using both qualitative and quantitative factors to determine whether these deficiencies are material weaknesses.

- **Remediation actions and plans.** As part of managing internal control reporting, management should disclose actions already taken to remediate the identified internal control material weaknesses.

- **Monitoring ICFR.** Management should utilize the *Guidance on Monitoring Internal Control Systems* released by the COSO intended to assist organizations monitoring the quality of their internal control systems.

Management may have incentives to mislead investors, and when opportunities are provided, they may attempt to manipulate financial information. Thus, there is a need for external verification and mechanisms to align the interests of agents with those of principals and to reduce the likelihood of opportunistic behavior and information asymmetries. There are a variety of mechanisms, including a vigilant board of directors, effective corporate governance, and external audits that may be used to align the interests of agents and principals and reduce divergent motivations and information asymmetries. The existence and persistence of information asymmetry can cause a moral hazard when shareholders take more risk from misstated financial information about long-term and sustainable economic performance. The moral hazard can occur when management has more information about sustainable economic performance and intentionally or unintentionally withholds such information from shareholders who bear the risk of unsustainable economic performance. As the agent of investors, management has more information about economic sustainability performance and may act inappropriately in withholding such information to investors if the principal (investors) fails to monitor the agent or if the interests of the agent are not aligned with those of the principal. This monitoring process is discussed in the next section of corporate governance. Executives (CEOs, CFOs) play an important role in influencing the quality of financial reports in many ways: first, executives must certify completeness and accuracy of financial statements in compliance with Sections 302 and 906 of SOX. Second, executives must certify and report on the effectiveness of internal control over financial reporting according to Section 404 of SOX. Third, executives also contribute to the "tone at the top" of achieving sustainable shareholder value creation. Management's roles in IFICR are:

- Designing and implementing appropriate disclosure controls and procedures to ensure reliable financial information is being disclosed

- Designing and maintaining adequate and effective internal control over financial reporting (ICFR) to ensure reliability of financial reports and fair presentation of financial statements in conformity with generally accepted accounting principles (GAAP)

- Evaluating the effectiveness of the company's disclosure controls and procedures and disclosing its conclusions as of the end of the reporting period

- Evaluating the effectiveness of ICFR as of the end of the reporting period and disclosing internal control significant deficiencies to the company's audit committee and independent auditor, and material weaknesses to shareholders

- Designing and maintaining an appropriate accounting system to ensure production of accurate and complete financial information

- Preparing and certifying financial statements that reflect fair presentation of the financial position and results of operation in conformity with GAAP

Management, in effectively fulfilling its financial sustainability performance responsibility, prepares and disseminates the following key performance indicators to all stakeholders:

- Price/earnings ratio

- Market value of future products

- Pro forma operative earning budget forecast

- Growth in sales/revenue/dividend/earnings

- Earnings forecast

- Decline in sales/revenue/dividend/earnings

- Cash flow forecast

- Interest rate sensitivity and analysis

- Structural/liquidity ratios

- Profitability ratios (reported earnings, return on assets, return on equity)
- Revenue for geographic unit
- Sales, volume for geographic unit
- Growth of certified partner
- Revenue for business unit (BU)
- Distribution by volume/sales
- Operating income
- Internal control effectiveness
- Risk assessment and management
- Segment performance information
- Financial reporting and internal control compliance (certifications under SOX)
- Compliance with accounting standards
- Average customer profile
- Delivery time
- Telephone waiting time
- Numbers of claims
- Mobility trends
- Compensation plans description investment in partnerships
- Nonfinancial incentives description
- Financial incentives description

4.7 Value relevance of economic sustainability performance and disclosures

As the number of public companies reporting their sustainability performance grows worldwide, the value relevance of sustainability performance disclosures has been addressed by regulators, investors, and the business community. In recent years, there has been an increased focus on sustainability performance disclosures, and researchers have used sustainability performance interchangeably with corporate social responsibility (CSR). Theoretically, management engagement in sustainability activities, performance, and disclosures can be viewed as value-increasing or value-decreasing for investors. On one hand, companies that effectively manage their business sustainability improve CSR performance, enhance their reputation, fulfill their social responsibility, and promote a corporate culture of integrity and competence. On the other hand, companies can only survive and generate sustainable performance when they continue to be profitable and are able to create shareholder value. However, financial and nonfinancial sustainability performance disclosures supplement each other and are not mutually exclusive. Companies that are governed effectively, are socially and environmentally responsible, and conduct themselves ethically are expected to produce sustainable financial performance, create shareholder value, and gain investor confidence and public trust. In this context, sustainability focuses on business activities that generate long-term financial performance of firm value maximization as well as voluntary activities that result in the achievement of nonfinancial sustainability performance (CSR) that concerns all stakeholders.

Although the conventional measures of cash flows, earnings, and return on investment are essential in evaluating financial performance, they don't reflect sustainable performance and future growth. Thus, key measures of sustainable performance such as operational efficiency, customer satisfaction, talent management, and innovation should be derived from internal factors of strategy, risk profile, strengths and weaknesses, and corporate culture as well as external factors of reputation, technology, completion, globalization, and utilization of natural resources. The use of these measures enables companies to create sustainable value for shareholders while protecting interests of other stakeholders such as creditors, employees, customers, suppliers, government, and society.

The value relevance of voluntary sustainability disclosures is determined by the firm-specific costs and benefits of providing such disclosures on the firm value. The firm value is expected to increase where the firm-specific benefits of sustainability disclosures exceed the costs of providing such disclosures. Market-wide effects of firm sustainability disclosures are important if net benefits at firm level affect the entire market or the net benefit is ignored or not fully internalized by firms. Market-wide effects of voluntary sustainability disclosures can be measured in terms of impacts on firm valuation. This suggests that investors are willing to pay premium for firms that engage in sustainability activities by assigning higher valuation to these firms in the financial markets.

In accordance with the agency theory, there is an inherent information imbalance (III), better known as asymmetric information risk (AIR), between management, investors, and their representative board of directors, which is a critical governance and accountability reporting challenge for many public companies and their stakeholders.[19] To mitigate the AIR, the board of directors and investors should receive transparent and relevant information on both financial and nonfinancial KPIs of dimensions of sustainability performance.

There are two costs associated with disclosure of sustainability information. First, the direct cost of producing sustainability reports and obtaining assurance on such reports. The second cost is the opportunity cost of managerial time and efforts spent organizing sustainability disclosures. Third, there are proprietary costs of voluntary disclosures if the firm reveals valuable information such as trade secrets, information about profitable customers and markets, or the exposure of operating, organization, or reporting weakness to unions, regulators, investors, customers, suppliers, or competitors.[20] Finally, the likelihood of litigation can increase when firms disclose voluntary information.

4.8 Conclusions

The economic dimension of sustainability performance is the most important dimension of sustainability performance. Business organizations must be economically and financially sustainable in creating shareholder value in order to survive and achieve other dimensions of sustainability performance, including social and environmental. Management's financial and internal control reporting systems must be robust, effective, and reliable in producing and disseminating high-quality financial information that properly reflects economic sustainability performance. The effectiveness of financial and internal controls systems requires management to identify significant risks that may cause material misstatements and design control activities to minimize the negative impacts. Management is primarily

---

19   KPMG, 2013a.
20   Leuz, 2004.

responsible for the achievement of sustainable economic performance and effective reporting of such performance to all stakeholders, particularly investors.

4.9 Action points

- Economic sustainability performance has and will continue to be the most vital component of business sustainability performance, as business organizations have to be financially stable before doing any good for the environment and society.

- Improving sustainability performance starts with a tone at the top commitment to effective sustainability performance, reporting, and assurance.

- Directors and executives should establish sustainability develop-ment systems and processes to promote achievement of all five EGSEE dimensions of sustainability in creating sustainable value for all stakeholders.

5
Nonfinancial dimensions of sustainability performance and reporting

Financial dimensions of sustainability performance and reporting were discussed in Chapter 4. This chapter presents nonfinancial dimensions of sustainability performance and reporting including governance, social, ethical, and environmental (GSEE). Regulators, investors, and business organizations worldwide are now interested in more information about GSEE. Socially responsible funds are approaching $4 trillion USD, and soon European corporations will be required to disclose GSEE sustainability performance information.

5.1 Introduction

There has been growing international interest in business sustainability, including corporate social responsibilities (CSR), environmental, ethical, and governance issues. Particularly, the CSR program is designed to minimize conflicts between corporations and society caused by differences between private and social costs and benefits and to align corporate goals with those of society. CSR requires business organizations to take the initiative to advance some social good beyond their own interests and compliance with applicable regulations. The true measure of success for corporations should be determined not only by reported earnings, but also by their governance, social responsibility, ethical behavior, and environmental (GSEE) initiatives. Business sustainability has received considerable attention from policy-makers, regulators, and the business and investment community for the past decade, and is expected to remain an important theme worldwide for decades to come. Consideration of nonfinancial GSEE sustainability activities can create both synergies and conflicts. These nonfinancial GSEE sustainability activities and performance can enhance the long-term value of the firm by fulfilling the firms' social responsibilities, meeting their environmental obligations, creating ethical workplaces, and improving their reputation. However, these sustainability activities may require considerable resource allocation that could conflict with shareholder wealth maximization objectives and encourage management to solely invest in sustainability initiatives that would result in long-term financial sustainability. This chapter describes in detail nonfinancial GSEE dimensions of sustainability performance, even though the synopsis of these dimensions was presented in Chapter 1.

5.2 Governance dimension of sustainability performance

Corporate governance has evolved as a central issue for regulators and public companies in the wake of the 2007–2009 global financial crisis. Companies have recently undergone a series of corporate governance reforms aimed at improving the effectiveness of their governance, internal controls, and financial reports. Effective corporate governance promotes accountability, improves the reliability and quality of financial information, and prevents financial statement fraud. Poor corporate governance adversely affects the company's potential, performance, financial reports, and accountability, and can pave the way for business failure and financial statement fraud. Corporate governance measures of the oversight function assumed by the board of directors, managerial function delegated to management, internal audit function conducted by internal auditors, external audit function performed by external auditors, and compliance function enforced by policy-makers, regulators, and standard-setters are vital to the quality of financial information. Corporate reputation, customer satisfaction, ethical workplaces, corporate social responsibility, and environmental initiatives are nonfinancial drivers of sustainable economic performance and long-term growth that are addressed in this and the following sections under the nonfinancial dimensions of sustainability performance. Business sustainability requires that the company be managed effectively through robust corporate governance mechanisms. Globalization and technological advances have promoted global convergence in corporate governance. The move toward convergence in corporate governance has become substantially more prevalent in the aftermath of the 2007–2009 global financial crisis. Corporate governance participants must structure the process to ensure the goals of both shareholder value creation and stakeholder value protection for public companies. The corporate governance structure is shaped by internal and external governance mechanisms, as well as policy interventions through regulations. Corporate governance mechanisms are viewed as a nexus of contracts designed to align the interests of management with those of the shareholders. The effectiveness of both internal and external corporate governance mechanisms depends on the cost–benefit trade-offs among these mechanisms and is related to their availability, the extent to which they are being used, whether their marginal benefits exceed their marginal costs, and the company's corporate governance structure. Several corporate governance reforms (e.g., Sarbanes-Oxley Act of 2002, Dodd-Frank Act of 2010) have changed the relationship between shareholders, management, and boards in the U.S.A. by creating an appropriate "balance of authority" exercised by boards, management, and shareholders in the corporate decision-making process and governance. Directors are now accountable to a wide range of stakeholders, including shareholders, creditors, employees, customers, suppliers, government, and communities in which the corporation operates.

There are several federal laws that affect corporate governance, with the most recent laws being the Sarbanes-Oxley Act of 2002[1] and the Dodd-Frank Act of 2010.[2] The primary purposes of both laws are to restore investor confidence and public trust in public financial information and the financial markets and to protect investors and consumers. Both Acts were passed by the U.S. Congress in response to the wave of financial scandals, irregularities, fraud, bad practices, and crises. Provisions of both Acts address different aspects of public companies, their governance, financial reports, and related financial markets, from consumer credit to investor protection

1   Sarbanes-Oxley Act, 2002.
2   Dodd-Frank Act, 2010.

and mandatory corporate governance practices to corporate governance education.

The primary role of corporate governance is to ensure that managers act in the best interest of the company and its stakeholders, not to themselves or to the majority shareholders. Good corporate governance ensures accountability of the board and management to stakeholders including shareholders. Strengthened accountability promotes transparency, which should lead to an increase in capital inflows from domestic and foreign investors and thus the potential for lower cost of capital. Governance performance measures establish policies and practices that address the conflict of interests between shareholders and managers. The strength of governance measures includes:

- Executive compensation linked to performance

- Ownership strength

- Transparency

Concerns of governance are:

- High compensation

- Ownership concern

- CEO duality

As the representative of shareholders, the board of directors plays an important role in corporate governance by overseeing managerial strategies, decisions, and actions. The board of directors is elected by shareholders and is responsible for hiring, compensating, overseeing, and firing executives who are appointed to manage the business organization for the benefit of shareholders. The board of directors should act in the best interest of the company and its stakeholders on an informed basis, with good faith and due diligence and care. The board is primarily responsible for protecting the interests of all stakeholders, particularly shareholders, in generating sustainable value. The board usually fulfills its responsibility through the effective work of board committees. Board committees normally function independently from each other, are provided with sufficient resources and authority, and are evaluated by the board of directors. The establishment of board committees can bring more focus to the board's oversight function by giving proper authority and responsibilities and by demanding accountability for these committees. Listing standards of national stock exchanges require that listed companies form at least three board committees that must include audit, compensation, and nominating committees. In addition to these three mandatory committees, public companies often have governance and other committees such as finance, IT, and disclosure.

Directors are normally classified as executive directors (inside directors), non-executive directors (outside directors), and independent non-executive directors (independent directors). One important issue relevant to the structure, leadership, and effectiveness of the board of directors has been whether or not the position of the board chairperson should be separated from that of the CEO. The global 2007–2009 financial crisis encouraged policy-makers, regulators, and the investing community to readdress the CEO's duality as part of board leadership and an independent structure. Corporate governance best practices in Europe support the separation of the chairperson and CEO roles (CEO duality).[3] The Dodd-Frank Act of 2010 and related SEC rules require listed companies to disclose their board leadership structure and explain why they have determined that such a leadership structure is appropriate, given their specific circumstances or characteristics.[4] The board of directors should meet regularly, at least on a monthly basis, to fulfill its oversight responsibilities, and thus directors should devote adequate time and efforts to board meeting attendance and preparation.

5.3 Audit committee

The audit committee is responsible for overseeing internal controls, financial statements, risk assessment, and external and internal auditor's activities. The effectiveness of the audit committee depends on its independence, financial expertise, qualifications, and resources. The audit committee should be composed of at least three independent directors with at least one financial expert member and have adequate resources for funding the independent auditor and any outside advisors engaged by the audit committee. The extended oversight responsibilities for the audit committee are:

- Appointment, compensation, and retention of registered public accounting firms
- Preapproval of audit services and permissible non-audit services

3   Financial Reporting Council, 2014.
4   Dodd-Frank Act, 2010.

- Review of the independent auditor's plan for an integrated audit of both internal control over financial reporting (ICFR) and annual financial statements

- Review audited annual financial statements and reviewed quarterly financial reports by the independent auditor

- Monitoring the auditor's independence

- Auditor rotation requirement

- Audit committee members to be independent

- Audit committee members to select and oversee the issuer's independent account

- Procedural process for handling complaints regarding the issuer's accounting practice

- The authority of the audit committee to engage advisors

The Global Auditor Investor Dialogue has made several suggestions for more transparent information flows to the audit committee. The effectiveness of the audit committee depends on the quality, timeliness, and reliability of information it receives from management, internal auditors, legal counsel, and external auditors regarding financial, internal control, risk, legal, and auditing issues. The Global Auditor Investor Dialogue suggests the following guidelines for more effective communication with the audit committee:[5]

- The audit committee should identify its information needs and verify the information received to ensure its reliability, completeness, and timeliness in making appropriate decisions

- The audit committee should receive adequate information about internal control and risk assessments to satisfy itself that internal control and risk assessment are sufficient and effective

5   Global Auditor Investor Dialogue, 2009.

5.4 Compensation committee

The compensation committee has the responsibility for evaluating executive and director performance and establishing top-management compensation and benefit programs. The purposes of the Compensation Committee[6] are to:

- Determine and approve the compensation of the Company's chief executive officer (the "CEO") and other executive officers

- Approve, or recommend to the Board that it approves, the Company's incentive compensation and equity-based plans

- Assist the Board in its oversight of the development, implementation, and effectiveness of the Company's policies and strategies relating to its human capital management function, including, but not limited to, those policies and strategies regarding recruiting, retention, career development and progression, management succession (other than that within the purview of the Corporate Governance and Nominating Committee), diversity, and employment practices

- Prepare any report on executive compensation required by the rules and regulations of the Securities and Exchange Commission (SEC)

The compensation committee is usually formed to determine the compensation and benefits of directors and executives. The committee should be composed of all independent directors, and they should rotate periodically. The committee is directly responsible for ensuring that all aspects of executive compensation are fully and fairly disclosed in the annual proxy statement.

Section 953(b) of the Dodd-Frank Wall Street Reform and Consumer Protection Act of 2010 mandates the reporting of the CEO-to-Employee Pay Ratio for publicly traded companies in disclosing the median of the annual total compensation of all employees (except the CEO) and the ratio of CEO compensation to median employee compensation.[7] This reporting requirement is intended to assist investors better understand the link between CEO compensation and the company's performance as well as compensation of other employees. The transparent CEO-to-Employee Pay Ratio enables the

---

6   Shearman & Sterling LLP, 2011.
7   Dodd-Frank Act, 2010.

board of directors, particularly the compensation committee, to be better informed in overseeing and approving the CEO compensation scheme that would encourage the CEO not to take excessive risks at the expense of shareholders.

5.5 Nominating committee

The primary responsibility of the nominating committee is to nominate directors who will fit in well in the boardroom, can fairly represent shareholders, and can effectively work with management. The nominating committee is usually responsible for identifying, evaluating, and nominating new directors for the board, renominating existing directors, and facilitating the election of new directors by shareholders. Ever-increasing corporate governance reforms, including the Sarbanes-Oxley Act of 2002, the Dodd-Frank Act of 2010, related SEC rules, and listing standards require the nominating committee to be composed of at least three independent directors. The independence of the nominating committee has reshaped the balance of power between the board and management (CEO), who traditionally had driven the nominating process at many public companies. The recent move toward the practice of the majority voting system in the election of directors enables the nominating committee to give more of a voice to shareholders.

In the post-2007 global financial crisis era, the board of directors' accountability and responsibility has become the central stage of corporate governance. An important issue relevant to board accountability is the method of electing the most competent and ethical directors. The prevailing and accepted regulatory method of director election in the U.S.A. has been the "plurality method." Under a plurality voting standard, the nominated director with the most votes "for" is elected, which means that a candidate can be elected as long as she/he receives one vote "for," irrespective of the number of votes "withheld," as shareholders cannot vote "against" a director nominee, they can only vote "for" or "withhold" support. Best practices of corporate governance in Europe advocate a "majority" voting standard in which a director would not be elected unless the majority of votes (above 50%) were cast in her/his favor. The use of a majority voting standard in bringing more democracy and accountability to the board has been considered and addressed by policy-makers, regulators, and the business community in the U.S.A. However, the Dodd-Frank Act of 2010 did not require the majority voting standard for director elections, which is inconsistent with the best practices of corporate governance adopted in European countries.

5.6 Executive compensation

Executive compensation decisions have received considerable attention in the aftermath of the 2007–2009 financial crisis. Executive compensation is defined as the total compensation, including salary, bonuses, the value of stock options, restricted stock, long-term incentive pay, and other compensation paid to CEOs and other top executives. Senior executives are typically paid a salary, an annual bonus, and long-term incentive compensation. Executive compensation decisions have received considerable attention post-Enron, other financial scandals, the recent financial crisis, and regulatory responses. Reported financial scandals and crises have raised serious concerns regarding the reasonableness and effectiveness of executive compensation in motivating management to create sustainable performance. The important issue of how executives should be compensated in order to align their interests with those of investors and to provide incentives for them to create shareholder value while refraining from taking excessive risks has been debated by policy-makers, regulators, and the business community.

Several provisions of SOX directly or indirectly affect executive compensation packages. These provisions are:[8]

- The prohibition of personal loans to directors and executives (Section 404)
- Reporting insider trading (Section 403)
- Insider trading during pension fund blackout periods
- The forfeiture of certain bonuses and profits

SOX is also intended to make directors and executives more vigilant and diligent, which may increase executives' liability (e.g., executive certification of financial statements and internal controls). Any increase in executives' liabilities should affect their compensation as well.

8 Sarbanes-Oxley Act, 2002.

In December 2009, the SEC amended Items 401, 402, and 407 of Regulation S-K to elicit enhanced disclosures regarding risk, compensation, and corporate governance matters. In particular, the new rules require disclosure about:

- The relationship of a company's compensation policies and practices to risk management

- The backgrounds and qualifications of directors and director-nominees

- How the board (or its nominating committee) considers diversity when identifying director candidates

- Board leadership structure (e.g., one person serving as both the chair of the board and the CEO vs. split roles)

- The board's role in risk oversight

- Revised reporting of stock and option awards to company executives and directors in the summary compensation table

- Potential conflicts of interests of compensation consultants

The Dodd-Frank Act is intended to improve corporate governance effectiveness and disclosures in many areas, including nonbinding or advisory shareholder votes on "say on pay" and "say on golden parachutes" that give payments to executives associated with mergers and acquisitions and major asset transactions. Dodd-Frank requires that at least once every three years shareholders vote on the executives' compensation and that at least once every six years a proxy firm or shareholders meet to discuss whether shareholder voting should occur every one, two, or three years.

According to the provisions of Dodd-Frank Act, say-on-pay means a nonbinding vote by shareholders of a publicly traded company for approval or disapproval of the executive compensation program at that company. Nonetheless, any negative say-on-pay vote should not be automatically interpreted as evidence of failure by the company' directors and officers to fulfill their fiduciary duties. Companies also are required to disclose:[9]

- The relationship between senior executives' compensation and the company's financial performance in terms of graphs and charts

---

9   Dodd-Frank Act, 2010.

- The ratio of CEO compensation and the median total compensation to employees, excluding CEO compensation

- Whether employees or directors are allowed to hedge against a decrease in value of options included in their compensation scheme.

The Dodd-Frank Act requires that all U.S. public companies incorporate so-called claw-back provisions into incentive compensation arrangements for executive officers. It expanded the provisions of SOX on claw-back practices by requiring companies to implement and report on their policies and practices for recouping payments to current and former executives when published financial statements are subsequently restated (restatements of financial statements) caused by material non-compliance with financial reporting standards. The recouped pay is the extra amount paid based on misstated financial statements and is recoverable for three years preceding the restatement date. The Dodd-Frank Act requires national securities exchanges and associations to revise their listing standards to prohibit listings for any company that does not implement a claw-back policy.

The federal securities laws require clear, concise, and understandable disclosure about compensation paid to CEOs, CFOs, and certainly other high-ranking executive officers of public companies. Several types of documents that a company files with the SEC include information about the company's executive compensation policies and practices. One widely accepted practice is that executive compensation should be closely tied to stock performance, in the form of both stock options and cash payouts in order to create adequate incentives to focus on achieving long-term performance while not taking excessive risks. Since the SEC mandated enhanced executive compensation disclosure in 2006, we have seen more attention paid to the fairness and disclosure of executive compensation. A study conducted by the ISS Corporate Services shows that the median value of total CEO compensation for S&P 500 companies decreased 4.8% in 2009 and then increased by 20% to $10.6 million in 2010, and a nearly similar trend was observed for smaller public companies.[10]

The Sarbanes-Oxley Act of 2002 (SOX) and the Dodd-Frank Act of 2010 address executive compensation in several provisions. The question of how executives should be compensated, particularly after reported financial scandals and congressional responses (SOX, Dodd-Frank Act), has also

10   Cheng, 2011.

received great attention. Prior studies present two streams of determining executive compensation. The first stream is performance-based compensation suggesting that companies use cash compensation (salary and bonuses) to reward executives for past performance.[11] The second stream is pay-for-performance compensation, indicating companies attempt to promote future performance by offering stock options (noncash compensation) to optimize executives' equity incentives.[12] The use of stock-based executive compensation has increased substantially during the past two decades to align executive incentives with the shareholders' goal of increasing firm value and ensuring sustainable performance. In particular, the new rules require disclosure about:

- The relationship of a company's compensation policies and practices to risk management

- Revised reporting of stock and option awards to company executives and directors in the Summary Compensation Table

- Potential conflicts of interests of compensation consultants

Several suggestions are provided for improving the effectiveness of executive compensation, including the following:[13]

- The dual problems of moral hazard and collective action should be curbed by creating new disclosure and compensation regimes

- The true losers in the financial crisis had little control over the incentives of risk managers on Wall Street and elsewhere, so policymakers need to address the basic human problems inherent in the trading firm on more than just economic grounds

- Public policy should not incentivize the better-informed financial elite to make decisions at the expense of the everyday investor

- The provisions in Dodd-Frank that affect the executive pay process quite arguably will have the broadest and most significant impact on that pay process of any set of new rules ever contained in one law

- The proxy statement continues many of the trends noted in prior years: enhanced attention to the risk profile of compensation

---

11   Murphy, 1999.
12   Core and Guav, 1999.
13   Edwards, 2010.

strategies; more companies adopting claw-back policies; increased acceptance of shareholder say-on-pay votes; and increased use of independent compensation consultants

- To prevent a situation in which executives' personal interests tumble a corporation and send ripples of pain elsewhere, independent compensation committees have been charged with creating appropriate incentives for the executives

- Effective board compensation committee oversight of executive compensation policies and practices

- To provide a direct linkage between executive compensation and overall long-term sustainable performance

- To design executive compensation schemes aligned with the company's risk appetite and tolerance

- To improve public disclosure of executive compensation schemes and their components

- To minimize non-performance-based pay

- To align management interests with those of shareholders by linking executive compensation to sustainable performance

Best practices of corporate governance suggest that executive compensation should be tied to sustainable performance. Nonetheless, corporate performance during the past two decades has declined while executive compensation has continued to increase substantially. Several ways are suggested in the aftermath of the 2007–2009 global financial crisis to align executive compensation with sustainable performance. One of the better-known ways is the concept of "pay for performance." There are six measures and interpretations of the concept of "pay for performance":[14]

1. **Pay versus target pay.** This measure of performance suggests that companies can achieve pay for performance when they award compensation above a target level when performance is good and below a target level when performance is poor. This measure can cause companies to award their executive even for poor performance to the level where it is not linked to performance.

---

14   Tonello, 2011.

2. **Performance and pay changes.** This measure determines pay for performance in terms of performance and pay changes without considering the market for executive compensation.

3. **Pay versus market pay.** This measure determines executive compensation based on pay opportunities that are competitive with those provided by peer companies in the same industry or the market. This measure does not directly tie pay to performance.

4. **Alignment of pay percentile with performance percentile.** This measure determines percentage of changes in executive compensation based on the percentage of changes in performance considering peer companies on a sustained basis.

5. **A comprehensive pay for performance.** This measure determines executive pay based on three factors of incentive strength, cost control, and alignment.

6. **Pay value leverage.** This measure determines executive compensation based on the ratio of percentage change in *relative* pay to percentage change in *relative* performance.

Companies should tailor one or a combination of the above measures into their executive compensation schemes that reward sustainable performance. The best executive pay-for-performance measure is the one that rewards good sustainable performance, provides incentives for executives to achieve the highest possible sustainable performance while taking justifiable prudent risk, minimizes the compensation cost to shareholders, attracts and maintains key talent, and promotes the culture of integrity and competence.

5.7 Emerging issues in global corporate governance

Corporate governance has played and will continue to play an important role in the quality of financial reports and the efficiency of financial markets and the way organizations manage their business affairs and activities. Each country has its own corporate governance reforms that are shaped by its economic, cultural, and legal circumstances. The worldwide responses to corporate scandals and the 2007–2009 global financial crisis promote convergence in corporate governance across borders. Convergence is particularly vital in the areas of investor rights and protections, board responsibilities, and financial disclosures. While total convergence in corporate governance reform may not be feasible, global corporate governance practices should be promoted to improve efficiency and liquidity in the global capital markets. In addition for the need of global convergence in corporate governance, the following are emerging issues:

- Corporate governance reforms should create an environment in which public companies can operate in creating shareholders' value, protecting the interests of other stakeholders, and rebuilding investors' trust through effective enforcement of these reforms

- Regulations must be cost-effective, efficient, and scalable

- New corporate governance reforms should:
  - Address the systematic risk of all business transactions and particularly the risk of business failures and potential insolvency
  - Protect the interests of all stakeholders (investors, government, customers, creditors, suppliers, employees, society)
  - Promote accountability for businesses and their directors and officers
  - Encourage convergence and global cooperation and co-ordination

Persisting challenges in corporate governance are:

- **Compliance.** Effective compliance with implementation rules of provisions of both SOX and DOF as related to whistle-blowing and FCPA (anti-bribery, anti-money laundering) is a major challenge for public companies.

- **Board leadership.** CEO duality and the efficacy of separating the roles of the chairman of the board and CEO in differentiating between leadership of management oversight and management function is gaining new attention.

- **CEO succession planning.** CEO succession planning is one of the most important and challenges responsibilities of the board of directors in the aftermath of the 2007–2009 global financial crisis.

- **Risk assessment and management.** Effective risk assessment and management continue to be important issues facing public companies in the aftermath of financial scandals and crises.

- **Executive compensation.** Executive compensation has been and will be an important agenda for the board of directors, particularly the compensation committee, as long as the compensation of executives is perceived to be excessive and corporations fail to implement "say on pay" non-binding votes by shareholders in approving executive pay.

5.8 Social dimension of sustainability performance

Social Responsibility is an ethical or ideological theory that suggests that entities, regardless of type or size, have a responsibility to protect the society in which they operate, and that such responsibility varies across countries and is influenced significantly by the culture's socioeconomic attributes. Social performance measures how well an entity has translated its social goals into practice and is measured through the principles, actions, and corrective measures implemented. Social performance (SP), or the social bottom line, is about making an organization's social mission a reality and aligning it with the interests of the society by adding accepted social values and fulfilling social responsibility. Not all companies present meaningful reports to shareholders and the general public on their social performance. A governing body providing regulations or standards for disclosures on social responsibility will enhance the transparency, accuracy, and usefulness of such reports. This chapter presents the social dimension of sustainability performance.

Corporate social responsibility (CSR) has emerged as important area of challenges and opportunities for corporations worldwide. Corporations face challenges of how to respond to CSR issues and the perceived pressure of localization and globalization in determining their CSR policies and procedures. Employee-related CSR initiatives are derived from and directed toward improving social, political, and economic opportunities for existing and potential employees, contract workers, society, and other stakeholders. These initiatives range from empowering employee participation in making strategic decisions, improving employee benefits, wages, and work conditions, giving voice to customer satisfaction, and being a good corporate citizen. In more detail, these initiatives can address specific issues of diversity in terms of female participation, ethnic make-up, or linguistic capabilities. Product- and marketing-related CSR initiatives and activities are garnering considerable attention from customers, suppliers, manufacturers, government, and society. Consumer-driven CSR includes product and process innovations, environmental issues, promotions, advertising, and distribution policies and practices.

Social performance measures how well a company has translated its social goals into practice. Social performance is about making the company's social mission a reality and aligning it with the interests of society. Variables in the social area are associated with the existence of corporate policies that are mainly community service-related or geared toward improving social conditions. Variables in the social arena are associated with the existence of corporate policies that are mainly community service-related. The strength of social measures include:

- Charitable giving
- Innovative giving
- Non-U.S. charitable giving
- Support for housing
- Support for education
- Other community strengths
- CEO diversity
- Promotion of minorities
- Board of directors diversity
- Work–life benefits
- Women and minority contracting
- Employment of the disabled
- Gay and lesbian policies
- Other diversity strength

Concerns include:

- Investment controversies
- Negative economic impact
- Tax disputes
- Other community concerns

- Diversity controversies

- Minority non-representation

- Other diversity concerns

Business organizations typically strive to promote social responsibility among all their stakeholders. Business organizations also try to focus their efforts toward building and maintaining a more diverse community of extremely engaged employees and establishing a good relationship with vendors and contractors. Businesses often offer global philanthropic activities in the U.S.A. and in other countries, particularly in those communities where the company has operations. Business organizations can contribute to their communities by engaging in social activities such as the World Food Program, which formed a school feeding program, and other community involvements in some shape, form, or fashion.

International Organization for Standardization (ISO) 26000 covers a broad range of an organization's activities from economic to social, governance, ethics, and environmental issues.[15] ISO 26000 is a globally accepted guidance document for social responsibility that assists organizations worldwide in fulfilling their CSR goals.[16] Social responsibility performance promoted in ISO 26000 is conceptually and practically associated with the development of achieving sustainable performance, because the fulfillment of social responsibility necessitates and ensures sustainability development. ISO 26000 goes beyond profit maximization by presenting a framework for organizations to contribute to sustainable development and the welfare of society. The core subject areas of ISO 26000 take into account all aspects of the triple bottom line's (TBL) key financial and nonfinancial performance relevant to people, planet, and profit as explained in details in Chapter 3.

Brockett and Rezaee discuss the following provisions of ISO 26000 designed to help business organizations operate in a socially responsible manner by providing guidance on:[17]

- Concepts, frameworks, terms, and definitions pertaining to CSR

- Backgrounds, trends, characteristics, and best practices of socially responsible organizations

---

15   International Organization for Standardization (ISO), 2010a.
16   International Organization for Standardization (ISO), 2010a.
17   Brockett and Rezaee, 2012.

- Principles, standards, and best practices relevant to CSR

- Policies, procedures, and best practices for integrating, implementing, and promoting CSR

- Engagement of all stakeholders, including shareholders, in socially responsible activities

- Disclosure of information and nonfinancial KPIs related to social responsibility

5.9 Best practices of CSR

Several models and best practices of CSR have been presented to hold business organizations accountable for fulfilling their CSR. Sethi suggests a three-level model for corporate social performance which reflects business organizations' behavior to society as:[18]

1. A social liability as demanded by regulatory constraints and market mechanisms

2. A social responsibility beyond the legal and market requirement to benefit society

3. Social accountability to all stakeholders, including shareholders, employees, customers, creditors, suppliers, government, the environment, and society

Carroll developed a CSR conceptual model that consists of four dimensions of economic, legal, moral, and philanthropic responsibilities.[19] The first dimension is economic responsibility, which includes a commitment to the desired return on investment for shareholders and creditors, job opportunities and proper compensation for employees, exploration of new resources, promotion of technology and innovation, and the production and offering of high-quality and safe services and products. The legal dimension of CSR responsibility includes compliance with all applicable laws, rules, regulations, policies, and standards. The moral dimension of CSR represents engagement in social activities above and beyond the legal requirements and personal benefits by maximizing social benefits and minimizing

---

18   Sethi, 1975.
19   Carroll, 1999.

costs to society. The philanthropic dimension of CSR suggests that involvement in activities and programs that provide financial and nonfinancial assistance to the community tend to be less strategic than other forms of CSR involvement in terms of adding social and business values.

CSR best practices are designed to minimize the conflicts between corporations and society caused by differences between private and social costs and benefits and to align corporate goals with those of society. Examples of conflicts between corporations and society are related to environmental issues (pollution, acid rain, global warming), wages paid by multinational corporations in poor countries and child labor in developing countries. Corporate governance measures, which include rules, regulations, and best practices of CSR programs, can raise companies' awareness of the social costs and benefits of their business activities. These CSR models and best practices assist business organizations in developing their own CSR program to achieve their social performance. The Organisation for Economic Co-operation and Development (OECD) defines the purpose of a CSR program as "to encourage the positive contributions that multinational enterprises can make to economics, environmental, and social progress and to minimize the difficulties to which their various operations may give rise.[20] This definition focuses on two important aspects of a CSR program, namely, the creation of social value through corporate activities (social value-added activities) and the avoidance of conflicts between corporate goals and societal goals (societal consensus).

The primary concepts of CSR programs are:

- The CSR programs are important ingredients of business sustainability, and companies must strive to make as small a footprint as possible on CSR.

- One of the most important investments a company can make is in its CSR programs, including its employees, investors, customers, and communities.

- Philanthropic programs are important in aiding those who are less fortunate and thus a common theme among companies with a global reach.

These CSR programs are not without costs and they should be viewed as corporate investments in employees, community, and society which should

20   Organisation for Economic Co-operation and Development, 2003.

generate long-term and sustainable financial performance. However, there are two differing views regarding the relationship between investing in CSR programs and firm financial performance:

1. Socially responsible behavior is costly due to increases in expenses, but no increase in benefits.

2. A positive association exists between CSR and firm performance because CSR programs and activities enhance employee morale and productivity, attract and retain high-quality employees, generate a positive corporate image, enhance product evaluation via an overall evaluation of the firm, and improve a firm's access to sources of capital.

Business organizations worldwide now recognize the importance of quality as it relates to CSR and the link between profitability and social behavior. Justifications for CSR are: moral obligation, maintaining a good reputation, ensuring sustainability, licensing to operate, and creating shared value. In a shared value approach, corporations identify potential social issues of concern and integrate them into their strategic planning. There are many factors determining whether a company should follow CSR, such as: the pressure of the labor movement, the development of moral values and social standards, the development of business education, and the change in public opinion about the role of business. Companies which are, or aspire to be, leaders in CSR are challenged by rising public expectations, increasing innovation, continuous quality improvement, and heightened social and environmental problems. Companies should fulfill their social responsibility due to: public image, consumer movements, government requirements, investors' education, tax benefits, better relations with stakeholders, employee satisfaction, a sense of pride, and an appropriate way to improve quality.

Globalization creates incentives and opportunities for multinational corporations (MNCs) and their stakeholders and executives to influence their CSR initiatives and strategies of the headquarters as well as subsidiaries. MNCs can choose from a variety of CSR initiatives with regard to the scope, extent, and types of CSR strategy that focus on different issues, functions, areas, and stakeholders that vary across their subsidiaries. Given that MNCs are also constrained by scarce resources, they have to be selective when deciding on the scope, extent, and types of CSR initiative. Subsidiaries' CSR initiatives typically have distinct "home country" characteristics that are pursued across subsidiaries. Nonetheless, global/local CSR initiatives often vary depending on the types of initiative and the CSR strategies pursued.

The ISO 26000 standards are voluntary and aspirational rather than prescriptive, providing a framework for incorporating CSR issues into business and investment decision-making and ownership practices. Compliance with ISO 26000 standards is expected to lead not only to a more sustainable financial return, but also to a close alignment of the interests of businesses and investors with those of the global society at large. Management should develop and maintain proper CSR programs that provide a common framework for the integration of CSR issues and activities that consist of:

- Integration of CSR issues into the business and investment analysis and decision-making process

- Incorporation of CSR issues and activities into business and investment policies and practices

- Promotion of appropriate disclosure on CSR issues and performance

- Collaboration among all stakeholders to enhance the effectiveness of implementing CSR programs

- Promotion of product innovation and quality, customer retention and attraction, and employee satisfaction and productivity through CSR programs

- Periodic disclosures of both financial and nonfinancial KPIs relevant to CSR activities to all stakeholders

In summary, the social dimension of sustainability performance requires business organizations to take initiatives to advance some social good beyond their own interests and compliance with applicable regulations. Simply put, CSR means enhancing corporations' positive impacts and minimizing their negative effects on society, as well as minimizing harm to society and the environment and creating positive impacts on the community, environment, employees, customers, and suppliers. The social dimension of sustainability performance requires that business organizations take initiatives to advance some social good beyond their own interests and compliance with applicable regulations. The true measure of success for corporations should be determined not only by their reported earnings, but also by their governance, social responsibility, ethical behavior, and environmental initiatives. The social dimension of sustainability performance and CSR has received considerable attention from policy-makers, regulators, and the business and investment community over the past decade and is expected to remain the main theme for decades to come. ISO 26000 standards and CSR policies, programs, activities, and best practices should assist business organizations worldwide in improving their KPIs as well as the quality of financial and nonfinancial social performance information disseminated to their stakeholders. The most commonly used and important social sustainability KPIs are presented in Chapter 2.

5.10 Ethical dimension of sustainability performance

Ethics are broadly described in literature as moral principles about right and wrong, honorable behavior reflecting values or standards of conduct. Honesty, openness, responsiveness, accountability, due diligence, and fairness are core ethical principles. Business ethics are a specialized study of moral right and wrong. An appropriate code of ethics that sets the right tone at the top by promoting ethical and professional conduct and establishing the moral structure for the entire organization is the backbone of effective corporate governance. Corporate culture and compliance rules should provide incentives and opportunities to maintain their honesty. Attributes of an ethical corporate culture or an integrity-based culture are a sense of employee responsibility, freedom to raise concerns, managers modeling ethical behavior, and expressing the importance of integrity. The company's directors and executives should demonstrate, through their actions as well as their policies, a firm commitment to ethical behavior throughout the company and a culture of trust within the company. Although a "right tone at the top" is very important in promoting an ethical culture, actions often speak louder than words.

Variables in the ethics area are related to employee relations and human rights. Strengths include:

- Strong union relation
- No-lay-off policy
- Cash-profit sharing
- Employee involvement
- Retirement benefits
- Health and safety
- Other employee relationship strengths

- Indigenous people relationship strengths

- Other human rights strengths

Concerns include:

- Weak union relations

- Health and safety policies

- Workforce reductions

- Retirement benefits

- Other employee relations concerns

- Labor rights concerns

- Indigenous people relations concerns

- Other human rights concerns

Ethics is a relatively broad concept and there are different aspects about ethics that can be disclosed. The strongest form of defense against business failure comes from an organization's ethical culture and behaviors. The effectiveness of ethics performance depends on employees' integrity and begins with the tone that management sets at the top and the workplace ethics. Attributes of an ethical corporate culture consist of the existence of codes of conduct for senior executives and employees, a sense of employee responsibility, accountability, honesty, mutual respect, and freedom to raise concerns. Appropriate ethical policies and procedures in the workplace can affect the integrity and quality of financial reporting and thus cost of capital. The KLD database includes in the ethics area disclosures that are related to employee relations and human rights.

Business sustainability in the ethical dimension provides information to debt and equity investors about the relationship between the corporation and employees. Such information is beneficial to both debt-holders and stockholders when they assess the expected return they must demand from holding securities issued by the firm. However, the effect of such an ethical dimension of business sustainability should be different for debt and equity holders. Bond holders should benefit more from such a dimension of business sustainability, as they can benefit from the improved employer–employee relationship between the firm and its workers, but do not need to bear the higher cost associated with the improved relationship, such as higher salary or cash-profit sharing.

Corporations should establish an ethical workplace culture of integrity and competence that encourages all employees to follow and exemplify. Some of the core cultural values that are intended to inspire a culture of integrity and competence in the workplace include:

- Upholding the highest ethical standards and integrity along with the culture of accountability in the workplace

- Promoting the culture of good citizenship by adding value to the organization, protecting employee health and safety, and managing natural resources responsibility

- Avoiding conflicts of interest by considering what is best for the entire organization when making decisions

- Focusing on producing safe and good quality products and services by achieving business results and customer success

- Being fair and treating others with dignity and respect and promoting diversity

- Promoting excellence by helping others reach their potentials

- Participating in developing objectives and embracing changes

Ethical actions are derived from the ethical theories that can be divided into two aspects of ethics of conduct and ethics of character. Ethics of conduct focuses on what sorts of actions a person should perform, whereas ethics of character focuses on what kind of person an individual should be. Ethics of conduct has two main theories: Consequentialism and Deontology. The Consequentialism theory advocates that ethical behavior or the moral rightness of one's actions are determined by the results of the act and its impact on either the individual (egoism) or all involved (utilitarianism).[21] The standard is that an action is right if it promotes the best consequences. The best consequences are those in which utility in terms of happiness and satisfaction is maximized.

The Deontology theory requires that ethical action and behavior should be in accordance with certain moral rules or principles. The standard is that an action is right if it is in accordance with a moral rule or principle and is rational.

The Aristotelianism theory, which is also called the Virtue theory, claims that a virtuous agent is one who acts virtuously, i.e., one who has and

---

21   Shaw, 1999.

exercises virtues. A virtue is a character or trait a human being needs in order to flourish or live well. The ethical standard is that an action is right if it is what a virtuous agent would do in the circumstances.

Metaethics focuses on ethical theories, their evolution, and the social, religious, spiritual, and cultural influences shaping those theories. Normative ethics emphasizes practical aspects by providing principles of appropriate behavior and guidance for what is right or wrong, good or bad in behavior (e.g., principles of justice, honesty, social benefits, and lawfulness). Applied ethics deals with the application of moral principles and reasoning as well as codes of conduct for a particular profession or segment of the society (e.g., business ethics, environmental ethics, and medical ethics).[22]

Business ethics is often interpreted as:

- Complying with all applicable laws, rules, regulations, and standards

- Refraining from breaking the criminal law relevant to all business activities

- Avoiding any actions that may result in civil lawsuits against the company

- Refraining from actions that are bad for the company image and reputation

Businesses are especially concerned with all actual and perceived unethical business activities that may involve loss of money and reputation. Public companies are required by the SEC to have business codes of conduct that address these and other ethical issues. Public companies also retain corporate attorneys and public relations experts to monitor that employees observe the established codes of conduct in their daily activities. Alternatively, public companies can hire philosophers to instruct employees on becoming "moral." Philosophers can teach employees a basic understanding of morality, keep them out of trouble, and systematically address the issue of right and wrong conduct. Although being moral may prevent a company from some legal and public relations challenges, morality in business is not without cost. A morally responsible company should invest in employee satisfaction, product safety, environmental impact, truthful advertising, and scrupulous marketing.

22   Rezaee, 2009.

There is always a conflict between the ethical interests of the money-minded businessperson and the ideal-minded philosopher. A business-oriented individual may argue that there is a symbiotic relation between ethics and business in which ethics naturally emerges from a profit-oriented business. In this context, good ethics results in good business, which simply means that moral businesses practices are profitable and sustainable. For example, it is profitable to make safe products since this will reduce product liability lawsuits. Similarly, it may be in the best financial interests of businesses to respect employee privacy, since this will improve morale and thus improve work efficiency. Some moral business practices may not be economically viable, even in the long run. For example, this might be the case with retaining older workers who are inefficient, as opposed to replacing them with younger and more efficient workers. It can also be argued that in a competitive and free market, the profit motive will in fact bring about a morally proper environment. That is, when customers demand safe products, or workers demand privacy, then they will buy from or work for only those businesses that meet their expectations. Businesses that do not meet these demands will not be sustainable.

Another approach to business ethics is that moral obligations will comply with all applicable laws, rules, and regulations. Corporations that assume an obligation beyond the mere compliance with law, either in their corporate codes or in practice, take on responsibilities that are normally considered optional. Strictly following this legal approach to business ethics may indeed prompt businesses to do the right thing, as prescribed by law. There are, however, overriding challenges with restricting morality solely to what the law requires. First, even in the best legal context, the law will lag behind our moral condemnation of certain unscrupulous, yet legal, business practices. For example, drug companies could previously make exaggerated claims about the miraculous curative properties of their products. Now government regulations prohibit any exaggerated claims. Thus, prior to the enactment of a law, there will be a period of time when a business practice will be deemed immoral, yet the practice will be legal. This will be a continuing problem since changes in products, technology, and marketing strategies will present new questionable practices that cannot be addressed by existing legislation. A second problem with the law-based approach is that, at best, it applies only to countries such as our own whose business-related laws are morally conscientious. The situation may be different for developing countries that lack sophisticated laws and regulatory agencies.

Corporate codes of ethics are often viewed as attempts to foster good public relations or to reduce legal liability. Corporate codes of ethics are also a reasonable model for understanding how moral principles can be articulated and introduced into business practice. The practical advantage of this approach is that it directly stipulates the morality of certain action types, without becoming ensnared in the problem of deriving particular actions from more abstract principles. But, the limitation of the corporate code model is that the principles offered will appear to be merely rules of prudence or good manners unless we can establish their distinct *moral* character.

Values are important and often interpreted in relation to the organization's vision and ethical culture. An organization's vision must be based on and consistent with their core values of integrity, honesty, transparency, and fairness. These are not the only values that should determine business culture and character, but are the ones that are central to the sustainability of an organization. Values are the embodiment of what an organization stands for, and thus guide the behavior of its members. Any disconnect between individual and organizational values or differences between stated values and practiced values will be dysfunctional. Values are directly related to ethics because values that guide a person to do the right (wrong) can also be viewed as being ethical (unethical). Thus, the challenge is in determining what is right or wrong. Perhaps the first place to look in determining what is right or wrong is society. Ultimately, every society makes some determination of morally acceptable behavior in light of a set of generally accepted guidelines. Experience often leads societies to develop beliefs about what is of value for the common good. One example is the notion of reciprocity; one good deed deserves another. Organizations, to some extent, define what is right or wrong for the members of the organization.

Norms are also important, for a discussion of ethics and values as norms may allow or even encourage certain behaviors as "appropriate" that are not in compliance with society's or an organization's stated values. When there is a discrepancy between stated and operating values, it may be difficult to determine what is "right." An example might be a company that has among its stated values to treat everyone with dignity and respect, but whose norms have permitted (and perhaps even encouraged) a pattern of sexual harassment over a number of years. Many organizations have participated in the ethics and compliance program to create an ethical and competent culture. In addition, the Ethics and Compliance Hotline provides a way for partners and employees to report their concerns – anonymously, if they wish – without fear of retaliation. The hotline intake process is administered by a third-party vendor that specialized in hotline reporting and tracking services, which helps to provide confidentiality and anonymity if requested.

5.11 Professional codes of conduct

Organizations communicate their values, accepted standards for decision-making, and all other rules of behavior. Actually, all organizations have a standard of conduct, explicitly or implicitly. Some of them publish a code of conduct or ethics, which helps organizations deal with the underlying values, commitment to employees, standards for doing business, and their relationship with wider society.

These codes of conduct not only demand profit maximization and transparency, but also increased focus on ethics, corporate governance, and corporate responsibility. These codes are required even by laws and regulations in some countries. Some codes are also prompted by market mechanisms such as movements in share price, or a combination of market forces and regulation. There also are some codes that are published by psychological organizations or other organizations.

Here are some examples of professional codes of conduct:

- The American Psychological Association (APA) has the APA Ethical Principles of Psychologists and Code of Conduct.[23]

- The Canadian Psychological Association (CPA) articulates ethical principles, values, and standards to guide all members of the Canadian Psychological Association, whether scientists, practitioners, or scientist practitioners, or whether acting in research, direct service, teaching, student, trainee, administrative, management, employer, employee, supervisory, consultative, peer review, editorial, expert witness, social policy, or any other role related to discipline of psychology.[24]

- The Society for Research in Child Development (SRCD) provides ethical standards for research with children.[25]

---

23 American Psychological Association, 2015.
24 Canadian Psychological Association, 2000.
25 Society for Research in Child Development, 2007.

- The Association for Computing Machinery (ACM) Code of Ethics and Professional Conduct is another professional code of conduct which is expected of every member (voting members, associate members, and student members) of the ACM.[26]

By implementing codes of conduct effectively and consistently, organizational performance and control could be improved. Irregularities and corporate scandals would be fewer and fewer. Trust would build up gradually between organizations and their stakeholders. The corporate Code of Business Ethics should define what is appropriate behavior and what is not. It describes corporate core values, principles, and a culture of integrity and competence. That is a profound statement for any corporation to make as a primary focus of their everyday business operations.

The code of ethics should be developed and approved by the board of directors, communicated to all employees, enforced by management, and require certifications of compliance from all employees. Every employee is responsible for the code of ethics, and it must taken very seriously if violated in any manner, as it will reflect on the corporation as a whole. The corporate code of conduct extends beyond compliance with the law; it is about integrity in business practices and overall commitment to operational excellence in business. In addition, the code should require adherence to all applicable laws, rules, regulations, standards, and best practices including the antitrust laws, Foreign Corrupt Practices Act (FCPA) and Bribery Act.

5.12 Environmental dimension of sustainability performance

In 2010, the SEC released guidance reiterating the relevance and importance of adequate disclosures of material risk associated with climate change by public companies.[27] Current and future legislation, coupled with society's increasing sensitivity to the environment (especially toward pollution, hazardous waste, human health, and other general environmental concerns), necessitate the need for high level management to pay attention to their companies' environmental practices and obligations. ISO 14000 requires executive management to conduct regular evaluations of

26   Association for Computing Machinery, 2015.
27   Securities and Exchange Commission, 2010.

the EMS to ensure the system is realizing the set goals and missions of the environmental practices. The main goal for management's review of the EMS is to identify deficiencies and successes to improve environmental practices in the future. A company will benefit economically and socially through the implementation and continual usage of an EMS that is relevant, accurate, and sustainable in monitoring and developing environmental best practices, missions, and goals.

The environmental dimension of sustainability performance includes reducing an organization's carbon footprint, creating a better work environment, and improving the air and water quality of the property and the surrounding community. Many of the business disasters (e.g., BP oil spill) that occurred in the past decade prove that corporate environmental responsibilities are vital to economic sustainability, the wellbeing of society, and future generations. Sustainability disclosures with respect to the environmental dimension are mainly related to effects on natural resources and environment that could directly or indirectly affect living conditions of human beings. Environmental strengths in environmental areas include:

- Beneficial products and services
- Pollution policies
- Recycling
- Clean energy

Concerns include:

- Hazardous waste
- Regulatory problems
- Ozone depleting chemicals
- Substantial emissions
- Agricultural chemicals
- Climate changes

Widening sensitivities to the environment (e.g., pollution, hazardous waste, human health, and other general environmental concerns) along with ever-increasing environmental laws and regulations force corporations to pay attention to their environmental practices and obligations. Reporting environmental performance in the U.S.A. in a corporate setting has been built on regulations and a societal demand for accurate environmental reporting. Corporations have developed environmental reporting tools through voluntary and standards enforced by various social and governmental initiatives. Environmental initiatives and regulations have far reaching consequences on how corporations are viewed in society and held liable for inadequate environmental consideration. Environmental business sustainability created through best practices, regulations, or accounting standards forces Corporate America to rethink how business is conducted. Moreover, corporations are developing or adapting voluntary reporting tools to be compliant with regulatory bodies and to enhance their social view. The U.S. Congress has recognized that human activities have a dramatic impact on natural ecosystems, through population growth, urbanization, industrialization, resource use, and technological advancements.[28] It is critical that continuing systems are put into place to maintain environmental, social, and economic sustainability to ensure the success and livelihood of future generations. Furthermore, the U.S. Congress stresses the adoption and cooperation of state and local governments, as well as public and private organizations, to facilitate the creation of solutions for environmental, social, and economic issues.

Developing an environmental strategy for the company is only the beginning. Companies with large supplier relationships must insure the integrity of the specific suppliers' environmental KPIs to ensure sustainability throughout their value chain. Implementing these practices is voluntary in the U.S.A.; however, the increase in environmental regulations has induced the federal government to enforce the regulations, through the Environmental Protection Agency (EPA). The EPA is responsible for identifying and enforcing environmental laws and regulations and forcing companies to clean up a contaminated site or to seek recovery costs from cleaning up a contaminated site. Companies that do not comply will be liable for:

- Clean-up costs
- Reducing or eliminating future contamination
- Degradation to natural resources
- Societal litigation
- Criminal charges

28   National Environmental Policy Act, 1969.

Effective compliance with environmental laws and regulations requires full commitment by companies to initiate environmental management systems, accounting, and auditing practices.[29]

In general, corporations involved in resource intensive industries are required to follow environmental requirements, laws, and regulations (e.g., the Clean Air Act and the Superfund Act). On a broad scale, the EPA issues and enforces health and environmental regulations such as the clean air act, clean water act, the solid waste act, and the Superfund Amendment and Reauthorization Act (SARA), as well as other regulations affecting environmental reporting. For specific industries, such as construction, the EPA has developed a set of environmental KPIs for businesses to use as a guideline. The six basic guidelines are as follows: diesel emission reduction strategies, smart energy practices, green remediation, green building/construction practices, water management, and environmentally preferable purchasing. The EPA uses a National Priorities List (NPL) to identify contaminated sites that need or potentially need to be cleaned up. A NPL site is defined as having a release of hazardous materials, pollutants, or contaminants that have negative effects on the environment and human health. At the end of 2009 the NPL consisted of 1,111 seriously contaminated (nonfederal sites).[30] In 2009 the EPA spent over $4 billion on clean-up efforts on sites that had severe human exposure or unknown exposure. From 2010 to 2014 the EPA expects to spend $335-$681 million each year on contaminated sites. As of April 1, 2011, the EPA has identified 1,132 nonfederal sites and 158 federal sites that are in immediate need of clean-up with no direct cost estimations.[31]

In June 2009, CERES and the Environmental Defense Fund released a joint report on their analysis of climate risk disclosures of 100 companies in five sectors for the 2007 fiscal year SEC filings and concluded that investors are not receiving adequate climate information from corporate fillings with the SEC.[32] The report on an examination of climate change disclosures of about 6,400 10-K filings by S&P 500 companies during 1995–2009 reveals that there was "an alarming pattern of non-disclosure by corporations regarding climate risks."[33] A survey conducted by Ernst & Young in 2010 suggests the following four global themes regarding climate change:[34]

29   United States Environmental Protection Agency, 2015a.
30   United States Government Accountability Office, 2010.
31   United States Environmental Protection Agency, 2015b.
32   CERES and Environmental Defense Fund, 2009.
33   CERES *et al.*, 2009.
34   Ernst & Young, 2010.

1. Executive leadership is critical to effective governance of fully understanding and realizing the full potential of the business response to climate change. More than 90% of executives surveyed indicate that climate change governance should be addressed at the board and top management level.

2. Business drivers dominated by top-line and bottom-line impacts of climate change initiatives with the keen focus on meeting changes in customer demand.

3. Business executives are committed to addressing the ever-increasing challenges of climate change.

4. Climate change investments have increased despite regulatory uncertainty.

In 2010, the SEC released guidance reiterating the relevance and importance of adequate disclosure of material risks associated with climate change by public companies.[35] Items in filing SEC documents S-K or S-X that could trigger climate related disclosure are items 101, 103, 503(c), and 303. Item 101 pertains to any material capital expenditures on facilities environmental controls during the company's current fiscal year and previous periods where the company finds it material.[36] Item 103 requires a company or its subsidiaries to describe any material legal proceedings it may be involved in.[37] Item 503(c) gives guidance on what risk factors a company should review and disclose regarding existing or pending regulation on climate change.[38] Item 303 requires public companies to determine the effect any enacted climate change legislation or regulation will have on the company's financial position.[39] For example, pending legislation or regulations on climate change can affect costs of purchasing or improving facilities and demand for products and services.

In another survey conducted by Ernst & Young in 2010, respondents reported that the top three factors driving their climate change initiatives were:[40]

---

35   Securities and Exchange Commission, 2010.
36   Securities and Exchange Commission, 2010, pp. 6295-6296.
37   Securities and Exchange Commission, 2010, p. 6293.
38   Securities and Exchange Commission, 2010, p. 6296.
39   Securities and Exchange Commission, 2010, p. 6296.
40   Ernst & Young, 2010.

1. Energy costs

2. Changes in customer demand

3. New revenue opportunities

Current and future legislation, coupled with societies' increasing sensitivity to the environment (especially toward pollution, hazardous waste, human health, and other general environmental concerns), necessitate the need for high level management to pay attention to their companies' environmental practices and obligations. A list of EPA acts relevant to environmental issues can be found on the Website of the EPA.[41]

The EPA has other programs which are voluntary and are helping to drive industry wide adoption and awareness of environmental practices. The voluntary programs are: Green Lights, Climate Wise, Waste Wise, and Energy Star. Corporations in the U.S.A. are not required to issue environmental reports or follow ISO 14000 environmental accounting standards, however, but are liable for environmental degradation their company or subsidies inflict (e.g. BP oil spill). Many large corporations such as IBM, Pfizer, and Apple have developed their own tools in developing environmental KPI reporting variables. The reports are produced annually and include tailored KPIs and goals, which include energy conservation, waste reduction, increased recycling, and use of environmentally friendly materials.

The U.K. and the U.S.A. both have large corporations or conglomerates that operate throughout the globe. The U.K. has developed environmental law that enforces environmental practices, where the U.S.A. has regulations that govern industries involved in the use of natural resources. Although both countries have laws and regulations to ensure public safety now and in the future, neither have standards on how to disclose environmental practices. Furthermore, such disclosure is voluntary but increasing in popularity stemming from societal demand. In the U.S.A., the SEC and the Financial Accounting Standards Board (FASB) have given corporations some support in developing reporting standards; however, the major increase in reporting is mainly attributed to the increase in social awareness and governmental regulation.[42] The EPA has influenced what types of KPI are monitored and used throughout the business world. Moreover, systems have been developed to help report environmental information. The EPA has put through several acts to control and monitor environmental degradation, which

---

41   United States Environmental Protection Agency, 2015c.
42   Holland and Foo, 2003.

enables them to enforce the regulations when companies fail to adhere to the regulations.

General guidelines for implementing ISO 14000 are as follows:[43]

- **ISO 14001.** Environmental Management Systems – Specification with Guidance for Use

- **ISO 14004.** Environmental Management Systems – General Guidelines on Principles Systems, and Supporting Techniques

- **ISO 14010.** Guidelines for Environmental Auditing – General Principles

- **ISO 14011.** Guidelines for Environmental Auditing – Audit Procedures – Auditing of Environmental Management Systems

- **ISO 14012.** Guidelines for Environmental Auditing – Qualification Criteria for Environmental Auditors

- **ISO 14020.** Environmental Labeling – General Principles

- **ISO 14021.** Environmental Labels and Declarations – Self-declaration Environmental Claims – Guidelines and Definition and Usage of Terms

- **ISO 14022.** Environmental Labels and Declarations – Self-declaration Environmental Claims – Symbols

- **ISO 14024.** Environmental Labels and Declarations – Environmental Labeling Type 1 – Guiding Principles and Procedures

- **ISO 14031.** Environmental Management – Environmental Performance Evaluation – Guidelines

- **ISO 14040.** Environmental Management – Life Cycle Assessment – Principles and Framework

- **ISO 14041.** Environmental Management – Life Cycle Assessment – Goal and Scope Definition and Inventory Analysis

- **ISO 14050.** Environmental Management – Vocabulary

Environmental sustainability has become a strategic focus of corporations worldwide. The response to environmental challenges and pursuit of opportunities has resulted in policies and practices that seek to safeguard

---

43   Rezaee and Elam, 2000.

the environment and improve the wellbeing of society. Global environmental calamities such as the Union Carbide Bhopal chemical leak in 1984 and the 2010 British Petroleum oil spill in the Gulf of Mexico are examples of events that have forever changed the affected environments, corporations, and communities.

Public awareness of both corporate and individual responsibilities has increased, as has stakeholder input. Environmental risk mitigation is an integral part of economic sustainability, both present and future. Brockett and Rezaee define environmental sustainability as "a process of preserving the quality of the environment in the long term and creating a better environment for future generations."[44]

Increased CO_2 levels from greenhouse gases (coal, oil, and natural gas) are linked to atmospheric temperature; this will affect weather patterns. Volatility in climate patterns increases uncertainly about future demand, supply chains, and the stability of infrastructure. Hence business policy will evolve as these patterns become better understood. Extreme weather conditions are well understood and responded to on most cases and is generally part of an organization's business continuity plan. Both extreme weather and climate change impact sustainability. Energy and fuel supply uncertainties increase volatility in fossil fuel markets. Managing one's corporate reputation, customer expectations, and efficiency drives interest more than legal compliance in most cases. Independent ranking agencies rate companies on emissions and goals. Carbon footprints are found in supply chains, recognized as waste, and are hence an efficiency and risk measure, a liability that demands stakeholder management. Materially scarce resources will increase in line with population growth and urbanization. Shareholders have become more educated about these challenges and recognize the corporate investment required to meet long-term sustainability. Several sustainability indices are being developed by agencies such as Bloomberg to provide valuation tools for the measurement and comparison of indices.

5.13 Environmental key performance indicators (KPIs)

To help reduce the environmental footprint, corporations are adopting formal evaluation processes to measure their impacts on the planet. Various

44   Brockett and Rezaee, 2012a.

environmental KPI measures are being developed and adopted. The best practices of the adopted environmental KPIs are:

- Production and delivery of environmentally safer products by using biodegradable, non-toxic, and naturally derived materials in production

- Efficient and effective utilization of scarce natural resources such as power, energy, and scarce natural materials

- Efficient and effective use of recycled materials

- Leveraging technology to maximize utilization of scare resources and replacement of nonrenewable resources

- Effective and efficient utilization of non-waste technologies

- Minimization of the use of harmful and unsafe materials and products

- Assessment of environmental risks and management of environmental risks including providing for appropriate insurance of risks and environmental remediation and disposal efforts

- Environmental reporting that discloses environmental risk assessment and management, compliance with environmental requirements, and measurement of environmental liabilities

- Environmental external auditing and assurance on environmental reports

5.14 Global environmental initiatives

The stresses placed on the natural environment over the last century have increased strains and crises worldwide. In addition to the identification of ozone depletion in the late 20th century, the identification of climate change is a manifestation for this deterioration. Initiatives such as the Kyoto Protocol, the European Union Emission Trading System (EU ETS), Carbon Reduction Commitment (CRC), and the Montreal Protocol are all efforts to gain consensus on mechanisms to measure impacts on the environment and set limits on activities deemed detrimental. Specifically, the Kyoto Protocol sets Greenhouse Gas emission limits and provides signature nations three mechanisms by which to meet the necessary output levels; emission trading, clean development mechanisms, and joint implementation.

In addition to the numerous organizations such as the Alliance for Global Sustainability (which seeks to improve the scientific understanding of global environmental challenges as well as the education of a new generation of leaders committed to sustainable development), the International Organization for Standardization (ISO) has established global standards to assist firms in developing adequate environmental management systems.

The global success of ISO 9000 quality assurance standards serves as the model for the ISO 14000 series standards. While not mandatory, many organizations are required by their customers to be ISO 14000 certified prior to conducting business. Meeting ISO 14000 standards is increasingly becoming a prerequisite for competition in the global market. Further, the 14000 series standards can serve as the framework for environmentally sustainable business plans and mission statements, which if built and adhered to, will likely limit a company's future liability and will limit the cost of enforcement. As energy dependence rises, expect further visibility and development of ISO 50001 standards, which specifically address energy management throughout organizations.

There are numerous initiatives and organizations committed to creating sustainable business practices. Regardless of the mechanism by which any organization or nation decides to participate and measure compliance with established protocols, the simple act of adopting and attempting adherence to any of the protocols makes members keenly aware of how their activities impact the environment. This awareness and understanding furthers advancements in technology which can negate or offset the harmful impacts of daily activities.

5.15 Environmental management systems

The Environmental Management Systems (EMS) within a corporation are programs established by the corporation to improve the environmental performance of the company. EMS programs allow companies to achieve environmental goals based on the company's control of its processes. It is believed that when a company controls its environmental impact through goals, the company will improve its environmental performance. Most companies benefit from EMS programs through the savings of becoming energy-efficient. EMS programs maintain themselves through mission statements and company policies. These policies and goals are available to all the stakeholders.

The management team is responsible for determining the policies and goals for the EMS programs. Once the goals and policies have been established, a plan is developed to attain the goals set by the corporation. The company must then implement the plan and develop a monitoring system to determine the effectiveness and completion of the goals and policies. This ultimately comes to the review of management to further develop goals and policies. The documentation for EMS programs are specific, based on ISO 14000 standards. ISO 14001 is the leading standard for EMS programs. It requires extensive documentation as well as regular review of documentation by executive management.

The corporation establishes their EMS programs and applies for ISO 14000 certification. The company will then be audited regarding their goals and policies. Once the company gains certification they will be subject to periodic review. Some benefits of becoming certified include: new market customers, increased employee morale, increased efficiency, and a better public image. Some are the best practices and goals of an effective EMS are:

- Appropriate tone at the top set by the board of directors and senior executives to provide the leadership and commit adequate resources necessary for responsible environmental management

- The compliance board committee and/or compliance officers assigned the primary responsibility for the environmental performance of the operations within their control

- Proper education of all employees regarding environmental laws, regulations, and best practices

- Development of environmental policies and procedures in compliance with environmental rules and regulations

- Assignment of qualified officers and staff in charge of compliance with environmental policies to advance the corporation's knowledge of environmental protection

- Assessment and management of environmental risks and evaluation of environmental performance in an ongoing monitoring process

- Certification of compliance with established operating environmental procedures to ensure maintenance of environmental regulatory compliance and ensure responsible environmental management

- Establishment of an environmental audit program to ensure periodic review of each environmental KPI's operation

- Proper disclosure of environmental policies, procedures, reporting, and auditing to all stakeholders

5.16 Environmental reporting

Environmental KPIs should be managed, measured, and reported in compliance with the GRI reporting framework. Environmental reporting is often referred to as "green accounting" or "green reporting." Environmental information can be included in the corporate annual reports, provided in Management Discussion and Analysis (MD&A), or presented in a stand-alone environmental report. Environmental information has traditionally been disclosed in both annual reports and MD&A. The GRI framework developed a set of principles to establish whether or not the type of information the company wants to report will be included in the sustainability report.[45] The basic principles are as follows:

- **Materiality.** The organization should report information that has the greatest impact on short- and long-term operations, societal impacts, and environmental influences, fulfilling all dimensions of EGSEE. The materiality of reporting sustainability information should reflect the organizations overall mission, vision, strategies, stakeholder welfare, society impacts, and environmental issues.

- **Stakeholders.** The reports should disclose all major stakeholders' expectations and address any concerns or interests. A stakeholder is any entity (living or not) that can be affected by an organization's operations.

45   Global Reporting Initiative, 2006.

- **Sustainability context.** The objective is to disseminate sustainability information across all areas of EGSEE performance, and can be prepared in a format that best reflects all of these areas.

- **Completeness.** The report should reflect all areas of EGSEE in order to properly and transparently reflect the organization's overall sustainability performance.

There are a growing number of companies worldwide issuing separate environmental reports. For example: "2,500 organizations in some 60 countries around the world now measure and disclose their greenhouse gas emissions and climate change strategies through the climate disclosure project (CDP), and over 1,300 organizations published a GRI based report in 2009."[46] There are numerous reporting and certification processes and guidelines to develop proper reporting tools for government agencies and other stakeholders. Industry-led initiatives such as ISO 14000, ISO 26000, and Leadership in Energy and Environmental Design (LEED) are all certification processes in the U.S.A. and globally that can be used to track sustainable business development. These initiatives require companies to develop environmental management systems as discussed in the previous section, but do not require mandatory environmental accounting and reporting. A more convincing argument for encouraging the issuance of separate environmental reports is that the existing annual reports presenting financial statements are already very complicated and complex, and adding environmental disclosures in the annual reports would add to the already complex financial statements. More importantly, by producing a separate environmental report the organization can signal that it considers and values environmental disclosures as important as financial information.

The Statement of Financial Accounting Standards (SFAS No. 5) on contingent gains or contingent losses discusses how gains and losses are accounted for on financial statements. A contingent gain or loss is defined as a set of circumstances that leads to uncertain gains or losses in the future. The resolution of the uncertainty can induce the organization to purchase an asset, reduce a liability, incur a liability, or have a loss or impairment on an asset. However, not all uncertainties in the organization's accounting give rise to a contingent gain or loss. For example, depreciation, even though estimates are used to allocate costs over the life of a depreciable asset, is not a contingency. An example of a loss contingency defined by SFAS No. 5 is as

---

46   Global Reporting Initiative and Carbon Disclosure Project, 2010.

follows: collection of receivables; responsibility for warranties; risk of loss or damage of an organization's property from hazards; threat of expropriation of assets; litigation (current or future); risk of loss from catastrophes; agreement to repurchase receivables; etc.[47] To record an accrual for a loss contingency, these two conditions must be met: [48]

1. It is probable in the future that either an asset has been or is likely to be impaired before the financial statement issuance, or a liability has been incurred at the date of occurrence

2. The amount of loss can be reasonably estimated

5.17 Financial Reporting Standard 12

Financial Reporting Standard 12 (FRS-12) sets the principles for accounting provisions, contingent liabilities, and contingent assets. In most cases, organizations faced with transforming their environmental management activities will encounter reporting environmental provisions, contingent liabilities, and contingent assets. FRS-12 provides accounting guidance on such issues. FRS-12 defines a provision as a liability, which has uncertain timing or cash flow, and will be settled through an economic transaction.[49] A contingent liability is a potential obligation stemming from past activities whose existence can only be confirmed by future events the firm may not control, or a present obligation occurring from past events whose economic outcome cannot be established through reliable measurement.[50] A contingent asset is a potential asset coming to existence from past events not in the control of the entity.[51]

FRS-12 looks at several aspects of accounting for provisions, contingent liabilities, and contingent assets as follows:

- **Scope.** FRS-12 applies to all financial statements other than those that have financial instruments carried at fair value, have executor contracts (except where onerous), arise in insurance organizations

47   Financial Accounting Standards Board, 1975, p. 5.
48   Financial Accounting Standards Board, 1975, p. 6.
49   Accounting Standards Board, 1998.
50   Accounting Standards Board, 1998.
51   Accounting Standards Board, 1998.

contracts with policy-holders, and are covered by a more specific requirement in another FRS or SSAP rule.

- **Recognition.** A provision should be recognized when an organization has a legal or constructive obligation to a past event that has a possible transfer of economic benefits (a quantifiable estimate must be made on the amount of the obligation). If these conditions are not met the provision should not be recognized.

- **Measurement.** The amount to be recognized should be a reliable estimate of the expenditure required to settle the obligation at a given date on the balance sheet. The provision is measured before tax; changes in the tax consequences are dealt with under SSAP 15 "Accounting for deferred tax."

- **Reimbursement.** If some or all of the expenditure is obligated to be paid in settling the provision, the reimbursement should only be recognized when it is certain the reimbursement will be received by the party if the obligation is settled.

- **Changes in provisions.** Provisions should be examined each balance sheet date and updated to reflect the current best estimate. If the probability of transferring economic benefits reduces or is eliminated the provision should be reversed. If discounted, the size of the provision will change with respect to time. The change is recognized as an interest expense separate from other interest accounts on the profit and loss account.

- **Use of provision.** A provision should only be used for expenditures under the originally recognized provision.

- **Disclosure.** The following are the classes of provisions an organization should disclose: the carrying amount (the beginning and end of a period); increases to existing provisions and additions; amounts used; amounts reversed unused; change in discounted amount through time and the change in discount rate.

FRS-12 guidelines will help an organization deal with and accurately report difficult accounting situations when dealing with environmental reporting in accordance with generally accepted accounting principles (GAAP).

Financial Reporting Standard (FRS)-12 gives specific guidelines on reporting contingent liabilities and assets. Moreover, it is imperative that an organization seeking an EMS develops the necessary tools to report and track environmental performance using recognized certification processes. Through scientific advancement (e.g., global climate modeling, modeling ecosystems, and alternative energy sources), society's awareness regarding humans impact on the environment has increased, which multiplies the costs and obligations organizations will have to bear. Environmental laws and regulation will increase as well, and will force organizations to take a more hands-on approach to voluntary environmental challenges. Voluntary disclosures of environmental information can create diversity and dispersion in the format, structure, and content of environmental reporting, whereas mandatory standardized environmental reporting promotes comparability and uniformity in environmental disclosures.

5.18 Environmental auditing and assurance

Environmental assurance and auditing is a broad term used to encompass environmental compliance, assessments of risks, and company environmental sustainability and audits. ISO 14010 is a systematic verification process that evaluates the effectiveness of the EMS. The audit provides assurance that the company is complying with regulations, reducing insurance costs, and is appropriately assessing the operational environmental liabilities. There is a growing trend to have the sustainability report assured in part or whole as the value of these efforts become embedded in business strategy and stakeholder value. To ensure that the company is always improving its risk-reduction efforts, a third-party independent assurance provider can be hired to provide assurance reports on compliance with applicable environmental rules, laws, and regulations. The third-party assurance provider can examine chemical hazards and security vulnerabilities, facilitate and apply the appropriate risk-analysis technique for the risk identified, and recommend, prioritize, and review options to manage risk to a level appropriate for each company's specific risk tolerance.

5.19 Environmental best practices

Best practices are standards set informally through methods or processes that have proven successful over a period of time. Generally common sense plays a role in developing best practices, and such standards as ISO 9000 and ISO 14000 are good examples of voluntary best practices. Environmental best practices are standards such as ISO 14000 that establish an EMS in the organization to fully integrate environmental best practices, which leads to an environmentally sustainable organization. Some organizations choose to use reports based on KPIs in annual or quarterly reports on company specific missions, goals, and accomplishments. Some examples are CO_2 output, energy consumption, recycled material, raw material used, recycled material used, employee health in the workplace, etc. However useful internal KPIs may be, ISO 14000 sets global standards for management to use to become leaders in environmental sustainability.

5.19.1 ISO 14000

In 1996, the ISO created the ISO 14000 standards to help organizations globally develop adequate environmental management systems. The ISO was established in 1946 to encourage the development and execution of uniform standards throughout international trade. ISO 9000 standards on Quality Assurance and Quality Management are the best-known standards with over 1 million certified members.[52] Globalization creates competitive pressures throughout all globally competitive companies and is a driving force behind the staggering number of companies being certified in ISO 9000.

ISO 14000 standards are not mandatory; however, they are essential tools and guidelines to help organizations manage, monitor, and comply with external stakeholder demands on their environmental actions, as well as government laws and regulations. This certification ensures that organizations will meet the forthcoming environmental challenges faced by businesses and societies worldwide by providing a set of global standards for EMS. The ISO 14000 standards are viewed by organizations as a way to improve environmental performance while reducing their impact on the environment and to provide a tool for organizations to use instead of reacting to governmental laws and regulations. ISO 14000 certification can also help prevent future government litigation (or the passage of laws and regulations), and minimize their exposure to environmental costs enforced by governing bodies (e.g., the EPA). Since the ISO 14000 standards are not mandatory and strictly voluntary, environmental groups, governments, legal representatives, accountants, and other stakeholders should become familiar with the ISO 14000 standards and their impact.

---

52 International Organization for Standardization (ISO), 2010b.

ISO 14000 standards have six specific guidance areas that help an organization deal with the environmental revolution:

1. **ISO 14004.** Guidance on implementing an EMS

2. **ISO 14010.** Auditing principles and guidance

3. **ISO 14031.** Performance evaluation guidance

4. **ISO 14020.** Labeling guidance (merchandise)

5. **ISO 14040.** Life-cycle assessment principles and guidance

6. **ISO 14050.** Terms and definitions

ISO 14000 standards are becoming a necessity for competing in the global market and are helping organizations develop environmentally sustainable business plans, missions, and goals. For example, Apple has eliminated toxic chemicals and substances from its products such as arsenic, brominated flame retardants (BFRs), mercury, phthalates, and polyvinyl chloride (PVC); reduced the size of packaging for its computers by 40%, and offers complete recycling programs for old computers.[53] Many organizations are becoming and will continue to be more vocal in their environmental achievements to satisfy the growing concern for environmental sustainability. Globally there are other standards that comply with or are compatible with ISO 14000 in developing a EMS. One such system is the British standard 7750 which helps describe an EMS in that particular region.

However, there are some objections to the efficacy of continued compliance to ISO 14000 after a company or a facility has been certified.[54] Studies have shown that certified organizations or facilities do not have better environmental performance than noncertified organizations or facilities.[55] However, a study conducted by Deepa Aravind and Petra Christmann shows that while there is little difference on average between facilities that have or have not been certified, facilities that have a high-quality implementation with the full commitment of management do have higher post-environmental performance.[56] This illustrates the need for a regular auditing system that eliminates conflicts of interest while implementing proper interim monitoring systems to ensure ISO 14000 compliance and commitment. Despite some technical drawbacks, ISO 14001 certification

53 Apple, 2015.
54 O'Rourke, 2003.
55 Damall and Sides, 2008.
56 Aravind and Christmann, 2011.

does help organizations comply with government regulations and various waste reduction schemes and to reduce overall emissions.[57]

5.19.2 ISO 26000

ISO 26000 is a social responsibility (SR) standard complementary to ISO 14000 in creating a sustainable organization. ISO 26000 in general gives concepts and definitions of SR, past and future trends in SR, principles and practices of SR, develops a SR plan to integrate into the organization, engages stakeholders, and provides communication about SR practices put in place. ISO 26000 also sets guidelines for an organization to focus on the scope an organization needs to focus on understanding SR, principles of SR, recognizing SR, guidance on essential aspects of SR, and guidance on the integration process of SR.[58] ISO 26000 can be used in conjunction with ISO 14000 to ensure an organization is on the forefront of business environmental sustainability and social responsibility.

5.19.3 LEED certification

Leadership in Energy and Environmental Design (LEED) was developed in 2000 by the United States Green Building Council (USGBC) to provide building construction projects (existing building transformation or new construction) a framework and a quantification process for developing sustainable green design buildings, construction, or maintenance projects. LEED certification is useful in proving your organization is following environmentally sustainable development projects, which is audited and documented accurately. LEED measures:[59]

- **Sustainable sites.** Reduce the sites impact on the local ecosystem

- **Water efficiency.** Water use reduction inside and outside of the complex

- **Energy and atmosphere.** Sustainable design and energy monitoring systems

- **Materials and resources.** Recycled materials, sustainably grown and harvested

57   Aravind and Christmann, 2011.
58   International Organization for Standardization (ISO), 2010a.
59   United States Green Building Council, 2015.

- **Indoor environmental quality.** Improve indoor air quality

- **Locations and linkages.** Transportation efficiency to location

- **Awareness and education.** Provide necessary information about the use of green buildings.

- **Innovation in design.** Improve the buildings efficiency beyond what is necessary by LEED

These categories will lower the costs of operating the building, reduce waste, conserve energy and water, improve indoor and living quality, and reduce or eliminate GHG emissions. The certification process can also qualify for tax incentives from the U.S. government.[60] The certification process is based on a point system that can be seen here,[61] but in general the levels of certification are as follows: Certified (40–49), Silver (50–59), Gold (60–79) and Platinum (greater than 80 points), with platinum certification being the highest achievement. Such certification can help an organization document and achieve tangible sustainable development with monetary value. The certification can be a part of an organization's ISO 14000 and ISO 26000 standard system development to create a sustainable business.

The key environmental issues that impact our world today have become the key challenges of our time, the two main issues being the increase in world population and climate change. The increased need to reduce greenhouse gases in the atmosphere and the lack of natural resources make corporations vulnerable. Natural resources include water, energy, metals, rare earth minerals, and forest products. Best practices are evolving at this time, and companies are increasingly proud to share their efforts, meet regulations, and proactively lead the way in these practices. Non-compliance can be very costly, as was evidenced in the nearly $20 billion BP oil spill in the Gulf of Mexico.

5.20 Emerging opportunities and challenges of environmental performance, reporting, and assurance

There are many opportunities and challenges pertaining to environmental performance, reporting, and assurance. The 2014 revision of ISO 14001

---

60   United States Green Building Council, 2015.
61   United States Green Building Council, 2012.

addresses the following emerging changes in environmental management systems:[62]

- **Strategic environmental management.** The company's strategic plans and processes play an important role in the effective management of environmental performance. Proper environmental strategies can be mutually beneficial to the company and the environment. Effective strategies should identify and consider both opportunities and challenges facing the company in meeting its environmental responsibilities and ensuring sustainable environmental performance.

- **Leadership.** Proper leadership and tone at the top demonstrating commitments to sustainable environmental performance is the key to successful environmental management systems.

- **Protecting the environment.** Business organizations are expected to protect the environment by maximizing their positive impacts and minimizing the negative effects of their activities on the environment. Examples are prevention of pollution, protection of biodiversity and ecosystems, sustainable resource use, greenhouse gas initiatives, and climate change mitigation and adaptation.

- **Environmental performance.** Business organizations should strive to continuously improve their environmental performance by strengthening their environmental management systems and policy commitments to sustainable environmental performance.

- **Life-cycle thinking.** Business organizations need to not only manage their environmental aspects but also extend their environmental management systems and related controls and impacts on the environment.

- **Communication.** Business organizations should utilize environmental reporting as a channel of communication with all internal and external constituencies about their commitments to the environmental aspects of their business, effective management of environmental activities, and fulfillment of environmental responsibilities.

- **Documentation.** The technological advances enable business organizations to effectively and digitally document their environmental performance, reporting, and assurance.

62   International Organization for Standardization (ISO), 2014.

5.21 Conclusions

Stakeholder value creation can only be achieved when business organizations focus on all five EGSEE dimensions of sustainability. This chapter presents nonfinancial dimensions of sustainability performance, including governance, social, ethical, and environmental performance. Given that a company is the property of its owners and not stakeholders, the owners have the right to decide how to handle their property as either for profit or for social good, or both if they desired. However, there has been a move in recent years to a middle ground view of "doing well by doing good" by focusing on both financial and nonfinancial sustainability performance. Companies that are doing well financially have more slack resources to undertake social and environmental activities. By that same token, companies that are managed more effectively through robust corporate governance measures, operate ethically, and pay attention to their social and environmental initiatives are more sustainable in the long-term.

5.22 Action points

- Various incentives and pressures, driven by socially responsible investors and activists, have encouraged companies to focus on their nonfinancial governance, social, ethical, and environmental (GSEE) performance and thus increase their GSEE disclosures in corporate annual reports and the quantity and quality of such disclosures in integrated sustainability reports.

- External and independent verification of integrated sustainability reports reflecting both financial and nonfinancial information can lend objectivity and credibility to sustainability reports.

- Internal and external users of integrated sustainability reports need to have information on all five EGSEE dimensions of sustainability performance, and such information must be reliable, relevant, useful, high in quality, and verifiable.

6
Sustainability performance reporting and assurance

The primary goal of many business organizations has been and will continue to be the enhancement of shareholder value through producing sustainable economic performance as reflected in their audited financial statements. However, corporations should also effectively deal with ethical, social, governance, and environmental issues to ensure they add value for their shareholders and other stakeholders. The corporate reports to shareholders on financial sustainability performance are mandatory and standardized in the context of audited financial statements. The corporate reporting on the other four dimensions of sustainability performance of governance, social, ethical, and environmental (GSEE) has been on voluntary basis. It is expected that in the near future corporations worldwide will be required to disclose their GSEE sustainability performance information. This chapter presents mandatory reporting and assurance on financial economic sustainability performance (ESP) and nonfinancial GSEE sustainability performance.

6.1 Introduction

Sustainability reporting consists of reporting on both financial economic sustainability performance (ESP) and nonfinancial governance, social, ethical, and environmental (GSEE) sustainability performance. Public companies in the U.S.A. and throughout the world are required to produce financial statements (balance sheet, income statement, statement of cash flow, and statement of owners' equity) on ESP, have their financial statements audited by independent auditors, finalize their audited financial statements with regulators, and disseminate them to shareholders. In the past decade many (over 6,000) corporations worldwide have published voluntary sustainability reports on their GSEE sustainability performance. Starting in 2017, more than 6,000 large public companies in Europe will be required to produce sustainability reports on some GSEE to all stakeholders. A 2013 report by the Conference Board presents many cases in which GSEE nonfinancial sustainability actions and performance have a positive impacts on ESP financial sustainability performance.[1] The report also highlights the importance of establishing the link between financial and nonfinancial GSEE sustainability using KPIs. This chapter presents both mandatory reporting and assurance on financial ESP and voluntary reporting and assurance on nonfinancial GSEE sustainability performance.

The number of companies worldwide issuing stand-alone sustainability reports on various dimensions of their economic, governance, social, ethical, and environmental (EGSEE) performance has significantly increased in the past decade and is expected to grow significantly. Reliability, objectivity, and credibility of the issued sustainability reports can be substantially improved by providing assurance on these reports. This chapter examines the relevance and feasibility of external auditors' engagement in providing sustainability assurance by:

- Discussing sustainability reporting and assurance on all five EGSEE dimensions of sustainability performance

- Presenting new initiatives and guidelines for auditors in providing sustainability assurance services to their clients

6.2 Relevance of sustainability performance reporting

Sustainability reporting compels firms to evaluate the trade-offs among the competing, conflicting, or complementing interests of shareholders, society, creditors, employees, and the environment. Ioannou and Serafeim

---

1   Bertoneche and van der Lugt, 2013.

suggest that corporate sustainability reporting increases the social responsibility of business leaders and that both sustainable development and employee training have become a higher priority for companies.[2] In its G4 guidelines released in May 2013, the GRI promotes sustainability reporting as a standard practice of disclosing sustainability-related issues relevant to companies' business practices and to their stakeholders.[3] A more uniform and standardized disclosure of GSEE sustainability performance has received considerable attention recently from regulators (SEC), standard-setters (Sustainability Accounting Standard Board, SASB), investor activists (Investor Network on Climate Risk, INCR), and interest groups (Bloomberg, GRI, International Integrated Reporting Council, IIRC).

Socially Responsible Investors consisting of financial institutions and public pension funds have often shown preferences for both desired investment returns and social impacts. Socially responsible investing (SRI) refers to investment strategies that are designed to achieve both financial and social objectives by focusing on both financial return regarding ESP and nonfinancial performance about GSEE sustainability activities. Under SRI principles, investors consider various sustainability issues in their investment decisions. It is reported that SRI funds increased by more than 22% to $3.74 trillion in managed assets during the 2010–12 period.[4] Business organizations with good track records in and perceptions of sustainable value creation philosophy and practices have a higher likelihood of attracting SRI and generating sustainable value, which enables them to focus on activities that maximize sustainable economic performance.

In July 2011, the Singapore Exchange released its "Sustainability Reporting Guide" for its listed companies, requiring them to issue disclosures of accountability for conducting business in a sustainable manner.[5] The idea is that a company must extend its focus beyond profit maximization by considering the impact of its operation on the community, society, and the environment. The 2011 third annual sustainability global executive survey reports that sustainability initiatives are gaining importance, as the majority (over 75%) of over 4,700 executives said that sustainability-related strategies are necessary in order to improve their corporate image, reputation, and competitiveness.[6] Another recent survey also indicates that firms

2   Ioannou and Serafeim, 2011a.
3   Global Reporting Initiative, 2013a.
4   US SIF Foundation, 2012.
5   Singapore Exchange, 2011.
6   MIT Sloan Management Review and Boston Consulting Group, 2011.

that see sustainability as both a necessity and an opportunity, changing their business models in response, are finding success.[7] Despite the growing importance of nonfinancial sustainability GSEE for a firm's long-term financial performance, there is very little in the way of required sustainability disclosures and related research. A 2013 joint study by the Investor Responsibility Research Center Institute (IRRCI) and the Sustainable Investments Institute (Si2) reports that only 1.4% of the S&P companies (seven firms) issued a stand-alone sustainability report within their regulatory filing of 10-K reports, whereas almost all S&P companies (499) indirectly disclosed at least one piece of sustainability information, 74% placed monetary value on their sustainability-related disclosures and about 44% linked their executive compensation to some type of sustainability criteria.[8] Clearly, GSEE sustainability disclosures are expected to be value-relevant to both external and internal users of such reports. The link between sustainability performance disclosures and firm value is driven from the stakeholder theory, which suggests that the primary goal of a firm is to protect the interests of all stakeholders with a keen focus on achieving a long-term and enduring desired return on investment for shareholders.[9] More than 6,000 global public companies issued a stand-alone sustainability report in 2012 compared with less than 500 companies in 2005.[10] This trend is expected to continue as sustainability performance related resolutions by shareholders have significantly increased during the 2013 proxy season.[11] Global stock exchanges either require or recommend their listed firms to report sustainability performance,[12] and the European Parliament, in September, 2014, adopted a new directive that would require about 6,000 listed companies to disclose information on their nonfinancial GSEE sustainability performance.[13] Investors demand sustainability performance information, regulators require disclosure of EGSEE sustainability performance information, and companies prefer to disclose sustainability performance information to differentiate themselves from less sustainable, less socially, and environmentally responsible companies. Sustainability reports are deemed to be

7   Kiron *et al.*, 2013b.
8   IRRC Institute and Sustainable Investments Institute, 2013.
9   Jensen, 2001.
10   Global Reporting Initiative, 2012a.
11   Institutional Shareholder Services, 2013.
12   Toronto Stock Exchange and Chartered Professional Accountants of Canada, 2014.
13   European Commission, 2014.

useful when they are complete, accurate, and their reliability, objectivity, and credibility are ascertained by assurance providers (auditors).

6.3 Mandatory reporting

Traditionally, public companies have prepared their financial statements to reflect their financial position and results of operations on economic performance for the benefit of their shareholders. In recent decades, in compliance with provisions of the Sarbanes-Oxley Act of 2002 and related Securities and Exchange Commission (SEC), rules and auditing standards of the Public Company Accounting Oversight Board (PCAOB) have certified completeness and accuracy of their financial statements and effectiveness of internal controls over financial reporting (ICFR) as well as audit reports on both financial statements and ICFR as discussed in detail in Chapter 4. These financial and audit reports solely present economic performance to shareholders with the main goal of creating shareholder value. However, in recent years, stakeholders and the public increasingly scrutinize how corporations can maximize their positive impacts and minimize impacts of their operations by paying attention to socially and environmentally responsible initiatives. Public companies are now expected to protect the interests of all stakeholders, including shareholders, creditors, customers, suppliers, employees, government, environment, and society. Thus, corporate reporting has expanded to reflect not only economic performance but also the environmental and social impacts of the business.

The Sustainability Accounting Standards Board (SASB) establishes and creates sustainability accounting standards suitable for developing standards for disclosing material sustainability issues for 88 industries in ten sectors, launching the process for mandatory filings to the Securities and Exchange Commission (SEC), such as the Form 10-K and 20-F through the first quarter of 2015.[14] SASB's concern is creating standards that enable peer-to-peer comparison between companies, which can be useful for investment decisions and allocation of capital. In June 2011 the Global Initiative for Sustainability Ratings (GISR) developed environmental, social, and governance (ESG) ratings standard to conduct with an eye toward maximum harmonization with leading, complementary standard-setters, most

14   Sustainability Accounting Standards Board, 2013.

notably, the Global Reporting Initiative (GRI), the International Integrated Reporting Council (IIRC), the Carbon Disclosure Project (CDP), and SASB, informed by best practices among leading raters.[15] Harmonizing SASB standards with existing disclosure standards avoids additional costs for companies and aligns SASB's work with global corporate transparency efforts. The products of the SASB, GRI, and IIRC can be used in complementary ways for the development of a sustainability report for investors and all stakeholders. The SASB provides standards for mandatory filings, whereas the GRI and IIRC provide frameworks for voluntary reporting.

The move toward the issuance of mandatory GSEE sustainability reporting has been very slow. The Social Investment Forum (SIF), in 2009, requested that the Obama Administration take initiatives to restore investor confidence by strengthening corporate responsibility of mandatory reporting on corporate GSEE sustainability performance as discussed in the previous chapter.[16] The SIF has developed a proposal requesting the SEC to require public companies to:[17]

- Report annually their sustainability information in compliance with the GRI guidelines
- Disclose their short-term and long-term sustainability risks in the Management Discussion and Analysis (MD&A) section of the 10-K

Many countries (France, Malaysia, Sweden, the U.K., Singapore) are modernizing their corporate reporting systems to include ESG factors in compliance with GRI guidelines.[18] The European Commission (EC) recently adopted a directive that would require disclosure of nonfinancial information of GSEE sustainability performance.[19]

6.4 Voluntary reporting

There is no mandatory guidance at this time for sustainability reporting on GSEE sustainability performance. However, there are several voluntary

---

15   Global Initiative for Sustainability Ratings, 2013.
16   Social Investment Forum, 2009.
17   Social Investment Forum, 2009.
18   Toronto Stock Exchange and Chartered Professional Accountants of Canada, 2014.
19   European Commission, 2014.

guidelines for sustainability reporting, including the reporting frameworks released by GRI, the Connected Reporting Framework, and the reporting publications of AccountAbility and the Sustainability Accounting Standards Board (SASB). The fourth generation (G4) of GRI's Guidelines covers economic, governance, social, and environmental performance with keen focus on sustainability value creation and the perception that all stakeholders benefit from an integrated report on all five EGSEE dimensions of sustainability performance with the ethics dimension is embedded in the other four dimensions.[20]

The GRI reporting process enables organizations to disclose their stakeholder value creation performance by self-declaring sustainability performance information based on one of three application levels (A, B, or C) depending on the extent of information provided. The GRI initially focused on a triple bottom line of economic, social, and environmental performance, with version 3.1 (G3) of its sustainability framework. However, in 2011 the GRI developed version 4.1 or the fourth generation (G4) of guidelines, which covers economic, governance, social, and environmental performance. The G4 framework promotes a principles-based approach of creating maximum flexibility for business organizations to tailor integrated reporting into their corporate reporting strategies, compliance requirements, and stakeholder needs and demands for sustainable financial and nonfinancial performance. An integrated sustainability report can be issued as a stand-alone report or in conjunction with the existing mandatory financial and compliance reports.

6.5 Guiding principles of integrated reporting

The GRI framework identifies both financial and nonfinancial sustainability performance information that should be included in an integrated report of organizations of all types and sizes. The GRI G4 framework also provides guiding principles for preparing an integrated report. These guiding principles have a strategic focus and future orientation, connectivity of information, stakeholder relations, materiality, conciseness, reliability, and completeness, consistency, and comparability.[21] A 2013 joint study by the Investor Responsibility Research Center Institute (IRRCI) and the

---

20   Global Reporting Initiative, 2013a.
21   Global Reporting Initiative, 2013a.

Sustainable Investments Institute (Si2) reports that only 1.4% of the S&P companies (seven firms) issued a stand-alone sustainability report within their regulatory filing of 10-K reports, whereas almost all S&P companies (499) indirectly disclosed at least one piece of sustainability information, 74% placed monetary value on their sustainability-related disclosures and about 44% linked their executive compensation to some type of sustainability criteria[22]

Currently, sustainability reports are voluntary and normally not audited by external auditors. Existing sustainability reports bear different names (green reporting, corporate social responsibility reporting), serve different stakeholders in achieving a variety of purposes, and vary in terms of content, structure, format, accuracy, and assurance. A more standardized, integrated, and audited process is required to make sustainability reports on EGSEE performance comparable, commonly acceptable, and relevant to all corporate stakeholders. Recently, Global Reporting Initiatives provided a comprehensive Sustainability Reporting Framework to enable greater organizational transparency.[23] In 2013, the International Integrated Reporting Council (IIRC) developed the International Integrated Reporting Framework, which provides guidelines for companies to integrate financial and nonfinancial performance information to benefit all stakeholders.[24] The European Parliament, on May 15, 2014, issued a new directive that would require listed companies to disclose information on their environmental, social, environmental, and diversity in addition to financial information on economic performance.[25] It is expected that companies in other countries will follow suit, and thus in the future, sustainability reports should reflect both financial and nonfinancial information relevant to all five EGSEE dimensions of sustainability performance. Assurance should be provided on these reports to enhance their credibility and reliability.

A comprehensive integrated report should include four key parts:[26]

1. **Inputs.** These are what the company brings in to create stakeholder value. In effect, this is the company's capital (i.e., the "six capitals," as defined by the IIRC: Financial, Human, Intellectual, Manufactured, Natural, and Social and Relationships). With more

22   IRRC Institute and Sustainable Investments Institute, 2013.
23   Global Reporting Initiative, 2012b.
24   International Integrated Reporting Council, 2012.
25   European Commission, 2014.
26   Topazio, 2014a.

knowledge about the ways in which capital comes into the company, stakeholders can better formulate that capital into more profitable ventures. In addition, certain stakeholders may know how best to utilize said capital in different manners to affect better growth than if it were utilized solely by prevailing measures.

2. **Business activities.** These are activities that the company performs using the aforementioned inputs to create value for the company. They entail all financial and nonfinancial dimensions of sustainability performance of the company and should be linked into the company's mission.

3. **Outputs.** These are the end results of the company's business activities. These include the products and services offered as well as any of their by-products. Each of these outputs has a certain price point attached to it, and that price is different for each stakeholder. For example, pollution may have zero consideration for a customer interested solely in the end-product, a very high cost for a stakeholder interested in the environment, and an economic benefit for a supplier who can recycle the waste into another product.

4. **Outcomes.** Outcomes are the consequences of disclosing the five EGSEE dimensions of sustainability performance and can be financial or nonfinancial, positive or negative. Outcomes should reflect strengths and concerns of the company's activities and sustainability performance in all five EGSEE dimensions.

6.6 Sustainability reporting assurance

Objectivity, reliability, transparency, credibility, and usefulness of sustainability reports are important to both internal and external users of these reports and can be enhanced by providing assurance on sustainability reports. Sustainability assurance can be provided internally by internal auditors or external assurance providers. While internal auditors are well qualified to assist management in the preparation of sustainability reports and providing assurance, external users of sustainability reports may demand more independent and objective assurance on sustainability reports. This type of assurance can be provided by certified public accountants (CPAs), professional assurance providers, or equivalent accredited individuals, groups, or bodies. Current auditing standards are intended to provide reasonable assurance on financial and internal control reports prepared by management. However, the degree of reliance placed on nonfinancial information such as sustainability reporting is not completely clear. Assurance standards on different dimensions of sustainability performance reports vary in terms of rigorousness and general acceptability. For example, auditing standards governing reporting and assurance on economics activities presented in the financial statements are well established and widely accepted and practiced. Assurance standards on other dimensions of sustainability including governance, ethics, social, and environmental standards are yet to be fully developed and globally accepted. Sustainability assurance in the form of audit reports has been issued on financial ESP by external and independent auditors. In order to audit financial statements and internal control over financial reporting attention, this study considers a standard published by Public Company Accounting Oversight Board (PCAOB) and applies it to the economic dimension. Unlike audit reports on financial statements, assurance reports on sustainability information are neither standardized, regulated, nor licensed. The International Federation of Accountants (IFAC) released its revised "International Standard on Assurance Engagements Other Than Audits or Reviews of Historical Financial Information," 3000 (ISAE 3000).[27] Specifically, ISAE 3410 deals with assurance engagements for an organization reporting greenhouse gas (GHG) statements.[28] ISAE 3410 addresses professional accountants' assurance practices pertaining to sustainability reports, including reports on carbon emissions information prepared for regulatory purposes or disclosures to the company's stakeholders.

The GRI also recommends that assurance be provided on sustainability reports by external assurance providers, which can be designated with a "+" added to the application level declared. Alternatively, the GRI can examine the content of detailed sustainability reports and express an opinion on the extent of compliance with GRI guidelines but not the quality and/or reliability of disclosed sustainability information.[29]

As the number of public companies worldwide issuing sustainability reports grows, these reports should be audited and/or reviewed by assurance

27   International Federation of Accountants, 2011.
28   International Federation of Accountants, 2012a.
29   Global Reporting Initiative, 2011.

service providers. Unlike audit reports on financial statements, assurance reports on sustainability information are neither standardized, regulated, nor licensed. A number of professionals, including internal auditors, external auditors, and other service providers, can offer assurance on sustainability reports. The "Big Four" accounting firms have developed expertise in sustainability reporting and assurance, and they are well equipped and trained to provide sustainability assurance services to their clients.

The International Standard on Assurance Engagements, "Other Than Audits or Reviews of Historical Financial Information," 3000 (ISAE 3000), and ISAE 3410 (Assurance Engagements on Greenhouse Gas Statements) assurance practice standards provide guidelines for assurance providers to engage in assurance sustainability services in expressing professional opinions on all five dimensions of EGSEE sustainability performance. These two standards suggest limited assurance engagements for nonfinancial dimensions of sustainability performance without specifying what audit procedures should be performed. However, a certain set of audit procedures such as inquiry, analytical procedures, and other procedures necessary in assessing the risks of material misstatements should be performed in order to provide reasonable assurance on accuracy, consistency, and completeness of the sustainability reports. The International Standards on Assurance Engagements (ISAE) 3000, issued by the IAAS Board in 2004, the AICPA's Attestation Standards (AT Section 101), CICA section 5025, and AA1000 Assurance Standards (AS) issued in 2008 by Accountability (AA) provide guidance for assurance on nonfinancial dimensions of sustainability.[30]

6.7 Best practices of sustainability reporting

The best practices of sustainability reporting are evolving as more business organizations disclose various dimensions of their sustainability performance on a voluntary basis. Table 6.1 presents a limited list of such best practices of sustainability reports, including the name of the company, its industry, country, the year of the report, and various EGSEE dimensions of sustainability performance, adopted sustainability reporting guidelines, recognized professional organizations, and best practices for sustainability

---

30   Brockett and Rezaee, 2012a.

Company	Industry	Country	Year of latest report	Recognizing body	EGSEE[1] focus	Adopted guidelines	Best practices for sustainability reporting
Varian Medical Systems	Medical devices	U.S.A.	2014	CERES[2]	G, S, E3	GRI	95% of hazardous waste recycled/reclaimed/treated
Keppel Land Limited	Real estate/development	Singapore	2013	SSA[3]	G, S, E3	GRI G4, UNGC 10, ISO 26000	ESG issues are considered and discussed at every board meeting and are a fundamental part of the company's objectives.
Sembcorp Marine Ltd.	Utilities, marine engineering, urban development	Singapore	2012	SSA	E1, G	GRI G4	Enacts a strict set of guidelines surrounding executive compensation, employee remuneration, and board composition
Repsol	Oil/gas	Spain	2013-14	SAM[4]	G, S, E2, E3	UN GPBHR, ISO 26000, OECD, IFC	Promotes education among youth to create a more sustainable business environment
Statoil	Oil/gas	Norway	2013	UNGC 100, CK,[5] DJSI[6]	E1, G, S, E2, E3	GRI G3	Promotes local development through education and investment programs
Eni	Energy	Italy	2013	UNGC LEAD, TI	G, E3	GRI G3.1	Pilot member of the UNGC LEAD program and ranked first in corporate transparency reporting
PTTEP	Energy/utilities	Thailand	2013	SET,[7] CH Asia	G, S	GRI G3.1	Constructed a pipeline to direct excess natural gas to locals for cheap fuel
Genting Singapore	Real estate/development	Singapore	2013	BritCham, SIAS[8]	G, S, E3	GRI G4	Discloses all related information to all stakeholders through SGXNET and its corporate website

NORMA Group[1]	Engineering/supply chain	Germany	2013	LACP[9]	E1, G, E3	GRI G4	Designs lightweight components to make end-products more environmentally friendly
Airport Authority Hong Kong	Management	Hong Kong	2014	BCI Asia	E1, S, E3	GRI G3.1	Holds many meetings, presentations, and talks to discuss EGSEE matters with stakeholders
Cobb-Vantress	Livestock	U.S.A.	2013	N/A	S, E3	GRI G3.1	Publishes biennial reports to effectively interact with their stakeholders, but not overwhelm with information
Bank Asia	Financial services	Bangladesh	2013	ICAB	E1, S, E3	GRI G3.1	Uses the TBL as its main guideline for action
CapitaLand	Real estate	Singapore	2013	CK, DJSI	G, S, E3	GRI G4	Instituted a sustainability management structure to ensure ESG progress
Novartis	Pharmaceuticals	Switzerland	2013	CK, DJSI	S, E3	GRI, UNGC 10	Uses its worldwide logistics connections to ascertain issues in all of its locales

TABLE 6.1   Best practices of sustainability performance

[1] E1: Economic, E2: Ethical, E3: Environmental
[2] Coalition for Environmentally Responsible Economies
[3] Singapore Sustainability Awards
[4] Sustainability Asset Management
[5] Corporate Knights
[6] Dow Jones Sustainability Index
[7] Stock Exchange of Thailand
[8] Securities Investors Association Singapore
[9] League of American Communication Professionals
[10] Institute of Chartered Accountants of Bangladesh

reporting. The information presented in Table 6.1 suggests the following best practices of sustainability reporting:

- Sustainability reports are prepared by types and sizes of business organizations operating in different industries ranging from medical to real estate, energy, and financial.

- The most prevailing reporting standards followed by the majority of these organizations are G4 of the Global Reporting Initiative.

- These reports disclose information regarding all five economic, governance, social, ethical, and environmental (EGSEE) sustainability performance, with a majority reporting their environmental, social, and governance (ESG) sustainability performance.

- These sustainability reports are recognized by professional organizations, security regulators, professional accountants, and investors associations.

- Sustainability reports are linked to the company's strategic decisions and plans on economic, social, and environmental activities.

- A balance between the economic prosperity and environmental and social responsibilities can lead to competitive advantages and a leadership position in the industry.

- A proactive business sustainability strategy with a keen focus on social, economic, and environmental performance is cost-effective with substantial financial rewards.

- Leaders in sustainability reporting effectively communicate their business sustainability strategies, decisions, actions, and performance to all stakeholders in demonstrating their commitment to the promotion of stakeholder value creation.

- Sustainability reports can be used as an important communication vehicle in building public trust, investor confidence, customer satisfactions and reputation, attracting and retaining talented employees, and earning the license to operate globally.

- The integrated reporting enables organizations to incorporate sustainability into their business decisions and identify, classify, measure, recognize, and disclose their EGSEE sustainability performance to all stakeholders.

6.8 Best practices of sustainability assurance

The best practices of sustainability assurance are evolving as more assurance providers engage in providing assurance services on various EGSEE dimensions of sustainability performance and as professional organizations and assurance standard-setters are developing more robust sustainability assurance guidelines. Table 6.2 presents a limited list of such best practices of sustainability assurance reports, including the name of the company, its industry, country, the year of the assurance report, assurance on various EGSEE dimensions of sustainability performance, adopted sustainability assurance guidelines, professional assurance providers, and best practices for sustainability assurance. The information presented in Table 6.2 suggests the following best practices of sustainability assurance:

- External assurance and independent review is an important component of sustainability reporting.

- Organizations of all sizes and types obtain external assurance on various dimensions of their sustainability performance.

- The majority of sustainability reports were examined by the Big Four international auditing firms of KPMG, PwC, EY, and Deloitte.

- Adopted auditing standards used in providing sustainability assurance services are limited to those issued by the GRI and IAAS.

- The scope of sustainability assurance services is limited to inquiry and analytical procedures or any other agreed audit procedures.

- The type of sustainability assurance report is of the negative assurance type, indicating that the assurance provider is not aware of any non-compliance with related standards or guidelines.

- Lack of a set of globally accepted assurance standards has caused inconsistency in sustainability assurance reports and a lack of uniformity in the type and scope of audit procedures applied.

- The most challenging assurance services are assurance engagements of ethical, social, and governance dimensions of sustainability performance.

- Sustainability assurance services usually consist of both internal and external engagements.

Company	Industry	Country	Year of latest report	Assurance provider	Scope of report given assurance	Adopted guidelines and standards	Best practices for assurance
BHP Billiton	Mining and metals	Australia	2014	KPMG	Entire report, GHG[1]	GRI G3, ISAE3000, ICMM	Over 300 senior management and key staff interviewed with the auditors to provide assurance
Votorantim Industrial S/A	Conglomerate	Brazil	2013	PwC	Limited: Social and Environmental	GRI G3	Included the Assurance Report, which indicates the auditor's opinion that the company did not comply with GRI guidelines on the scope investigated
Banco Galicia	Financial services	Argentina	2013	PwC	Limited: Key elements of sustainability reporting	GRI G3.1, AA1000AS, ISAE3000	Despite the assurance engagement being limited, each of the factors tested by the auditors was found to be compliant with guidelines and well done
Family Development Foundation	Nonprofit	UAE	2014	Humantelligence	Limited: Did not cover financial or supplier issues	GRI G3	Sought assurance on both the report itself and the company's progress since the previous year
Mineração Rio do Norte	Mining and metals	Brazil	2014	KPMG	Limited assurance on entire report	GRI G3.1, ISAE3000	Though the GRI compliance level was a low C+, the company still provided external assurance on the parts that it did cover
Larsen & Toubro Ltd.	Construction	India	2013	EY	Limited to sustainability performance and company collection protocols	GRI G3, AA1000AS, ISAE3000	The company has put into place people at all organizational levels and at its work sites to ensure sustainability management and reporting

Arçelik	Consumer durables	Turkey	2013	BSI	Limited: GHG only	GRI G3	In the absence of national standards on assurance providing, the company works with the assurance provider to enact its own standards to get reasonable, if not ultimate, assurance
Dell	Computers	U.S.A.	2013	Trucost	Limited: GHG only	GRI G3.1, AA1000APS	The company created a stakeholder map to ensure that their needs are met and that the most material KPIs are attended to.
Endesa Chile	Energy	Chile	2013	KPMG	Entire report	GRI G3.1, AA1000AS, ISAE3000	The company provided KPMG with access to key personnel and sites and reviewed internal controls and proprietary data.
Allergan	Healthcare products	U.S.A.	2014	ERM	Limited: GHG only	GRI G3.1, ISO 14064-1 & -3	Due to the breadth of facilities to audit, the company sought limited assurance on its GHG emissions overall and a detailed review of its main facility.
Kemira	Chemicals	Finland	2013	Deloitte	Limited assurance on entire report	GRI G4, ISAE3000	The company engaged the assurance provider to provide assurance for its quantifiable data, not data foreseen for the future.
Vivendi	Media	France	2014	KPMG, EY	Limited assurance on entire report	GRI G3.1, ISAE3000	The company sought assurance on all subsidiaries deemed material to company financial reporting.

TABLE 6.2   **Best practices of sustainability assurance**

1 Greenhouse Gas emissions
Source: The "Featured" section of the GRI sustainability disclosure database at http://database.globalreporting.org.

- Sustainability assurance engagements are effective in identifying areas of concern and improvement as well as the risk associated with achieving sustainability performance.

- Sustainability assurance reports are used for internal managerial decision-making purposes and enhancing credibility of sustainability performance reports submitted to the company's stakeholders or filed with regulatory agencies.

- Potential benefits of external sustainability assurance are enhancing credibility of sustainability reports on all five dimensions of sustainability performance, ensuring compliance with all applicable laws, rules, regulations, and standards, minimizing the risk of non-compliance, improving operational effectiveness and efficiency on all EGSEE dimensions, and reducing the risk of civil and criminal liabilities.

6.9 Conclusions

The type, format, and content of sustainability performance reports are evolving rapidly. More than 6,000 public companies worldwide now voluntarily disclose their various dimensions of sustainability performance information, and European companies will soon be required to report their sustainability performance in areas of social, environmental, governance, and diversity. The number of companies worldwide issuing stand-alone sustainability reports on various dimensions of their economic, governance, social, ethical, and environmental (EGSEE) performance has significantly increased in the past decade and is expected to grow significantly. The reliability, objectivity, and credibility of the issued sustainability reports can be substantially improved by providing assurance on these reports. This chapter suggests the development of a business sustainability information system that captures and consolidates the details necessary to prepare sustainability reports externally as well as monitor and control all five EGSEE dimensions of sustainability performance internally. This chapter also presents the best practices of sustainability reporting and assurance.

6.10 Action points

- Identify attributes, needs, and compliance requirements of sustainability reporting for both internal and external reporting purposes.

- Utilize an integrated sustainability report that reflects all five EGSEE dimensions of sustainability performance and their relevance to all stakeholders.

- Internal sustainability reporting is intended to promote sustainability development throughout the organization, provide important feedback for improving sustainability performance, and hold directors, executives, and employees accountable for achieving sustainable performance.

- Verification of information contained in sustainability reports can be accomplished with audits by sustainability assurance providers.

- To provide assurance on sustainability performance information and thus confidence among stakeholders, companies should demonstrate that their five EGSEE dimensions of sustainability performance metrics are accurately measured and representative of actual efforts and achievements.

- External sustainability reporting provides an opportunity for business organizations to communicate their sustainability value creation regarding all five EGSEE dimensions of sustainability performance to all stakeholders.

- Independent verification of external sustainability performance reports is an important component of sustainability reporting.

- Address challenges associated with an independent verification and audit of sustainability reports by external assurance providers. Correspondingly, there are no generally accepted worldwide auditing or reporting standards.

- Use existing guidelines and framework on reporting social, governance, ethical, and environmental sustainability performance provided by the GRI, AccountAbility, SASB, and IIRC.

- Corporate sustainability reporting and auditing processes require internal and external sustainability reports and audits.

- Corporate sustainability reports should reflect both strengths and weaknesses in all five EGSEE dimensions of sustainability performance.

- International public accounting firms are well trained, have adequate resources and the required expertise, and are independent to provide external assurance services on sustainability reports.

- External assurance on sustainability performance reports lends credibility to reports and increases stakeholder confidence in the quality and usefulness of sustainability reports.

7
Future of sustainability performance, reporting, and assurance

Business sustainability is gaining considerable attention as socially responsible investors prefer to invest in sustainable and socially responsible corporations while regulators worldwide recommend and/or demand that public companies disclose their nonfinancial dimensions of sustainability performance in areas of governance, social, environmental, and diversity activities. The format and content of sustainability performance reporting is also rapidly evolving. More than 6,000 public companies worldwide now voluntarily disclose some sustainability performance information, and European companies will soon be required to report their performance on sustainability. This chapter presents future trends in sustainability performance, reporting, and assurance by exploring the best practices of sustainability, the use of the Extensible Business Reporting Language (XBRL) in sustainability reporting, and the use of continuous auditing in providing sustainability assurance.

7.1 Introduction

Starting in 2017, more than 6,000 public companies in Europe will be required to disclose their sustainability performance information regarding governance, social, environmental, and diversity activities.[1] Other countries are expected to follow suit. This move toward sustainability performance, reporting, and assurance is inevitable as sustainability initiatives are integrated into corporate strategies, supply chain, decisions, actions, and performance.

The content and format of sustainability reporting is also shifting toward being online and in real time. The Extensible Business Reporting Language (XBRL) format is used in financial, tax, and statutory reporting, and its relevance to sustainability reporting is being explored by researchers. Continuous auditing techniques are being applied to audit the automated financial reporting process, and their applications in providing continuous assurance on sustainability reporting are examined in this chapter. The XBRL platform for sustainability reporting and the outline of the implementation methods for using XBRL-based architectures for sustainability reporting are viewed by many as the future of corporate reporting and assurance services.

7.2 Sustainability reporting guidelines

The terms: "sustainability reporting," "integrated reporting," "environmental, social, and governance (ESG) reporting," "corporate social responsibility (CSR) reporting," and "risk compliance and governance (RCG)," have been used interchangeably in business literature to describe reports with a wide range of coverage and different degrees of focus on risk, environmental, social, or governance issues. Rezaee and Brockett take a holistic and integrated approach to sustainability reporting by focusing on disclosing all five dimensions of sustainability performance of economic, governance, social, ethic, and environmental (EGSEE) issues.[2]

Sustainability reporting is a complex and not easily understood process. As such, many companies do not or have not yet begun to report on their sustainability practices. It is, however, not an insurmountable task, as Nick

---

1   European Commission, 2014.
2   Brockett and Rezaee, 2012a.

Topazio of the Chartered Institute of Management Accountants details. In his article titled, "6 Tips for Integrated Thinking," he lists a few ways that companies can more easily create these reports:[3]

1. **Value creation.** A business organization must understand what makes itself tick, what makes it stand above others, and what inputs and outputs come into and out of the organization. This is more inclusive than a simple production line, as all organizations are connected with multiple relationships that are important for many reasons, and they are all interconnected with each other. The main objective of integrated reporting is to reflect the company's stakeholder value creation.

2. **Current and future trends.** An organization should be familiar not only with the current environments in which it operates, but also with the environment in which it will operate in the future. This includes not only positive externalities such as sales/profit growth, new markets, and trends, but also negative externalities such as new competition, falling prices/sales, and agency issues. An organization should be able to explain why these are happening, how they affect the organization, and what will be done to increase or decrease their effects, as the case may be.

3. **Nonfinancial metrics.** Determine what nonfinancial measures may be in play for the organization, study them, and report them to the stakeholders as a main point, not just an appendix to the financial statements. If it is evident that the organization is not giving prominence to the ways in which it is promoting sustainability, then stakeholders cannot know to what extent their demands are being met. Typical nonfinancial dimensions of sustainability performance are environmental, social, and governance (ESG).

4. **The link between nonfinancial measures and long-term financial success.** Demonstrate to the stakeholders the importance of the above nonfinancial measures to the long-term financial stability of the organization. An investment in low-energy light bulbs, for instance, may be expensive in the short term, but the cost savings may be great over their life-span, as they last longer and use less electricity than do regular light bulbs.

3   Topazio, 2014b.

5. **Tone at the top commitments to sustainability performance reporting.** Give evidence to the entire board that all parts of the organization are linked to each other through the financial and nonfinancial information. The executive members should already be knowledgeable on the practice and theory behind these inter-actions, but that is not necessarily the case for all members. All members should be able to see, if at only a limited level, how each of these measures affects the others and have any questions they may have allayed. The ways in which new ventures help and will help the bottom line in the end should be explained in an easy-to-understand manner, not limited to those with advanced prior knowledge.

6. **Holistic and integrated sustainability reporting.** Be extensive when it comes to reporting. While few would read a report with every single piece of sustainability information that an organiza-tion has available, readers should be able to get a good overview of the measures that the organization is putting forth to create sustainable value. An important aspect of this is that the informa-tion should be easy to read and follow, as well as interconnected. This should help the organization make its decisions in a better manner.

The Global Reporting Initiative (GRI) releases guidelines to aid companies in their pursuit of sustainable reporting. The latest version, known as G4, was released in May 2013 and seeks to be the most comprehensive detail-ing of the steps companies should take to ensure their compliance with the best practices of sustainability reporting. The suggested methodology for generating a proper sustainability report is as follows:[4]

1. Obtain an overview of the G4 reporting guidelines

2. Choose whether to make the report comprehensive or focused solely on core issues

3. Prepare to disclose general standard disclosures used by all companies:
    – Identify the general standard disclosures to use for the appro-priate choice made in step 2 and check if any apply to their industry

4   Global Reporting Initiative, 2013a.

– Plan out the process to disclose these general standard disclosures in line with standards of quality

4. Prepare to disclose specific standard disclosures material to their company

5. Prepare the sustainability report

As these guidelines are followed and enacted, the companies that follow them should be well on the road to having a sustainable practice. The GRI requests that companies that release sustainability reports send these reports to the GRI to ensure that their guidelines are being followed in a proper manner. Below is a more detailed description of the various stages.[5]

7.2.1 Obtaining an overview of the G4 reporting guidelines

The G4 reporting guidelines are part of a very large corpus, totaling over 300 pages of material. As such, it is essential that a company understands them in a very general sense when they begin making the report and learns its parts in greater detail throughout the process. The first part of the guidelines details the reporting principles, standard disclosures, definitions of key terms, and how companies may determine whether their report is "in accordance" with the Guidelines. The Reporting Principles are used to define the content and the quality of the reports. These include the following aspects:

- Content:
  - **Stakeholder inclusiveness.** Stakeholders must be identified and explanations given regarding the extent to which their expectations and interests have been met.
  - **Sustainability context.** The context in which the company enacts its sustainability practices with regard to its environment, such as its industry, economic, environmental, or social conditions, or trends at the local, regional, or global level, must be detailed to form a metric to compare against others in the field.
  - **Materiality.** The content of the report is composed of topics that have significant economic, environmental, or social impacts and/or that significantly influence the assessments and decisions of stakeholders.

5   Global Reporting Initiative, 2013a.

- **Completeness.** Report writers should include the extent to which the material topics have been covered and their boundaries so that the stakeholders can assess the company's performance during the period under report.

- Quality:
  - **Balance.** The report must show a balanced and unbiased view of the company, ensuring that its good and bad aspects are brought to light in the appropriate measures and that there are no adverse selections or omissions.
  - **Comparability.** Companies must ensure that the data provided may be compared easily with the information previously disclosed by the company and by other companies in the industry so that a clear view may be had of the company's progress over time and of its relation to other companies in the industry.
  - **Accuracy.** It is vital that the information included in the report be accurate and detailed so that stakeholders can evaluate the company's performance and be better assured of their forecasts.
  - **Timeliness.** Companies must ensure that the reports are given at regular times and able to be used by stakeholders in making decisions. Timeliness is also an important factor in stakeholders' minds in their valuation of the company and their concerns regarding its practices; if a company takes too long to make a report or delays it for too long a time, that may reflect some issue with their sustainability and thus diminish their achievements in the eyes of the stakeholders.
  - **Clarity.** Reports should be easy to understand to stakeholders who follow the company's practices.
  - **Reliability.** Reports must be able to stand up to checks from stakeholders interested in the veracity of the information contained therein. If issues arise when examined closely, then stakeholders will have less confidence in the infrastructure of the company's sustainability initiatives.

These factors may take some time to understand and fully implement, but they should be a good starting point.

7.2.2 Prepare the integrated report

Once these factors are understood, the company can work toward the next step, deciding whether to use the **core** or **comprehensive** options to prepare their integrated report. Either approach can be used by any company of any size in any industry, but it is up to management to decide which to use. A company that issues a perfunctory report may choose the **core** option, or a company well-known for its sustainability practices already may choose the same option so as not to duplicate efforts. A company may choose the **comprehensive** option to emphasize its history of sustainability practices or because it is a newcomer wishing to impress potential new stakeholders. Either option denotes the respective quality of the report, as a well-done **core** report may be more valuable than a poorly done **comprehensive** report. The decision for which option to choose is made simply based on what the company chooses to focus on with its goals, resources, and attention.

7.2.3 Prepare to disclose general standard disclosures used by all companies

Once the choice has been made for the **core** or **comprehensive** option, a company must collate all of the information necessary for standard disclosures for that option. Not all of the following disclosures are appropriate for each industry, so companies must determine which affect them and pursue them accordingly. Below is an explanation of each of these disclosures:

- **Strategy and analysis.** This will be an overview of the company's short-, medium-, and long-term vision and strategy for ensuring sustainability in its practices. It should include not only information endemic to the company itself, but also information from the industry at large, local, and regional issues, targets, and challenges in the aforementioned time-periods and other items of note that may affect how the company achieves sustainability in the future.

- **Organizational profile.** This section is where the overall structure of the company is laid out. There are a total of 14 disclosures, which range from the company's name and address to its main markets, products, and brands to a breakdown of its legal state of incorporation (sole proprietorship, LLC, etc.) and capital structure. Of note here is that the G4 guidelines state that companies should include information on their employees broken down by their gender, employment contract, status (part-time or full-time employees, contract workers, or self-employed), region, and whether or not they are covered by collective bargaining agreements. The company should also include information here on the extent to which the company has external ties to initiatives or organizations. In essence, after reading this section, stakeholders should be able to understand, at least at a basic level, the ways in which the company does its business, with whom they work, how they pay for their business processes, and how tied they are to their resources and to the market in which they act.

- **Identified material aspects and boundaries.** At this point, with the overall image of the company and its strategy laid out, the company gets into the meat of the report. Here, the company lists all of its entities (the company itself and its affiliates, subsidiaries, partners, etc.) which it wishes to include in the report. They include all information on how they wish to define the report content and which material aspects to use, identifying for each the extent to which it is material both within each entity listed and to the outside market in which the company interacts. As is true with each of these disclosures, companies should also report any changes from past reports and the extent to which they may change the ongoing operation of the company.

- **Stakeholder engagement.** A company will list here the stakeholders with which it chooses to engage, the reasons why said stakeholders were chosen, the company's approach to engaging the stakeholders, and any matters and concerns of note that have resulted from engaging with the stakeholders. This shows the stakeholders not only in which other stakeholders the company holds interest, but also some view of the extent to which the company values their contributions.

- **Report profile.** This section states the general information about how the report is structured, such as its reporting period, frequency, and contact person, as well as the GRI Content Index for the option chosen for disclosure (**core** or **comprehensive**). The GRI Content Index is a list of the disclosures used, any omissions, and whether any external assurance has been used on each disclosure, as well as the report page numbers so that the stakeholders can easily see where this information is.

- **Governance.** Governance is a very big issue for many companies, so this section is extensive, with 22 disclosures. To be brief, this section encapsulates information that will be useful to determine how well governed the company is in its actions by detailing the way in which the company formulates its governance function, the competences of said function, the compensation and incentives given to those involved, and its role in establishing the company's purpose, values, and strategy, as well as the company's risk management, sustainability reporting, and evaluation of economic, environmental, and social performance.

- **Ethics and integrity.** Finally, this section reflects on the company values, principles, standards, and norms, as well as the ways in which they seek internal and external advice regarding both ethical/legal and unethical/illegal practices and behaviors.

Once all of these General Standard Disclosures are in place and the report is written, the stakeholders can determine the impacts of the company's decisions on their interests. There are many more Specific Standard Disclosures which the company can use in its reports, but these should suffice for the average report, and that is the goal toward which businesses currently should strive. The ultimate result should be that the report will increase the value of the company, or at least make it so that the stakeholders can more easily gauge the extent to which their valuation is correct. There are many ways in which the report will be used by the stakeholders and many ways to talk about the results, but the important thing is that there is sufficient standard information for companies to be compared against one another to ensure the sustainability of the marketplace.

7.3 Future trends in sustainability performance

Anecdotal evidence suggests that sustainability is paying off and that companies continue to gain from their sustainability initiatives of focusing on the achievement of long-term financial and nonfinancial key performance indicators.[6] More than 6,000 business organizations worldwide are disclosing some variations of their five EGSEE measures of sustainability performance. Some companies issue stand-alone sustainability reports,

---

6   Kiron *et al.*, 2013a.

sometimes under the title of corporate social responsibility performance reports. The 2014 survey of investors conducted by PricewaterhouseCoopers (PwC) finds that about 80% of responding investors said they considered ESG sustainability issues in their investment decisions when they were voting proxies and making investment portfolios in the past year. Among the top sustainability issues considered by investors are climate changes, resource scarcity, CSR, and good citizenship. Investors' primary drivers for considering sustainability issues, in the order of performance are risk reduction (73%), avoiding firms with unethical conduct (55%), performance enhancement (52%), cost reduction (36%), attracting new capital (30%), improving capability to create value (30%), and being responsive to interest groups (21%).[7]

Novartis has published annual corporate responsibility (CR) performance reports since 2000 to demonstrate its commitment to leadership in CSR. The 2013 Novartis CR performance report discloses that its CR works in two key areas:

1. Expanding access to healthcare for a large population of people worldwide

2. Doing business responsively

CSR at Novartis focuses on developing innovative products for underserved patients, employing CSR approaches to better serve low- and middle-income communities, operating with the utmost of ethical standards, and promoting environmental sustainability.[8] The Novartis 2013 CR performance report highlights:[9]

- Expanding access to healthcare (expanding social ventures programs, serving billions of patients)

- Doing business responsibly (responsible procurement, inclusion in the Dow Jones Sustainability World Index, being considered in the top 25 best places to work, reducing greenhouse gas emissions, being in the new UN 100 Index)

The 2013 CR report is prepared in compliance with the GRI G4 guidelines with disclosure at the Core application level and also reflects that the company is compliant with the GRI G4. The 2013 CR report also includes

7   PricewaterhouseCoopers, 2014a.
8   Novartis, 2014.
9   Novartis, 2014.

Action	General standard disclosure	Specific standard disclosure
Core business contribution to UN goals and issues	Strategy and analysis	Economic performance
Strategic social investments and philanthropy	Organizational profile	Market presence
Advocacy and public policy engagement	Identified material Aspects and Boundaries	Indirect economic impacts
Partnerships and collective action	Stakeholder engagement	Procurement practices
Local networks and subsidiary engagements	Report profile	Materials
Global and local working groups	Governance	Energy
Issue-based and sector initiatives	Ethics and integrity	Water
Promotion and support of the UNGC		Emissions
		Supplier environmental assessment
		Labor/management relations
		Occupational health and safety
		Training and education
		Diversity and equal opportunity
		Human rights grievance mechanisms
		Local communities
		Anticorruption

TABLE 7.1   Novartis corporate responsibility performance report

three other sustainability reports pertaining to CDP: the Investor Request Response, the CDP Water Information Request Response, and the Conflict Minerals Report.[10] Table 7.1 shows the Novartis CR report prepared in compliance with G4 Guidelines.

City Developments Limited (CDL) has issued stand-alone sustainability reports for several years, and its 2013 sustainability report details its commitment to long-term viability beyond just an opportunity to make a positive impact on the environment and society, which reflects its principles of

10   Novartis, 2014.

sustainability in creating enduring value for all stakeholders.[11] CDL's 2013 sustainability report provides detailed information related to financial, governance, social, and environmental performance in Singapore in 2013, prepared in compliance with the GRI guidelines.[12] This 2013 sustainability report enables CDL to take the lead in disclosing both financial and nonfinancial opportunities, challenges, and risks, and to integrate CSR strategies across all business operations in order to achieve balanced triple bottom line performance in all activities pertaining to people, planet, and profit.[13]

7.4 Future trends in sustainability reporting

Sustainability reporting has evolved from voluntarily disclosing some aspects of sustainability performance such as corporate social responsibility (CSR) in annual reports to issuing stand-alone voluntary sustainability reports on environmental, social, and governance (ESG) dimensions of sustainability performance to integrating both financial and nonfinancial (ESG) dimensions of sustainability performance into corporate reporting. The future of sustainability reporting will be either a mandatory stand-alone or an integrated report on all five EGSEE dimensions of sustainability performance along with the use of Extensible Business Reporting Language (XBRL) in sustainability reporting. The use of XBRL-formatted reporting is an important step in applying XBRL to all dimensions of sustainability performance reporting. Several professional organizations are now developing sustainability taxonomies and related instances that can be effectively used by both providers and users of sustainability performance and assurance reports. The future of sustainability reporting will be market-driven and/or regulatory-mandated integrated reports using XBRL in all dimensions of sustainability performance reporting by applying several existing taxonomies for financial and nonfinancial information relevant to the dimensions of sustainable performance. Many professional organizations, including the GRI, IIRC and SASB, are developing a business sustainability information system that captures and consolidates the details necessary to prepare reports externally as well as monitor and control internally using XBRL to facilitate the integration, consolidation, and audit trail of both conventional

---

11   City Developments Limited, 2014.
12   City Developments Limited, 2014.
13   City Developments Limited, 2014.

financial and emerging nonfinancial information. This and the next sections examine these initiatives and developments.

In 2012, the International Federation of Accountants (IFAC) issued a report titled "Investor Demand for Environmental, Social, and Governance Disclosures." In this report, the Professional Accountants in Business Committee considers trends in investor demand for ESG and recommends how professional accountants can better support their organizations in responding to these demands and ultimately improve the management and reporting of ESG performance. Professional accountants should work with their organizations in order to obtain the following objectives:[14]

- To implement a structured and systematic approach for engaging investors to determine their ESG information needs

- To implement governance processes that help embed ESG factors into management and reporting processes

- To enhance the understanding of the link between financial and nonfinancial drivers of performance and value

- To ensure that ESG disclosures meet investor needs by being material, timely, consistent, and comparable in order to improve the usefulness of reporting

- To connect processes, systems, and data across various organizational functions and within the extended supply chain

7.5 Integrated reporting

In 2013, the International Integrated Reporting Council (IIRC) developed the International Integrated Reporting Framework, which provides guidelines for companies to integrate financial and nonfinancial performance information to benefit all stakeholders.[15] The integrated reporting guidelines satisfy the information needs of long-term stakeholders including investors by reflecting the broader and longer-term consequences of decision-making. Integrated reporting provides the framework for disclosing the interactions between environmental, social, governance, ethical,

---

14   International Federation of Accountants, 2012b.
15   International Integrated Reporting Council, 2013b.

and financial performance. Existing sustainability reports show some of the five EGSEE dimensions of sustainability performance and often fall short of providing detailed sustainability information on all five EGSEE dimensions of sustainability performance. It is expected that the full implementation of integrated sustainability reporting guidelines encourage and enable business organizations to integrate all dimensions including biodiversity and ecosystem performance in corporate reporting. The integrated reporting should also provide standardized sustainability disclosures for all five EGSEE dimensions of sustainability performance. Integrated Reports should be much more than a compilation of financial statements and sustainability financial Key Performance Indicators (KPIs) within the same annual report.

The integrated report should disclose both financial and nonfinancial KPIs to enable stakeholders' access to relevant sustainability information. However, investors are often and significantly more dissatisfied than satisfied with the sustainability information provided by firms regarding the following topics (in the order of the level of dissatisfaction): identification and disclosure of material sustainability risk and opportunities (82%); comparability of sustainability reporting between firms in the same industry (79%); relevance and implications of sustainability risks (74%); impacts of social and environmental issues on the supply chain (69%); Sustainability KPIs (68%); sustainability strategy that is linked to business strategy (68%); internal governance of sustainability issues (62%); and processes used to identify material sustainability issues (57%).[16]

7.6 Electronic sustainability reports using XBRL

The Extensible Business Reporting Language (XBRL) format, a derivative language of the Extensible Markup Language (XML), recently has gained considerable attention and is becoming an integral component of corporate reporting.[17] XBRL is a consortium consisting of a series of technical specifications intended to make business information more accessible and more easily communicated electronically. XBRL also facilitates the timely and accurate analysis of both internal and external business information. Companies and users of business reports can electronically search, download, and analyze information that is "tagged" electronically. XBRL also facilitates

16   PricewaterhouseCoopers, 2014a.
17   XBRL, 2013.

the timely and accurate analysis of both internal and external business information. Companies and users of business reports can electronically search and download financial and nonfinancial information. The primary benefits of XBRL are the ability to retrieve and analyze data and to facilitate interparty interactions without human interference, as well as the formalization of labels, definitions, and interpretations. XBRL defines and tags data using standard definitions which provide a mechanism for consistent structure and the use of the XBRL US GAAP Financial Reporting Taxonomy and/or other taxonomies (such as the IFRS Taxonomy) or extended (customized) tags based on either national or international accounting standards. The SEC has encouraged public companies to tag financial statement information on the EDGAR reporting system using XBRL since 2005, as approximately 9,600 public companies are filing XBRL-formatted information with the SEC.[18] Since 2009, the SEC has required that public companies that use US GAAP file their financial statements in the XBRL format.

Business sustainability has extended the type and amount of financial and nonfinancial information that business organizations provide to their stakeholders regarding their EGSEE sustainability. XBRL can provide the technological foundation for the communication of both financial and nonfinancial information to stakeholders. Five EGSEE dimensions of sustainability performance can be integrated into XBRL GL instance documents that contain tagged KPIs on both financial and nonfinancial information. No single taxonomy exists at present that can cover the world's diverse need for financial and nonfinancial sustainability reporting, but XBRL enables companies to define proper taxonomies and incorporate them into corporate reporting.

The development of the XBRL taxonomy for EGSEE sustainability reports represents an important milestone in implementing the concept of EGSEE sustainability reporting. While the use of XBRL facilitates the standardization of EGSEE sustainability reporting, there are many challenges to be addressed as the financial reporting paradigm shifts from a paper-based to an information-based model. A variety of XBRL taxonomies have been proposed for use in EGSEE reporting in order to harmonize the document structure for online communication by organizations. The EGSEE taxonomies will enable organizations to communicate sustainability information in the XBRL format in a much faster and easier way.

---

18   Starr, 2012.

The mandatory use of XBRL-formatted financial reporting is an important step in applying XBRL to all five EGSEE dimensions of sustainability performance as well as the effective and efficient analysis by all participants (board of directors, management, auditors, legal counsel, financial analysts, regulators, and investors) involved in the corporate reporting process. The tags of EGSEE sustainability taxonomies describe each of the five EGSEE dimensions of sustainability performance data and have labels that are both human- and machine-readable and show their relation to other sustainability data elements and applicable sustainability frameworks (e.g., GRI v.4). XBRL-tagged sustainability reports, when made publicly available, can be used by all stakeholders interested in sustainability information. The global acceptance of XBRL-formatted sustainability reports requires the proper development of taxonomies for each of the five EGSEE dimensions of sustainability performance. Several organizations and interest groups are currently developing XBRL taxonomies, namely: the GRI; the Governance, Risk Management, and Compliance (GRC); the Central Scoreboard for Corporate Social Responsibility (CCI); the Carbon Disclosure (CDP); the Climate Standards Disclosure Board (CDSB); the Climate Change Reporting Taxonomy (CCRT); The Integrated Scoreboard – Financial, Environmental, Social, and Corporate Governance (IS-FESG); and the IIRC. CCRT is a joint project of the CDP and the CDSB and is currently working to provide a single CCRT in XBRL format.[19]

The essence of EGSEE reporting using XBRL is the integrated presentation of nonfinancial information and the relationships among different types of sustainability performance dimension. A single EGSEE report can provide financial and nonfinancial sustainability information of particular interest to various stakeholders, and XBRL makes it possible to provide users with the tools that enable them to analyze and compare performance dimensions. An integrated EGSEE sustainability report can improve corporate reporting and communication with all shareholders, thereby adding a much greater dimension to the idea of EGSEE reporting using XBRL.

The EGSEE Taxonomy Architecture is intended to integrate the XBRL frameworks (i.e., architectures) of the IFRS and US GAAP taxonomies and then supplement them with nonfinancial taxonomies (e.g., GRI, CCI, WICI, GRC, CDP, CCRT and IS-FESG). Once the benchmarking and best practice taxonomy have been completed, KPI metrics can be identified and integrated into the XBRL taxonomy. Existing XBRL taxonomies focus on

19   CDP Worldwide, 2013.

objective/factual items as the basis for taxonomy elements. XBRL GL is a unique technology suggested for integrating sustainability reporting and XBRL. XBRL-GL integrates taxonomies into EGSEE semantics.

7.7 Future trends in sustainability assurance

Sustainability reporting will be mandatory in Europe and other jurisdictions in the near future. Thus, the reliability, objectivity, transparency, and credibility of sustainability reports definitely can be improved by providing assurance on these reports. Unlike audit reports on the economic dimension of sustainability performance in the context of audit reports on financial statements and internal control over financial reporting, assurance opinions on nonfinancial dimensions (governance, social, ethical, and environmental) of sustainability information are neither standardized, regulated, nor licensed. A number of professionals, including internal auditors, external auditors, and other service providers, can offer assurance on nonfinancial sustainability information. International accounting firms have developed expertise in sustainability reporting and assurance, and they are well-equipped and trained to provide sustainability assurance services on financial and nonfinancial dimensions of sustainability performance reports.

The Sustainability Accounting Standards Board (SASB) establishes and creates sustainability accounting standards suitable for developing standards for disclosing material sustainability issues for 88 industries in ten sectors, launching the process for mandatory filings to the Securities and Exchange Commission (SEC), such as Forms 10-K and 20-F, through the first quarter of 2015.[20] The goal of the SASB is to create standards that enable peer-to-peer comparison between companies, which can be useful for investment decisions and capital allocation. In June 2011, the Global Initiative for Sustainability Ratings (GISR) developed an environmental, social, and governance (ESG) ratings standard to move toward maximum harmonization with leading, complementary standard-setters, most notably, the Global Reporting Initiative (GRI), the International Integrated Reporting Council (IIRC), the Carbon Disclosure Project (CDP), and the SASB, informed by best practices among leading raters.[21] Harmonizing SASB standards with

---

20   Sustainability Accounting Standards Board, 2013.
21   International Integrated Reporting Council, 2012.

existing disclosure standards avoids additional costs for companies and aligns the SASB's work with global corporate transparency efforts. The products of the SASB, GRI, and IIRC can be used in complementary ways for the development of a sustainability report for investors and all stakeholders. The SASB provides standards for mandatory filings, whereas the GRI and IIRC provide frameworks for voluntary reporting.

Currently, sustainability reports are voluntary and normally not audited by external auditors. Existing sustainability reports bear different names (green reporting, corporate social responsibility reporting), serve different stakeholders in achieving a variety of purposes, and vary in terms of content, structure, format, accuracy, and assurance. A more standardized, integrated, and audited process is required to make sustainability reports on EGSEE performance comparable, commonly acceptable, and relevant to all corporate stakeholders. Recently, the GRI provided a comprehensive Sustainability Reporting Framework to enable greater organizational transparency.[22] The European Parliament, on May 15, 2014, issued a new directive that would require listed companies to disclose information on their environmental, social, and diversity in addition to financial information on economic performance.[23] It is expected that companies in other countries will follow suit, and thus the future of sustainability reports reflect both financial and nonfinancial information relevant to all five EGSEE dimensions of sustainability performance, and assurance will be provided on these reports to enhance their credibility and reliability.

Accounting and auditing standards are long-established for financial reporting and auditing.[24] Standards also exist for measuring, recognizing, reporting, and auditing governance, ethics, social responsibility, and environmental activities and performance, but these are fairly new by comparison. These include GRI and AA1000 issued in 2008 by AccountAbility (AA). There is an AA1000 assurance standard, as well as ISO standards and accounting profession standards for auditing sustainability metrics. Furthermore, organizations may be concerned about presenting unaudited key performance indicators (KPIs) on their ethical, social, governance, and environmental activities, which may create expectations and further accountability for them to improve their performance in these areas. Another challenge is

22   Global Reporting Initiative, 2013a.
23   European Commission, 2014.
24   Brockett and Rezaee, 2012a.

to disclose concise, accurate, reliable, complete, comparable, and standardized sustainability reports that are relevant and useful to all stakeholders.[25]

Accordingly, the AICPA Assurance Executive Committee (ASEC) Sustainability Assurance and Advisory Task Force developed application guidance assurance services.[26] The AICPA issued Statement of Position (SOP) No. 13-1, which supersedes SOP No. 03-2, Attest Engagements on Greenhouse Gas Emissions Information, detailing how to apply the attestation standards for a review engagement to the specific subject matter of Greenhouse Gas Protocol (GHG) emissions information.[27] The Statement of Position (SOP) No. 03-2, is an essential resource, whether for examinations or reviews, and provides guidance on performance and reporting related to information about a GHG emissions inventory or a baseline GHG inventory, as well as a schedule or an assertion relating to information about a GHG emission reduction in connection with the recording of the reduction with a registry or a trade of that reduction or credit.[28] The Statement of Position (SOP 13-1) provides guidance on the types of analytics and inquiry that might be performed in a review engagement on Greenhouse Gas Emissions Information. Consequently, performing analytics and inquiries alone with respect to GHG emissions information might not yield sufficient evidence for the limited assurance conclusion to be formed (otherwise known as "negative assurance" in the U.S.A.).

Sustainability Accounting Standards Board (SASB) is working with the Public Company Accounting Oversight Board (PCAOB) to prepare standards for disclosing material sustainability issues for the external assurance of sustainability reporting.[29] The SASB and IIRC frameworks are fully aligned on many of the core concepts of integrated reporting, including materiality, boundary, a principles-based approach, and accounting for capital leases. In May 2013, SASB and CDP signed a memorandum of understanding (MOU) to deepen their partnership toward advancing corporate disclosure on material sustainability issues.[30] Under the MOU, SASB utilizes CDP's data as evidence for determining the materiality of climate change-related issues in certain industries. The materiality map presents the relative priority of sustainability issues within an industry, which uses

25   Brockett and Rezaee, 2012a.
26   American Institute of Certified Public Accountants, 2003.
27   American Institute of Certified Public Accountants, 2003.
28   American Institute of Certified Public Accountants, 2003.
29   Deloitte, 2013.
30   Deloitte, 2013.

these tools to evaluate risks and opportunities for their industry or portfolio. SASB encourages public companies as well as auditing firms to use the American Institute of Certified Public Accountants' (AICPA) Statements on Standards (AT Section 101) in attest engagements for nonfinancial data. The Public Company Accounting Oversight Board (formed out of the Sarbanes-Oxley Act and supervised by the SEC in order to set the final rules for auditing of publicly traded companies) has also adopted this as their "interim" standard for attestation engagements.[31]

The Global Reporting Initiative in April 2001 released its working paper entitled *Overarching Principles for Providing Independent Assurance on Sustainability Reports*.[32] The standard was developed by an international and interdisciplinary multi-stakeholder working group headed by Canadian Alan Willis, a Chartered Accountant. Their standard is divided into five general principles:

1. **Business case for independent assurance.** Discusses the need for companies to evaluate the business case for engaging an assurance provider for their sustainability report. Included in the evaluation are: the need to ensure clarity of goals and expectations; definition of scope; definition of objectives; determination of benefits and costs.

2. **Prerequisite conditions for assurance engagements.** Sets out the primary requirements for a successful assurance engagement, including: evidence to support reported information, criteria against which to evaluate the evidence, resources to carry out the assignment, and cooperation in carrying out the assignment.

3. **Approaches and procedures.** Discusses at a high level the planning and execution of the assurance engagement, including: determining the approach and work plan, obtaining and evaluating evidence, and documenting the assignment.

4. **Communication of results.** Provides guidance on the reporting stage of the engagement, specifically: Communicating the results of the assignment, and providing comments and recommendations.

31   Deloitte, 2013.
32   Global Reporting Initiative, 2002.

5. **Attributes of assurance providers.** Focuses on the assurance providers themselves and discusses: independence, integrity, due care, confidentiality, competence, and accountability.[33]

The International Auditing and Assurance Standards Board provided an exposure draft of a new standard of assurance, called ISAE 3410 "Assurance on a Greenhouse Gas Statement" in reaction to existing and growing requests for assurance on greenhouse gas statements, and intended to serve as inclusive guidance on these greenhouse gas assurance engagements.[34] About half of greenhouse gas statements (50%) are independently assured internationally. In the competitive assurance market, those inside or outside the accounting profession now hold roughly identical shares. The characteristics of greenhouse gas assurance engagements are highlighted in this paper, those of which warrant multidisciplinary cooperation, the interdependent and exceptional skill sets that different individuals take to the engagements, and the market forces that bring about a request for varied providers. Internationally, assurance on greenhouse gas information is topical, as it is evident from recent exposure drafts of the International Auditing and Assurance Standards Board on a new standard of assurance, International Standard for Assurance Engagements 3410, "Assurance on a Greenhouse Gas Statement," which is envisioned to work as an inclusive assurance guidance for on both types of greenhouse gas information.

The proposed revised ISAE 3000 (Revised), provides requirements and guidance on assurance engagements. In conducting an assurance engagement, the objectives of the practitioner are:

- To obtain either reasonable assurance or limited assurance, as appropriate, about whether the subject matter information (that is, the reported outcome of the measurement or evaluation of the underlying subject matter) is free from material misstatement

- To express a conclusion regarding the outcome of the measurement or evaluation of the underlying subject matter through a written report that clearly conveys either reasonable or limited assurance and describes the basis for the conclusion

- To communicate further as required by relevant ISAE

---

33   Global Reporting Initiative, 2002.
34   International Federation of Accountants, 2011.

ISAE 3410 was approved by the IAASB and issued in 2009. It was accompanied by a working draft of a proposed standard dealing with reasonable assurance (RA) engagements only. The working draft received considerable support, but:

- There was strong support for expanding the scope of the proposed standard to also include limited assurance (LA) engagements

- A small number of other issues were identified as needing further refinement

The major issues in the revision are better distinction between reasonable and limited levels of assurance. Two levels of assurance, namely reasonable assurance and limited assurance, are recognized by ISAE 3000. The standard helps companies better understand the similarities and differences between the two levels of assurance. The levels of assurance include the explicit statement that professional judgment about materiality for a reasonable assurance engagement is the same as for a limited assurance engagement. This is because materiality is based on the information needs of intended users.

Several existing assurance standards have been developed for both financial and nonfinancial dimensions of sustainability preformation information. Applicable sustainability assurance standards on all (EGSEE) are ISAE 3000 and 3400, GRI, AA1000, and FEE guidance as discussed below:

- **Assurance on economic dimension and performance indicators.** The IFRS, US GAAP, and MD&A guidance are considered as a backbone structure for the assurance of the economic dimension.

- **Assurance on governance dimension and performance indicators.** The SOX Act and PCAOB statements are considered guidance for governance auditing. Sustainability governance assurance can be provided on all seven functions of corporate governance:

  1. Oversight function

  2. Managerial function

  3. Compliance function

  4. Internal audit function

  5. External audit function

  6. Legal and financial advisory function

7. Monitoring function

As an important gatekeeper, auditors should communicate with other gatekeepers, including the board of directors and corporate legal counsel.[35] The Auditing Standards Board (ASB) of the American Institute of Certified Public Accountants issued Statement of Auditing Standards (SAS) No. 114 entitled *The Auditor's Communication with Those Charged with Governance*, which superseded SAS No. 61, *Communication with Audit Committees*.[36] SAS No. 114 requires auditors to conduct more robust two-way communication with those charged with governance concerning certain significant matters pertaining to the audit of financial statements of all non-issuers.

- **Assurance on society dimension and performance indicators.** The ISAE 3000 and 3400, GRI, AA1000, and ISO 26000 are considered guidance for social auditing. The objective of social auditing is to make an organization more transparent and accountable. Social auditing is a dynamic process which an organization follows to account for and enhance its performance, consisting of planning, accounting, reporting, auditing, and stakeholder engagement.

- **Assurance on ethical dimension.** The AICPA, GRI, and AA1000 are considered guidance for the ethics dimension. The International Ethics Standards Board for Accountants (IESBA) serves the public interest by facilitating the convergence of international and national ethical standards through the development of a robust, internationally appropriate code of ethics. In June 2005, the International Ethics Standards Board for Accountants (IESBA), part of the International Federation of Accountants (IFAC), issued its revised code of ethics for use by professional accountants worldwide. The key principles of the IESBA's code are:[37]

  - Integrity
  - Objectivity
  - Professional competence and due care
  - Confidentiality
  - Professional behavior

---

35   Rezaee, 2007.
36   American Institute of Certified Public Accountants, 2006.
37   International Federation of Accountants, 2010.

- **Assurance on the environmental dimension and performance indicators.** The ISAE 3000 and 3400, GRI, AA1000, CCRT guidance (GHG), and ISO 14010 and ISO 14001 are considered a backbone structure for environmental auditing. There is now an emerging consensus that environmental audits represent a practical and effective way of relating environmental problems and issues directly to the workplace. The environmental audit process encapsulates the concept of cradle to grave responsibility, assessing a company by its supplies, processes, and products. The report resulting from the audit process should give the current status of compliance and suggest a program of further action. Environmental assurance is a general term that houses a range of activities that include environmental compliance, company environmental sustainability, environmental risk, and environmental audits.[38]

Sustainability assurance reports prepared based on the AICPA Assurance Framework and Statement of Position, SOP 13-2, can be used to address the completeness, mapping, consistency, or structure of EESG sustainability information and includes planning, performing evidence-gathering procedures, and reporting audit findings on all five EGSEE dimensions of sustainability performance in an integrated audit report or a separate audit report on individual EGSEE dimensions. The end-product of a sustainability assurance engagement is the sustainability report reflecting the auditor's either positive or negative opinion in the context of either reasonable or limited assurance on sustainability performance reports.

In general, the extent of test procedures performed differs between levels of assurance. Depending on the standards applied, these levels of assurance are described differently but represent the same things. The highest level of assurance is described as reasonable (ISAE 3000), examination (AT 101), or audit (CICA 5025) level of assurance. The lower level of assurance can be described as limited (ISAE 3000), moderate (AT 101), or review (CICA 5025) level assurance.[39] A reasonable assurance engagement provides a positive opinion on whether the subject matter is, in all material respects, appropriately stated and the work performed is, of course, greater than under the limit assurance engagement. A limited assurance engagement provides what is called a negative opinion-"nothing has come to our attention to cause us to believe that the subject matter is not, in all material aspects,

---

38 International Organization for Standardization (ISO), 2015b.
39 Brockett and Rezaee, 2012a.

appropriately stated." A limited assurance engagement requires a lower level of work and consists primarily of inquiry and analytical procedures.

Aspects of test procedures in a limited assurance engagement, including timing, nature, and extent, are determined based on the practitioners' understanding of the engagement's circumstances, underlying subject matters, critical events, risk of significant misstatement of information, the materiality of information presented, the level of meaningful and relevant assurance for intended users, and professional judgment. The common understanding is that applied evidence-gathering procedures in a limited assurance engagement include an understanding of the client's subject matter (social, governance, ethics, environmental performance); inquiries of management, board of directors, and personnel; and analytical procedures. The assessment of the effectiveness of internal control concerning subject matter information is recommended but not required. Additional test procedures may be performed if the practitioner becomes aware of matters that cause him or her to believe the information may be materiality misstated. Evidence gathered by performing additional procedures should assist the practitioners in concluding that the area of concern is not likely to cause the subject matter information to be materiality misstated. Appropriate working papers should be presented for both reasonable assurance and limited assurance engagements. Working papers should document the types of engagement, considered subject matter and related information, engagement standard applied, test procedures performed, evidence gathered, and conclusions reached.[40]

The audit risk model consisting of inherent, control, and detection risks should be used in assessing sustainability risks and their impacts on the credibility of sustainability reports. The risk assessment is performed both at the level of EGSEE sustainability statement (calculating performance materiality) and the declaration level for every line item of statement. The EGSEE sustainability statement has a similar nature to an income statement as it is a statement of EGSEE sustainability performance at a certain time. Therefore, similar assertions such as accuracy, occurrence, cut-off, completeness, and classification, as well as assertions regarding disclosure and presentation of the EGSEE sustainability performance (e.g., consistency, occurrence and responsibility, accuracy and quantification, classification and understandability, completeness) are used (ISAE 3410.A78). The report structure of EGSEE sustainability performance statement is comparable

---

40   Brockett and Rezaee, 2012a.

to financial statement audit reports. The IASSB released ISAE 3410.[41] The proposed ISAE standard allows both limited and reasonable assurance GHG engagements. In the case of a limited assurance engagement, basic evidence-gathering procedures (e.g., inquiry, analytical procedures) form the basis for reaching a conclusion. In the case of a reasonable assurance engagement, a much broader range of evidence-gathering procedures, including assessment of risk of material misstatement, are applied.[42]

The level of assurance provided by auditors on sustainability performance is determined by the type of sustainability category. The level of assurance from low to high depends on the type of assurance from social to economic, as well as the extent and nature of evidence-gathering procedures. In general, obtaining assurance requires an objective examination of subject matter and gathering of sufficient and competent evidence to provide an impartial assurance on the subject matter.[43] Audits on financial statements reflecting the economic dimension of business sustainability have a high to reasonable level of assurance, whereas the review of social dimension of sustainability performance can offer only a low to limited level. Examination of corporate social responsibility performance requires assurance providers to offer limited assurance indicating that the third-party provider is not aware of non-compliance with state social criteria.[44]

In the opinion-formulation stage: audit evidence includes information relating to the completeness, validity, and accuracy of the financial statements as a whole, such as information relating to the consistency of the financial statements with the auditor's knowledge of the business. The audit report is the most common and highest level of assurance provided by an independent auditor to those interested in a company's financial information. The company's financial statements are the most common assertion on which assurance is expressed. The preparation of the audit report is also the final phase of the auditing process, and to meet these responsibilities, auditors must have a thorough understanding of the auditing standards pertaining to auditors' reports. This includes knowledge of the contents of the audit report regarding different types of opinions and the conditions that must be made for them to be issued. Independent auditors provide various levels of assurance about different types of assertion. Performing attestation is the most important way they add credibility to an assertion of the

41   International Auditing and Assurance Standards Board, 2009.
42   International Auditing and Assurance Standards Board, 2009.
43   Brockett and Rezaee, 2012a.
44   Brockett and Rezaee, 2012a.

financial statements prepared by the company's management. The credibility added is in the form of an audit report that expresses assurance about the assertion. This report is often the only formal means of communicating to interested parties a conclusion about a company's financial statements.

In performing audit procedures, the auditor makes sure that the evidence is consistent, complete, and fully supports the overall conclusions. After evaluating the audit findings and formulating an opinion on the overall financial statements, the auditor communicates his or her opinion to the users of the financial statements. The independent auditor's report can take various forms under different conditions. The sustainability assurance on EGSEE sustainability performance reports based on the degree of assurance and content are as follows:[45]

- Positive assurance on financial statements reflecting economic performance

- Positive assurance on internal control over financial reporting (ICFR)

- Positive or negative assurance on sustainability reports pertaining to governance, social, ethical, and environmental performance

The content and format of the sustainability assurance reports that should be addressed to either the entity's board of directors, management, or intended users may vary and in general should include the following:[46]

- Reference to sustainability information presented by management.

- The assurance provider should use the criteria as a benchmark in assessing the effectiveness, efficiency, completeness, reliability, and transparency of sustainability EGSEE performance.

- Responsibilities of management and assurance: management is primarily responsible for the preparation, content, completeness, and reliability of information in sustainability reports. The assurance provider is responsible for the assurance conclusion provided on the reports.

- The scope of work done by the assurance provider should include the criteria used, analytical procedures, inquiries, and other evidence-gathering procedures performed to assess the risk of

45   Brockett and Rezaee, 2012a.
46   Brockett and Rezaee, 2012a.

material misstatements in sustainability reports. Evidence gathering should be documented and used as a basis in reaching sustainability conclusions.

The main difference among the audit objectives of sustainability reports is related internal controls. This presents challenges to auditors in preparing assurance on sustainability reporting and internal control reports. The aim of an integrated audit on EGSEE is the same as other financial statement audits: to state an opinion on the effectiveness of both the design and the posting of sustainability reporting, the operation of internal controls over sustainability reports, and the fair presentation of sustainability reporting in conformity with the EGSEE. Auditors who provide sustainability assurance service should measure and evaluate the sustainability against established and performed criteria. The selected criteria should be commonly acceptable, relevant, reliable, understandable, transparent, applicable, suitable, enforceable, and consistent. The assurance service providers should take the following steps:[47]

- Obtain an understanding of the organization's five EGSEE sustainability performance measures

- Obtain an understanding of the organizations' current and prospective sustainability initiatives

- Perform analytical procedures designed to enhance the understanding of the relationships among different components of EGSEE sustainability performance and identify areas of high risk that might affect the reliability of financial statements

- Conduct assessment of sustainability risk

- Encourage communication among the audit engagement team members regarding EGSEE sustainability dimensions that might affect the risks of material misstatement of financial statements

- Test effectiveness of internal control system used to collect, compile, process, and disclose EGSEE sustainability performance

- Perform audit procedures to gather sufficient and appropriate evidence on reported sustainability information

47   Brockett and Rezaee, 2012a.

Assurance Statement on the Management of City Developments Limited (CDL)

Introductory Paragraph
We have performed limited assurance procedures in relation to CDL's Sustainability Report 2014 ("the Report").

Management Responsibility
CDL's Sustainability Report 2014 has been prepared by the Management of City Developments Limited, which is responsible for the collection and presentation of the information it contains and for maintaining adequate records and internal controls that are designed to support the sustainability reporting process.

Auditor Responsibility
Our responsibility in performing our limited assurance activities is to the Management of CDL only and in accordance with the terms of reference agreed with them. We do not accept or assume any responsibility for any other purpose or to any other person or organisation.

Reporting criteria
As a basis for the assurance engagement, we have used relevant criteria in the sustainability reporting guidelines of the Global Reporting Initiative (GRI G3.1)

Assurance standard used and level of Assurance
Our limited assurance engagement has been planned and performed in accordance with the ISAE 300030 Assurance Engagement Other Than Audits or Reviews of Historical Financial Information. A limited assurance engagement consists of making enquiries and applying analytical and other limited assurance procedures.

Scope of work
We have been engaged by the Management of CDL to perform limited assurance on selected indicators of the Report as set out in Subject Matter environmental, labor practices and decent work, human rights, society, product responsibility, economic, construction and real estate sector supplement.

What we did to form our conclusions
The procedures performed aim to verify the plausibility of information. We designed our procedures in order to state whether anything has come to our attention to suggest that the Subject Matter detailed above has not been reported in accordance with the reporting criteria cited earlier.

Our independence
EY has provided independent assurance services in relation to CDL's Sustainability Report 2014. In conducting our assurance engagement we have met the independence requirements of the Institute of Singapore Chartered Accountants, Code of Professional Conduct and Ethics. Our EY independence policies prohibit any financial interests in our clients that would or might be seen to impair independence. Each year, partners and staff are required to confirm their compliance with the firm's policies.

Observations and areas for improvement
Our observations and areas for improvement will be raised in an internal report to CDL's Management. These observations do not affect our conclusions on the Report set out below.

Conclusion
Based on the procedures performed and evidence obtained, nothing has come to our attention that causes us to believe that the information in the Report was not presented fairly, and calculated in all material respects in accordance with the reporting criteria detailed above.

Signed for Ernst & Young LLP by
Singapore, 29 April 2014

FIGURE 7.1   Independent limited assurance on sustainability report

Source: Adapted from City Developments Limited, 2014.

- Interview the board of directors, management, and other personnel charged with the preparation of EGSEE sustainability reports

- Confirm certain sustainability information with outside parties where applicable (donations, environmental initiatives)

- Review important documents relevant to business sustainability mission, objectives, strategies, policies, and procedures

- Decide on the type and level of assurance that can be given on each dimension of EGSEE sustainability performance

Business organizations that produce a stand-alone sustainability report must also have their report audited/reviewed by external assurance providers, in many cases an independent auditor. In 2014, CDL engaged Ernst & Young (EY) as its auditor to provide independent limited assurance on its 2013 sustainability report.[48] The CDL 2013 assurance covers information in its sustainability report related to the subject matter agreed as per the Assurance Statement. EY deemed the company to be in compliance with ISAE 3000 "Assurance Engagement Other than Audits and Reviews of Historical Financial Information" after reviewing the underlying systems and processes that support the Subject Matters in the Sustainability Report and presenting the scope of the work and conclusions.[49] Figure 7.1 presents 2014 CDL's Assurance Statement.

7.8 Opportunities and challenges in sustainability reporting and assurance

This section presents challenges and opportunities in identifying, classifying, measuring, recognizing EGSEE dimensions of sustainability performance, reporting sustainability performance, and providing external assurance on sustainability reports. Sustainability performance reporting should be aligned with strategic management decisions through the balanced scorecard system using all five EGSEE dimensions of sustainability performance while focusing on both financial and nonfinancial sustainability performance metrics. Thus, the balanced scorecard system should be used to link both financial and nonfinancial sustainability KPIs to

48   City Developments Limited, 2014.
49   City Developments Limited, 2014.

corporate objectives. Given that the main corporate objective is to improve stakeholder value creation, the balanced scorecard system should be used to maximize the economic value of the company, which benefits all stakeholders. Increasing concerns for better and timelier assurance in corporate reporting have dominated debates within the business community for many years. The widespread use of sustainability reporting has been a major factor persuading market regulators and companies to emphasize the quality of information, suitable internal controls, and reasonable assurance on the reliability and relevance of sustainability reports. The need for a new reporting model to address fundamentals, due to the current environment's effect on corporate governance and financial reporting, is an important issue for regulators and management. Updating the reporting function has become an imperative in most organizations in demonstrating commitments to sustainable and long-term economic performance, effective corporate governance, ethical corporate culture, corporate social responsibility, and environmental conscientiousness.

In line with ever-increasing sustainability developments, corporate reporting has evolved from reporting financial information to just shareholders to reporting financial and nonfinancial information on KPIs in all five EGSEE sustainability dimensions to all stakeholders. The audit process has also evolved from the traditional manual audit to continuous auditing and assurance on all five EGSEE dimensions of sustainability performance. Sustainability assurance enables auditors to assess risk, evaluate internal controls, and perform a variety of audit procedures, including extracting KPI data for sustainability, footing ledgers, counting records, selecting samples for tests of controls and substantive tests, identifying exceptions and unusual transactions, and performing confirmations. However, the emergence of sustainability reporting and assurance raises fundamental challenges as well. These challenges pertain to whether an assurer is independent and how the assurer should be remunerated. Although sustainability reporting has brought some complexity to corporate reporting and the audit function, they have contributed to accounting and auditing overall. The success of business sustainability depends on the development of effective sustainability strategies to assess the financial and nonfinancial KPI drivers affecting the inputs and processes and to evaluate the achievement of objectives affected by the outputs and outcomes of the implemented sustainability strategies.

The growing market for sustainability assurance has created a competitive marketplace in which practitioners outside and within the accounting profession perform engagements. The EGSEE information needing assurance is sometimes presented as a fragment of more extensive sustainability reports. Assuring EGSEE sustainability information by multidisciplinary teams has benefits, which is principally important for specific types of sustainability assurance engagement, such as engagements that entail both subject matter expertise and assurance expertise, and less significant for other sustainability engagement types. In conclusion, we emphasize that there are forces that can convert this type of assurance to the natural domain of the accounting profession. When sustainability information disclosures are integrated into corporate reporting, there is a higher possibility that this information will be assured by the accounting profession. A distinguished trend is the integrated reporting aimed at combining the reporting of nonfinancial and financial information into one report. Reducing the differences between the key rival assurance standards presently used by non-accounting and accounting assurers, the ISO 14064-3 and proposed ISAE 3410, respectively, may have implications for future directions.

These assurance standards share some characteristics, and a promising dialogue is ongoing between the bodies responsible for standard setting that could eliminate redundant dissimilarities between the two standards. The factors motivating selection of assurers by entities and assurance standard especially warrant further exploration. Further rich research areas include investigation of the required procedures for a partial assurance engagement in comparison to a judicious assurance engagement, and the method of reporting this in the assurance report to share the obtained assurance level. The suitably significant role of the auditing profession in this developing field (multidisciplinary teams of sustainability assurance) has been reinforced by this discussion from a practitioner's standpoint. Moreover, the discussion accentuates the current dichotomy of this market. It is beneficial for practitioners to consider the factors that have produced and maintained this dichotomy as their engagements in this new market are increased. To create stakeholder value and provide confidence among all stakeholders, companies should highlight that their sustainability performance covers all five EGSEE dimensions, their sustainability reporting is integrated and reflects achievements of EGSEE sustainability performance, and external assurance providers have validated the integrated sustainability report.

7.9 Conclusions

The content, format, and method of disseminating sustainability reporting are evolving, and the optimal disclosure of sustainability information varies across countries and companies. However, a balance between economic sustainability performance and other ESG dimensions of sustainability performance can lead to competitive advantage, as stakeholders value sustainability disclosures. Reliable and useful sustainability information on all five EGSEE dimensions of sustainability performance enables all stakeholders to make sound decisions regarding operating, financing, and investing activities. The use of XBRL platform and continuous auditing improves the relevance and credibility of sustainability reports.

7.10 Action points

- Sustainability should be integrated into day-to-day management decision processes and particularly into operational, financing, and capital investment decisions, as well as supply chain management.

- Identify all stakeholders who affect and will be affected by your business sustainability and its success.

- There are primary stakeholders and secondary stakeholders. Primary stakeholders are visible and able to influence corporate decisions, whereas secondary stakeholders are disconnected from the company due to lack of interest and remoteness. Typical stakeholders include shareholders, creditors, customers, suppliers, employees, regulators, the environment, and the community.

- Develop the business sustainability model that fits your organization and stakeholders' needs. This model should integrate all five EGSEE dimensions of sustainability performance.

- Achievement of successful business sustainability performance requires firm commitment of the board of directors and executives to an integrated and comprehensive approach in promoting sustainability.

8
Sustainability performance, reporting, and assurance in action

Business sustainability (with a keen focus on the achievement of long-term stakeholder value creation) is gaining momentum with investors with long-term investment horizons and business organizations that value their customers' satisfaction, employees' welfare, and social and environmental responsibilities. Business organizations worldwide will be encouraged and/or required to disclose their nonfinancial environmental, ethical, social, and governance performance along with financial economic sustainability performance. Management should develop and maintain proper sustainability programs that provide a common framework for the integration of all five EGSEE dimensions of sustainability into their management processes, and establish an integrated sustainability report to effectively communicate the achievement of sustainability performance to all stakeholders. The emergence of benefit corporations in promoting the goal of stakeholder value creation in the U.S.A. is a move in the right direction toward promoting business sustainability performance, reporting, and assurance.

8.1 Introduction

This chapter presents the status of business sustainability performance as well as sustainability reporting and assurance. More than 6,000 European companies will soon be required to disclose their nonfinancial sustainability performance in the areas of the environment, social aspects, governance, and diversity. Several stock exchanges worldwide require their listed companies to disclose sustainability performance information. The best practices of business sustainability developments, programs, and performance are being initiated, and their reporting and assurance are being established. This chapter discusses the best practices of sustainability performance, reporting, and assurance in actions.

8.2 Effective implementation of sustainability performance and accountability reporting

Identifying and prioritizing key stakeholders to support the sustainable development of a Multiple Bottom line (MBL) will focus on the development of Economic, Governance, Social, Ethics, and Environmental (EGSEE) aspects of the business. The implementation of environmental management systems (either through ISO 14000 and other ISO standards or by other means) will provide insight and direction for identifying and prioritizing key stakeholders, and how they can and do affect the organization. Developing the knowledge base of key stakeholders will come easily through a basic identification process. The standard sets of stakeholders that can influence an organization are shareholders, governments, employees, environment, suppliers, customers, society, and future generations, as discussed in previous chapters. The primary objective of business sustainability should be the promotion of sustainable stakeholder value creation. To effectively achieve this objective, business organizations worldwide should focus on enhancing shareholder wealth, customer satisfaction, talented employee retention, operational efficiency, innovation, long-term growth, and engagement in social and environmental responsibility.

Collaborative efforts by the board of directors, management, and auditors are very important in sustaining sustainability by setting a tone at the top in promoting business sustainability and committing to sustaining sustainability performance, reporting, and assurance. New research by *MIT Sloan Management Review*, the Boston Consulting Group, and the UN Global Compact shows that a growing number of companies are turning to collaborations – with suppliers, NGOs, industry alliances, governments, and even competitors – to become more sustainable.[1] The study also looked at board engagement as a driver of sustainability success. Overall, 86% of respondents believe that the board of directors should play a strong role in driving their company's sustainability efforts, but only 42% of respondents see their boards as moderately or more engaged with the company's sustainability agenda. This disconnect affects performance, as in companies whose boards are perceived as active supporters, 67% of respondents rate collaborations as very or quite successful. In companies whose boards are not engaged, the reported rate of success is less than half of that.

Corporate executives should refocus their efforts from short-term performance and earnings management to long-term growth and performance in creating value for all stakeholders. Management should utilize integrated reporting that provides all stakeholders with a long-term and broad perspective on stakeholder value creation. The integrated reporting framework developed by the International Integrated Reporting Council (IIRC) enables business organizations to articulate their stakeholder value creation and related investment value prospects, establish business strategies, EGSEE sustainability performance, and prospects, and engage with all stakeholders to make business sustainability a reality and priority. Integrated reporting should build on conventional financial reporting and expand to include nonfinancial information on all five EGSEE dimensions of sustainability performance. Management should identify and fully utilize all financial and nonfinancial drivers of the five EGSEE dimensions of sustainability performance. Management should also use appropriate KPIs and their related metrics and assess and manage the risks associated with sustainability performance, as discussed in the next section.

8.3 Sustainability risk assessment and management

Global business is constantly changing and becoming more volatile, unpredictable, and complex. In this challenging business environment, the use of Enterprise Risk Management (ERM) is vital in turning challenges into opportunities. The global financial crises of 2007–2009 can be attributed to many factors, including an inadequate risk assessment of business transactions. Risk management has become an integral component of managerial

1   Kiron *et al.*, 2015.

functions affecting all transactions and economic events. The move toward sustainability reporting underscores the importance of an adequate ERM in improving the effectiveness of all five EGSEE dimensions of sustainability performance. ERM is a risk-based approach to managing an enterprise, integrating concepts of strategic planning, operations management, sustainability, and internal controls. The goal of implementing ERM is to maximize the value of the firm by managing overall risks through identifying and reducing the possibility of events which create operational surprises and losses.[2] Managers should identify challenges and opportunities and use methods and processes to enable them to take advantage of opportunities in managing related risks. The 2015 EMR survey conducted by the ERM Initiative at North Carolina State University reveals that a majority of surveyed executives say that risk management is not an important strategic tool at their organizations, and most have not managed their risk appetite in pursuit of objectives, and only 25% of companies have a formal ERM process in place.[3]

The International Organization for Standardization (ISO) published its new standard: ISO 31000: Risk Management – Principles and Guidelines in 2009, which provides principles and guidelines on risk management.[4] These ISO 31000 risk guidelines assist business organizations in developing, implementing, maintaining, assessing, monitoring, and continuously improving their risk management system to minimize the negative effects of strategic, operations, financial, compliance, and reputation risks.[5] All of these risks are interrelated and thus should be properly assessed and managed. For example, an excessive strategic risk can also cause operations, financial, compliance, and reputational risks. The compliance risk directly or indirectly associated with business sustainability, including non-compliance with regulatory reforms, health and safety, human rights and labor laws, corporate governance measures, anti-bribery, and environmental risks can vary among organizations and across countries. For example, environmental risks can include direct effects (e.g., emissions trading cost exposures) and indirect consequences (e.g., energy price increases and accompanying reporting and compliance costs) of non-compliance with environmental laws, rules, and regulations. Business organizations also assess and manage their financial risk of producing and disclosing materially misstated

2   Committee of Sponsoring Organizations of the Treadway Commission, 2004.
3   Beasley *et al.*, 2015.
4   International Organization for Standardization (ISO), 2009.
5   International Organization for Standardization (ISO), 2009.

financial reports. Minimization of reputational risk is vital to the success of sustainability programs and related performance, as stakeholder satisfaction is essential to sustainable business.

Developing an environmental risk management system is essential for addressing environmental problems, reducing or eliminating waste, and mitigating negative risks with society, the government, and other key stakeholders. This enables the company to retain the necessary tools to develop sustainable products and programs. The development of sustainable programs moves the company from being reactive to social and government pressures to reactive, moving beyond economic performance and toward EGSEE performance and risk management.

8.4 Sustainability risk identification and assessment

A 2014 survey of institutional investors reveals that the primary driver for investors in considering ESG sustainability issues is mitigating risk, as about three-quarters of responding investors believe that consideration of ESG sustainability issues reduces investment risk. Other drivers are enhancing performance and avoiding firms with unethical conduct.[6] An annual top-risks survey conducted for several years by North Carolina State University EMR Initiative and Protiviti, a global consulting firm, has ranked regulatory risks first for the past three years.[7] The 2015 top ten business risks, in the order of ranking, are:[8]

1. Regulatory concerns of the risk associated with compliance with laws, rules, and regulations affecting the company's operations, governance, and financial reporting

2. Economic conditions that may affect the company's growth opportunities and market conditions

3. Cyber threats due to the risk of not being adequately and effectively prepared to mitigate the effects of cyberattacks

---

6   PricewaterhouseCoopers, 2014a.
7   Protiviti, 2015.
8   Protiviti, 2015.

4. Succession/recruitment planning of the risk of challenges associated with attracting and maintaining top executives and talented employees

5. Cultural response to risk that corporate culture is not sufficiently and promptly responding to challenges affecting the company's operations and achievement of its strategic goals

6. Aversion to change of the risk of resistance to change that may have detrimental effects on business model and core operations

7. IT security and privacy costs including the risk of not adequately investing in IT and privacy initiatives

8. Reputational risk of not being able to respond to events and crises that affect the company's reputation

9. Changes in customer preferences of not being able to satisfy customers demands and changes in their preferences and the associated risks of not sustaining customer loyalty

10. Not meeting performance expectations as related to quality, innovation, delivery, and competition

Brockett and Rezaee present five risks (strategic, operations, compliance, financial, and reputation) relevant to sustainability performance.[9] One more emerging risk currently threatening the sustainability of all types and sizes of organization is the risk of potential cyberattacks and security breaches. Consideration of and proper assessment and management of these six risks are becoming increasingly important, and play an integral role in achieving EGSEE sustainability performance. Figure 8.1 presents these six risks and their interactions, and the following sub-sections briefly describe these risks individually.

8.4.1 Strategic risk

There are several strategic risks triggered by business sustainability performance, reporting, and assurance, including threats to survival and achievement of long-term performance, uncertainty of marketing position and volatility in stock prices, abnormal changes in consumer demand, and risks associated with strategic investments, stakeholder communications, and investor relations. Of course, these strategic risks also create opportunities

9   Brockett and Rezaee, 2012b.

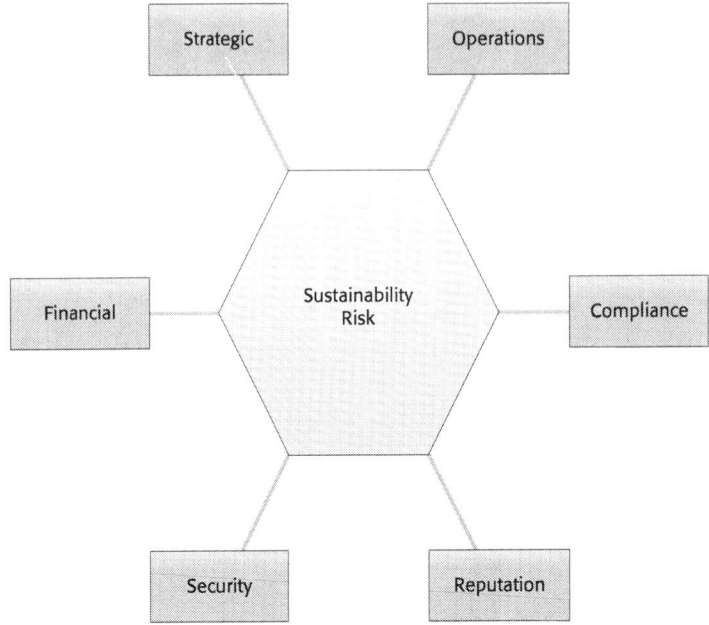

FIGURE 8.1 Sustainability risks

for possible improvements in operating, investing, financing activities and proper communication with all stakeholders. Strategic risks should be identified, assessed, and managed with a keen focus on minimizing their negative effects and building on the opportunities provided by addressing these risks.

8.4.2 Operations risk

Operations risks are associated with all five EGSEE dimensions of sustainability performance, the integration of all sustainability performance dimensions into operating activities across operational units, operational technology, supply chain, information technology, and other functional areas. One of the greatest challenges for companies in implementing their sustainability strategy revolves around collaboration and integration across operational business units and key functional areas. Operating risks associated with both conventional financial key performance indicators (KPIs) such as earnings and return on investment and conceptualization KPIs such as social and natural performance need to be assessed, managed, and their negative impacts minimized.

8.4.3 Compliance risk

Business organizations are required to comply with a set of national and international laws, rules, regulations, standards, and best practices. Many companies face the challenges of complying with these regulatory measures, and non-compliance may cause significant risks of interruption and/or discontinuation of their business. Compliance risks need to be assessed, managed, and their negative impacts minimized. To achieve this objective, many companies have created either the board compliance committee or an executive position as compliance and risk officer.

8.4.4 Reputation risk

Maintaining a good business reputation and meeting and exceeding expectations of corporate stakeholders from investors to creditors, suppliers, customers, employees, the environment, and society is a major challenge for many businesses. All five EGSEE dimensions of sustainability performance are associated with business reputation, customer satisfaction, and the ethical workplace. The company's reputation and its related risk should be evaluated on an ongoing basis and any damages to the reputation minimized.

8.4.5 Financial risk

Nonfinancial dimensions of sustainability performance (including ethical, social, governance, and environmental) affect financial performance. The financial risk of issuing materially misstated financial reports is detrimental to the sustainability of corporations. Sustainability reports are expected to be value-relevant to both external and internal users of such reports. Investors and other stakeholders including suppliers, customers, government, and society can have more transparent information about economic, governance, social, ethics, and environmental (EGSEE) performance, which enables them to make more informed decisions. Sustainability reporting can also improve internal management practices by enabling companies to establish better relationships with investors, customers, suppliers, employees, regulators, and society. Sustainability reporting can also create more incentives for management to refocus its goals, strategic decisions, and actions from a short-term to a long-term perpective.

Sustainability reporting can be used as a tool for more effective risk management by identifying both opportunities and risks associated with operations. Thus, more transparent sustainability disclosures on EGSEE performance create opportunities to identify and correct operational inefficiencies and reputational and financial risks that would improve economic performance. Best practices of sustainability suggest that companies that ignore their social, governance, ethics and environmental issues and responsibilities will:

- Not be sustainable in the long term

- Be subject to higher risk of regulatory action

- Lose their license to operate

- Lose customer reputation and confidence in their products and services

- Not be able to attract the most qualified and talented human capital and workforce

- Incur a higher cost of capital both debt and equity

- Have a smaller analyst following, which may affect their market valuation

- Not attract investors with long-term horizons

- Encourage managerial practices of not being sensitive or accountable for multi-dimensional EGSEE performance

- Not set an appropriate tone at the top by directors, officers, and corporate leaders promoting ethical, accountable, socially, and environmentally responsible behavior and practices throughout the organization

8.4.6 Cyberattacks and security breaches risk

Destructive cyberattacks such as the Sony Pictures incident are considered the most damaging cyberattacks outside the norms of cyber practices and can be detrimental to the sustainability of public companies. Thus, cyber security should be on the top agenda of the board of directors and executives. While the U.S.A. has accused the Government of North Korea for the Sony cyberattack, the group identifying itself as the Guardians of Peace has claimed responsibility for the attack. The U.S government is considering "proportional response" against those responsible for the Sony

Cyberattack.[10] Cyber hacking and security breaches of information systems are becoming a reality for many businesses (e.g., Sony, Target, Morgan Chase, Home Depot), and their risk assessment and controls demand significant IT investment and commitment by directors and officers to prevent. The purpose of ISO 27001 is to offer organizations guidance on keeping information assets secure by providing requirements for an information security management system (ISMS). Using this family of standards will help your organization manage the security of assets such as financial information, intellectual property, employee details, or information entrusted to you by third parties.[11] An ISMS is a systematic approach to managing sensitive company information so that it remains protected. Furthermore, it helps identify the risks associated with important information and put in place the appropriate controls to aid in reducing the risk. It includes people, processes, and IT systems, applying a risk management process. This standard is available to help any size organization, whether small, medium, or large, in any sector.

The 2013 Global Information Security Survey conducted by Ernst & Young indicates four reasons for the increase in cyberattacks:[12]

1. **Centralization of operations and information systems.** Centralization of operations and information system Internet-based technologies to improve cost efficiency and effectiveness across the supply chain creates security risks, high exposure, and dependence on the Internet, which provides opportunities for cyber hackers to engage in rewarding cyberattacks. Centralization across organizational functions requires the use of sophisticated operations technology (OT) and information technology (IT) with related network infrastructure to connect geographically diverse functions. Thus, both OT and IT securities and controls have become increasingly important under centralized systems to prevent hackers from penetrating the system and engaging in costly cyberattacks.

2. **Government-led/state-sponsored cyberattacks.** The ever-increasing cyber warfare activities by intelligence agencies and the military of sovereign states have made the practice of cyber warfare a game at the international level, exacerbated by the Stuxnet

10   Baker, 2014.
11   International Organization for Standardization (ISO), 2015d.
12   Ernst & Young, 2014.

attack on the Iranian nuclear facilities. The alleged cyberattack on Sony Pictures by the government of North Korea is another example of government-led cyberattack. Many countries have developed capabilities for launching major cyberattacks on other IT infrastructures, causing significant economic, social, and political damages. Thus, there should be a treaty for all countries to not engage in cyber warfare, which is detrimental to the global society.

3. **The rise of the informal activists.** Activists with social, political, and economic agenda find it justifiable in their own mind to engage in cyberattacks to advance their agenda at any cost to businesses and society.

4. **Outdated security programs.** Many OT and IT security programs are old, underdeveloped, and outdated, giving motivation and opportunity to cyber attackers to perpetrate these programs and engage in costly cyber hacking activities. These programs are initially designed to identify the emerging cyberhacks or information security threats, but have no risk assessment and internal control procedures to immediately respond to such hacks and security breaches.

The risk associated with cyberattacks should be assessed, and information security strategies must be developed to combat cyberattacks. Management's strategic cyber policies and procedures should include the following as a minimum for preventing, detecting, and deterring cyberattacks:[13]

- Establishing a tone at the top of making information security a board level and senior management priority

- Developing an integrated strategy to immediately respond to potential and real security threats

- Assessing the risk of cyberattacks and security breaches

- Establishing effective internal control activities relevant to the assessed threat risks to prevent and detect cyberattacks and security breaches

13   Ernst & Young, 2014.

- Using big data and data analytics to identify security breaches and cyberattacks and test the readiness of OT and IT programs to respond to the threats

- Assessing the current OT and IT systems and understanding their vulnerabilities and where a breach could likely occur

- Understanding the applicable laws, rules, and regulations pertaining to cyberattacks and security breaches and how they can help to protect your organization from cyberattacks and security breaches

- Integrating control activities and response protocol for cyberattacks and security breaches into sustainable supply chain management

- Establishing a committee consisting of risk and compliance directors/officers, senior management, risk advisors, internal auditors, and information systems analysts to assess the existing OT and IT programs and their readiness and effectiveness in responding to potential cyberattacks and security breaches

- Using big data and data analytics to identify and assess the threats and pattern of attacks

- Conducting attack and penetration tests on an ongoing and continuous basis

8.5 Emergence of benefit corporations in the U.S.A.

The primary goal of corporations has evolved from maximizing profit to increasing shareholder wealth. The goalpost has recently been advanced to creating shareholder value while protecting the interests of other stakeholders, including society and the environment.[14] Until recently, under corporate law and in accordance with the shareholder theory, it has been well defined and commonly accepted that shareholders are the owners of the firm and that the board of directors and management have a fiduciary duty to act in their best interests.[15] In the past decade, a number of firms (over 6,000 globally) that voluntary focus on profit-seeking and social mission have emerged as social enterprises or hybrid-corporations (HCs) in

---

14   Brockett and Rezaee, 2012a.
15   Jensen and Meckling, 1976.

pursuing their sustainability performance in all five EGSEE dimensions of sustainability performance. Recently, "benefit corporations" (BCs) have been formed as legal entities by legislation in 21 states, including the Delaware General Corporation Law, which since August 1, 2013, has authorized the formation of public BCs.[16] This pursuit of a mixed commercial and social mission creates a unique research opportunity to compare the financial performance and quality of BCs with both groups of CCs and HCs.

BCs should be viewed in a broader framework of the free enterprise system by considering the firms as points of contact between the company and its stakeholders with often conflicting interests. Potential conflicts of interest can create information asymmetries and unique empirical settings to investigate differences among three groups of firms:

1. Those with mandatory disclosures of their financial reports under the legal doctrine of "shareholder primacy and wealth maximization" and no disclosure of their environmental, social, and governance (ESG) sustainability performance beyond financial reporting disclosures (CCs)

2. Those with mandatory disclosures of financial performance as well as voluntary disclosures of their ESG disclosures (HCs)

3. Those with mandatory disclosures of both financial and nonfinancial sustainability key performance indicators (KPIs) under benefit corporation law (BCs)

There has been growing international interest in corporate social responsibilities, including an increased focus on long-term EGSEE dimensions of sustainability performance. EGSEE issues can affect the company's performance, supply chain management, and investment portfolios, and thus should be considered when assessing operating and investment decisions. Business sustainability is developing rapidly as a means of improving the investment and social enterprise sectors. However, for-profit entities are governed by an existing legal doctrine of "shareholder primacy and profit maximization" that does not provide incentives and opportunities for these firms to engage in social missions and activities. The BC is an alternative legal entity that addresses the requirements of entrepreneurs and investors for creating shareholder value while protecting the interests of identified stakeholders, including society.

16   Delaware Law Series, 2013.

Benefit corporations are legally for-profit entities incorporated as CCs under state law that have also chosen to adopt other ESG missions in their articles of incorporation. BCs are intended to minimize the conflicts between corporations and society caused by differences between private and social costs and benefits, and to align corporate goals with those of society under both the state corporate model and the benefit statute. Examples of conflicts between corporations and society are related to environmental issues (pollution, acid rain, global warming), wages paid by multinational corporations in poor countries, and child labor in developing countries. In perusing their mission of protecting interests of all stakeholders, BCs can raise companies' awareness of the social costs and benefits of their business activities. The major characteristics of the BCs' form are:

- A requirement that a BC must have a corporate purpose to create a material positive impact on society and the environment

- An expansion of the duties of directors to require the consideration of nonfinancial stakeholders as well as the financial interests of shareholders

- An obligation to report on their overall social and environmental performance using a comprehensive, credible, independent, and transparent third-party standard.

Several benefits of BCs are the ability to:

- Gain the attention and market share of socially conscious investors

- Use the power of business and resources to solve social and environmental challenges

- Spur more trust in businesses by the public, shareholders, and potential employees, and attract more customers to companies' brands and products

- Improve business, operational, and investment efficacy

- Assess, manage, and minimize their strategic, operational, financial, reputational, and compliance risks.

These benefits can improve the financial and nonfinancial performance of BCs, which is reflected in their financial reporting quality, cost of capital, and firm value.

The BCs' structure is administered on a state-by-state basis by allowing the state's benefit corporation statutes be placed within existing state corporation codes. The justification for BCs is that existing law prevents boards of directors from considering the impact of corporate decisions on other stakeholders, the environment, or society at large. Thus, boards of directors of BCs are required to consider the impact of their decisions on specific corporate constituencies, including shareholders, employees, suppliers, and the community, as well as on the local and global environment. In the past several years, 21 states, including New York, New Jersey, California, Louisiana, Maryland, Vermont, Virginia, South Carolina, and Hawaii have enacted laws allowing the creation of BCs for businesses that wish to simultaneously pursue profit and benefit society.[17] Since August 1, 2013, the Delaware General Corporation Law has authorized the formation of public benefit corporations. This Law:

- Allows entrepreneurs and investors to create for-profit Delaware corporations that are charged with promoting public benefits

- Modifies the fiduciary duties of directors of BCs by requiring them to balance public benefits with the economic interests of shareholders

- Requires BCs to report to their shareholders with respect to the advancement of public benefits and/or other benefits to non-shareholders

Other requirements are:

- The certificate of incorporation of a BC must identify one or more specific public benefits to be promoted

- The board of directors of a BC has a fiduciary duty of establishing a right balance between shareholders' economic interests, the specific public benefits listed in the company's certificate of incorporation, and the best interests of those materially affected by the corporation's conduct

- BCs must provide a biennial report to their shareholders disclosing the promotion of their specific public benefits and the best interests of those materially affected by their conduct

- The board of directors of a BC does not have fiduciary duty to any non-stockholder

---

17   Hiller, 2013.

- CCs can opt into BC status by merger or charter amendment with approval of 90% of the outstanding shares of each class of stock, and shareholders who do not vote in favor of the change will be entitled to appraisal rights

In summary, BCs are established to advance some social good beyond their own interests and comply with applicable regulations. BCs are intended to maximize positive impacts, minimize negative effects and harm on society and environment, and create positive impacts on the community, environment, employees, customers, and suppliers. The true measure of success for BCs should not only be determined by reported earnings, but also by their governance, social responsibility, ethical behavior, and environmental initiatives. BCs have received considerable attention from policy-makers, regulators, and the business investment community during the past decade, and it is expected to remain the main theme of the 21st century.

Lack of global acceptance of BCs is to a large extent due to less convincing theoretical frameworks and robust empirical settings, as explained below. There are two theories that can explain the economic function of BCs in maximizing positive and minimizing negative externalities of sustainability activities. First, the stakeholder theory that suggests that BCs' sustainability activities and performance enhance the long-term profits of the firm by promoting corporate governance effectiveness, CSR policies, and environmental initiatives. For example, BCs that employ robust internal and external corporate governance mechanisms are managed more effectively and ethically, which enables them to be sustainable. Likewise, any environmental initiatives pertaining to reducing pollution levels or saving energy costs may reduce contingent and actual environmental liabilities. Similarly, CSR activities may generate profit by establishing a better work environment and creating goodwill and reputation with consumers and society. More importantly, BCs can attract socially responsible investors (SRI). The stakeholder theory can be aligned with the profit-maximization philosophy if BC management considers the interests of all stakeholders and society at large. The shareholders' theory of CCs, on the other hand, suggests that management maximizes the interests of shareholders by engaging in activities that create shareholder value. Under the shareholder theory, management invests in all projects where the expected return exceeds the cost of capital. However, under the stakeholder theory, management of BCs is required to balance the interests of all stakeholders in such a way as to maximize a firm's aggregate welfare of all stakeholders, assuming that maximizing welfare is in line with maximizing firm long-term value.

In the U.S.A., Jensen states that "A firm cannot maximize value if it ignores the interests of its stakeholders"[18] and offers a theory of "enlightened value maximization" which recognizes "maximization of the long run value of the firm as the criterion for making the requisite trade-offs among its stakeholders."[19] Given that the objective function of a manager is well defined under the shareholder theory for CCs and to some extent for HCs as creating shareholder value, management incentives and related performance-based compensation are better defined and determined. However, such an objective function is not well defined in the stakeholder theory for BCs and thus, management performance becomes unaccountable, which may result in fewer performance-based managerial compensation contracts.

8.6 Future of business sustainability

To maintain sustainability in this global competitive business environment, companies should employ integrated thinking, decisions, actions, and performance by focusing on the consequences of their integrated sustainability performance that create value for all stakeholders. Business organizations must move away from focusing solely on economic performance (as reflected in the current historical financial model) and move toward an integrated reporting model that presents forward-looking financial and nonfinancial information about all five EGSEE dimensions of sustainability performance.

8.6.1 Total impact measurement and management (TIMM)

The TIMM was developed by PwC as a framework to focus on the impact of a company's strategies, decisions, and actions on all stakeholders, particularly the economy, environment, and society, which enables the company to think, act, and report on an integrated basis of creating sustainable value. The word "total" means an integrated and holistic consideration of all five EGSEE dimensions of sustainability performance, particularly economic, social, and environmental performance. The word "impact" signifies the ultimate consequences of this EGSEE sustainability performance

---

18 Jensen, 2001.
19 Jensen, 2001.

on sustainable value creation for all stakeholders. Measurement reflects the process of qualifying and monetizing the impacts, and management is the process of assessing options, optimizing, and making the best decisions. Business sustainability promotes the achievement of long-term financial performance that generates enduring future cash flows for investors to maximize their long-term share value and thus maximize overall firm value.

8.6.2 Value-adding sustainability development

Focusing on EGSEE sustainability performance enables achievement of long-term firm value maximization by creating value for shareholders and meeting the claims of other stakeholders. To create sustainable stakeholder value, the value of the firm's outputs measured in terms of the five EGSEE dimensions of sustainability performance should exceed the total value of its inputs measured in terms of both financial and nonfinancial utilized resources. Conventional performance measurements often focus on the one-dimensional and short-term performance of total return to shareholders (TRS). This measurement of TRS is influenced by many financial attributes (e.g., return on investment, profit, and cash flows) and nonfinancial variables. The proper measurement of sustainability performance should address:

- The time-horizon of balancing short-term and long-term performance with a keen focus on long-term performance

- The multi-dimensional nature of sustainability performance in all EGSEE areas

The selection of an appropriate time-horizon (period) to measure sustainability performance is very important and should be linked to the length of factors that drive sustainability performance. The overriding factors that derive sustainability performance are reaching the maturity stage of competitive positioning, efficient utilization of resources, and completing at least one business cycle. Achievement of this level of sustainable performance can take ten or more years.

The multi-dimensional EGSEE sustainability performance is interrelated. The relative importance of the dimensions with respect to each other and their contribution to the overall firm's long-term value maximization is affected by whether these EGSEE dimensions are viewed as competing, conflicting, or complementing. We argue that these EGSEE dimensions are complementary because a firm that is governed effectively, adheres to ethical principles, and commits to CSR and environmental obligations is well-equipped to sustain the generation of long-term financial performance. Furthermore, firms must do well financially in the long-term to be able to do good in terms of CSR and environmental activities. Firms that engage in business sustainability can develop a long-term focus on sustainable economic performance, as well as establishing other capabilities, resources, and competencies to build up better customer/supplier relationships, employees' workplace, and environmental and CSR initiatives.

The main goal under sustainability is to maximize firm value by improving sustainable economic performance. The debate over the merit of all other sustainability performance, be it governance, social, ethical, or environmental (GSEE), revolves around whether any investments and managerial efforts on GSEE are viewed by shareholders as value-enhancing or value-destroying activities. Investments in achieving sustainable (GSEE) performance can be considered from a risk management perspective, arguing that management should use sustainability as a tool to manage risk. Business sustainability enables management to develop better long-term focus, skills, and processes to manage risks associated with financial, compliance, strategic, operating, and reputation.[20]

8.7 Integrated thinking

The ultimate success of business sustainability development, performance, and reporting depends on the corporate culture of integrated thinking and tone at the top commitments to the promotion of all five EGSEE dimensions of sustainability performance and the reporting of both financial and nonfinancial sustainability performance information reflecting sustainable value creation for all stakeholders. Integrated thinking and reporting require focus on sustainable and forward-looking financial and nonfinancial information. Topazio, the head of corporate reporting research at the Chartered Institute of Management Accountants (CIMA), suggests the following six tips for the proper and effective adoption of integrated thinking and integrated reporting on all five EGSEE dimensions of sustainability performance:[21]

---

20   Brockett and Rezaee, 2012b.
21   Topazio, 2014b.

1. Sustainability value creation: define sustainability value creation in your organization and what this value means in the context of the organization, strategic decisions, and performance, and how your business model creates value. Sustainability value creation business models should identify and assess inputs, processes, and outputs for all five EGSEE dimensions of sustainability performance and their integrated effects on creating sustainable value for all stakeholders.

2. Strengths and concerns of sustainability performance: identify and assess the positive and negative impact of trends shaping your organization's five EGSEE dimensions of sustainability performance as suggested by the International Integrated Reporting Council and related to financial, social and relationship, intellectual, natural, and human.

3. Identify nonfinancial metrics on nonfinancial dimensions of sustainability performance (governance, social, ethical, and environmental) that are important in creating sustainable value, and use them along with financial sustainability performance metrics in making decisions.

4. Link nonfinancial sustainability performance metrics to the sustainable financial success of the business. An integrated financial and nonfinancial sustainability performance report is the key to the goal of achieving sustainable value creation.

5. Integrate strategy, strategic objectives, performance, risk, and incentives across financial and nonfinancial information dimensions of sustainability activities and promote this linkage throughout the organization.

6. Use holistic and integrated internal and external reports in effectively communicating your business sustainability strategic decisions, actions and performance to both internal and external users of sustainability reports.

8.8 Shareholder value creation of business sustainability

The primary objective of business sustainability is to create stakeholder value, particularly by enabling investors to make sound investment decisions. State Street Global Advisors (SSGA), an Australian Financial Services provider, considers sustainability disclosures (particularly environmental, social, and governance (ESG) matters) in assessing and engaging with investee companies.[22] SSGA believes that sustainability performance disclosures (ESG) can significantly impact the reputation of companies and also cause operational risks and costs to businesses.[23] Nonetheless, well-developed and effective sustainability development programs can promote efficiencies, improve productivity, mitigate risks, and thus contribute to shareholder value creation. SSGA engages with investee companies throughout the year (especially during the proxy season) on many sustainability issues affecting investors' investment decisions by developing proprietary in-house screening tools to help companies focus on all dimensions of sustainability performance and enable investors to assess and manage both opportunities and challenges associated with sustainability performance reporting and assurance discussed throughout this chapter. Particularly, the broad framework suggested by SSGA for evaluating business sustainability consists of analyzing the following business sustainability factors:[24]

- The quality of a company's sustainability performance, reporting, and assurance

- Consideration of key sustainability opportunities, challenges, and risks by the company and their relation to its overall core business

- The relative quality of a company's sustainability performance compared to that of its peers

- The underlying economics of its sustainability development and programs

- The importance of tone at the top and the level of commitments by the company's board of directors and executives to its sustainability initiatives, programs, and practices

22   Kumar and Honick, 2014.
23   Kumar and Honick, 2014.
24   Kumar and Honick, 2014.

- The importance of shareholder proposals on sustainability-related issues and their impacts on voting decisions

- Consideration of sustainability-related risks (reputation, financial, strategic, compliance) in the overall company's risk assessment and management and thus sustainable shareholder value creation

SSGA presents the following guiding questions for management in developing sustainability programs and for directors in reviewing such programs:[25]

- Questions for management to consider when developing sustainability programs, especially ESG policies and procedures:
  - What are the processes used to identify the potential material sustainability risks?
  - What are the sustainability opportunities and how they can be leveraged in creating shareholder value?
  - What are the strategic objectives for addressing the identified sustainability opportunities, challenges, and risks?
  - Are these identified sustainability objectives effectively communicated to all stakeholders?
  - What policies and procedures are established for effectively achieving the sustainability objectives?
  - How are these sustainability policies and procedures implemented?
  - How does the company monitor and measure the progress toward its sustainability goal of achieving stakeholder value creation?
  - How are the sustainability value creation goals and achievements being communicated to investors?

- Suggested guidelines questions for directors reviewing sustainability programs including ESG policies and procedures:
  - Is the board setting an appropriate tone at the top for promoting sustainable performance?
  - Are commitments by the board toward achieving sustainability performance in all dimensions of sustainability including ESG

25   Kumar and Honick, 2014.

communicated and effectively enforced throughout the company?

– Are there appropriate skills and commitments on the board to effectively oversee the company's sustainability programs?

– Does the board review sustainability opportunities, challenges, and risks facing the company?

– Do the company's sustainability programs address the key sustainability risks, opportunities, and challenges identified by the board?

– How does the board keep abreast of evolving sustainability initiatives, regulations, and best practices that can affect the company's sustainability programs, including the ESG risks?

– How are the long-term strategy and goals of the business integrated into the company's sustainability program?

– Are the company's sustainability programs comparable to that of its peers?

– How are the company's sustainability strategic objectives linked to its executive compensation?

8.9 Measuring sustainability value creation

The primary goal of business sustainability is to create sustainable value for all stakeholders including shareholders. The accounting and finance literature has suggested many models for measuring sustainable value creation for shareholders including the market-based (capital market performance metrics such as market capitalization, market liquidity and stock returns) and financial-based (operating performance metrics such as return on assets, return on equity, and earnings growth). The most common used measures of capital market performance are total shareholder return (TSR) and relative TSR.[26] TSR is defined as the percentage gain or loss to shareholders measured in terms of the share price at the end of the period minus the share price at the beginning of the period, plus dividends, divided by the share price at the beginning of the period, whereas relative TSR is defined as the company's TSR as compared with peers. TSR does not directly measure

26   IRRC Institute, 2014.

business strategy success or management performance because it is substantially affected by market and industry factors. Relative TSR, while better reflecting the company's performance in comparison with its peers, does not provide much relevant performance information about sustainable value creation. Financial-based performance measures such as reported earnings, EPS, ROA, and ROE while directly measuring accounting performance, fail to capture the level of invested capital and cost of capital in creating sustainable value. Thus, the economic profit as constructed below is a better measure for shareholder sustainable value creation because it measures sustainable profit after accounting for the desired cost of both equity and debt capital:[27]

- Economic profit = net operating profit after tax (NOPAT) *minus* capital charge

- Net operating profit after tax = EBIT *minus* cash taxes paid

- Capital charge in dollars = invested capital *times* weighted average cost of capital

The above calculated economic profit is a good proxy for measuring sustainable value creation for only one group of stakeholders, namely shareholders, by focusing on both current and future economic sustainability performance. To fully and comprehensively measure stakeholder sustainability value creation, the other four dimensions of sustainability performance, namely, governance, social, ethical and environmental (GSEE) performance, should also be measured. These GSEE dimensions of sustainability performance are typically nonfinancial and difficult to analytically measure. Thus, global business organization should view economic sustainability performance and its financial measures (economic profit, market-based or financial-based) as the main objective function for achieving shareholder value creation, and nonfinancial KPIs on GSEE sustainability performance for measuring the achievement of sustainable value creation for stakeholders other than shareholders.

27   IRRC Institute, 2014.

8.10 Business sustainability for new ventures and IPOs

Business sustainability performance and reporting is as important to new ventures and Initial Public Offerings (IPOs) as well-established and mature business organizations. New business ventures and IPOs often have more challenges attracting new investors to invest in their business. One pool of potential investors is the socially responsible investment funds (SRI). The United Nations Principles of Responsible Investing (UN PRI) was initiated in 2005 to promote global investors to integrate ESG into their investment decisions.[28] The UN PRI covers nine jurisdictions including the U.S.A., the U.K., and Canada, and has over 1,100 signatories representing more than $32 trillion (USD) in assets under management. Investors consider various sustainability issues on both financial economic sustainability and nonfinancial ESG sustainability in their investment analysis, as SRI increased by more than 22% to $3.74 trillion in managed assets during the 2010–12 period.[29] IPOs that desire to go public must comply with the listing standards of stock exchanges. A report issued by the Toronto Stock Exchange (TSX), in March 2014, discusses mandatory and voluntary corporate reporting on ESG and suggests several investment implications of ESG disclosures, including opportunity and competitive advantages of social and environmental issues and their investment risk management.[30] Academic research, in general, finds a positive relation between firm value and stakeholder welfare scores constructed to measure the extent to which firms meet the expectation of their stakeholders, including SRI funds.[31] Nonfinancial ESG sustainability performance is more relevant to entrepreneurs and joint ventures that have reached the maturity and survival stage. Business sustainability makes it easier for emerging growth companies (EGCs) to make it to their IPO, thus providing these companies access to the significant funding opportunities related to public capital markets.

28   United Nations Environment Programme Finance Initiative, 2005.
29   US SIF Foundation, 2012.
30   Toronto Stock Exchange and Chartered Professional Accountants of Canada, 2014.
31   Jiao, 2010.

8.11 The role of the chief sustainability officer

A business organization's success in effective achievement of all five EGSEE dimensions of sustainability performance demands "tone at the top" commitments to business sustainability strategies and actions. Commitment by the board of directors and top executives is essential in effectively co-ordinating all sustainability strategies and activities and successfully implementing sustainability strategies. There is an urgent need for the establishment of the position of chief sustainability officer (CSO) among the C-suite executives of business organizations.

Miller and Serafeim, in conducting a survey and interview to try to determine how CSOs' authority and responsibilities differ across business organizations, find that companies are often at different stages of sustainability commitment and find that CSOs have increased authority in companies that are in more advanced stages of sustainability.[32] They also find that while CSOs assume more responsibilities initially, as the organization's commitment to sustainability increases, CSOs decentralize decision rights and allocate responsibilities to the different functions and business units. Results of this study can be summarized as:

- As CSOs gain more authority, they become less central in the organization by allocating decision rights and responsibilities to the functions and business units.

- In the earlier stages of implementing sustainability strategies, business organizations typically have fairly generic sustainability strategies.

- In the more advanced stages of sustainability strategies, business organizations normally customize their sustainability strategy to the needs of the organization.

- Sustainability strategies are often driven by the demands of the markets where an organization has a presence or plans to expand in the future.

The changes that occur at a company regarding its commitment to sustainability are not readily discernible to C-suite executives. The desire for change can come from the inside (endogenous), such as the CEO or an employee group, or from the outside (exogenous), such as shareholders and

32   Miller and Serafeim, 2014.

regulators. Regardless of the originating factor of the change, it is important that there be a CSO in charge of serving all stakeholders and mediating the ambitions of projects and the reality of the company's abilities to meet them.

More so than other C-suite executive positions, the CSO position will need to expand and evolve more quickly as time goes on. Though companies may now hire people to fill the position nowadays as a result of pent-up demand for such a role from stakeholders, their true value will come once the market realizes the utility that they provide in normalizing the functions of the company in the long-term. In view of the Pareto principle, CSOs early on will earn easy rent for the company through their actions. Once the mechanisms are in place, however, the CSOs will need to increase efforts to ensure that their function remains a profitable venture for the company. The study by Miller and Serafeim has shown that this is currently a losing battle, as most CSOs hold their positions for four or fewer years. To show that the position is valid for the long-term, CSOs must:[33]

- Seek profit from increasingly difficult avenues of growth

- Be multidisciplinary in both their own knowledge and that of their staff

- Find ways to reach out to new stakeholders or increase the participation of and communication with existing ones

- Demonstrate flexibility in new endeavors that seek to increase the company's future growth aspects

- Communicate effectively with other officers and employees about best practices in sustainability and enforce compliance with the same

- Learn to leverage company strengths, such as technology, manpower, expertise, resources, and market positions

By meeting these goals, as well as others that may apply to particular companies or industries or which may come about as markets evolve, CSOs can ensure that their companies remain at the optimal position for sustained development and will continue operating into the future. Though the outlook is currently a bit foggy, what is clear is that this position is here to stay, albeit perhaps in a different incarnation than when companies began

33   Miller and Serafeim, 2014.

including the role in their corporate hierarchy. A company that is sustainable in the long-term will be able to face hardships without compromising other parts of the business, and to do that the company needs someone who can "do well by doing good."

8.12 Management accountants' role in sustainability

Corporations worldwide now recognize the importance of both financial and nonfinancial performance and their links to profitability and social goals. Justifications for the improved sustainability are: enhancing financial sustainability, moral obligations, maintaining a good reputation, ensuring CSR, licensing to operate, and creating value for all stakeholders. In a shared value approach, corporations identify potential sustainability issues of concern and integrate them into their strategic planning. There are many factors as to why a company should focus on sustainability: the pressure of the labor movement, development of moral values and social standards, the development of business education, and the change in public opinion about the role of business. Companies which are, or aspire to be, leaders in sustainability are challenged by rising public expectations, increasing innovation, continuous quality improvement, and heightened social and environmental problems.

Globalization has created incentives and opportunities for multinational corporations (MNCs) and their stakeholders and executives to influence the sustainability initiatives and strategies of the headquarters as well as subsidiaries. MNCs can choose from a variety of sustainability initiatives with regard to the scope, extent, and types of strategy that focus on different issues, functions, areas, and stakeholders. Management should develop and maintain proper sustainability programs that provide a common framework for the integration of sustainability into their strategies and operations that consist of:

- Integration of sustainability developments and programs into the business and investment analysis and decision-making process

- Incorporation of all five EGSEE dimensions of sustainability performance into business and investment policies, activities, and practices

- Promotion of appropriate reporting of sustainability performance

- Collaboration among all stakeholders to enhance the effectiveness of implementing sustainability programs

- Promotion of product innovation and quality, customer retention and attraction, employee satisfaction and productivity through sustainability programs

Several recent reports released by Chartered Global Management Accountants (CGMA) suggest that companies underutilize the knowledge and skills of their management accountants in advancing sustainability programs and developments and in reporting the impacts of environmental, social, ethical, and governance factors on financial performance. These reports suggest the following ways in which management accountants can assist their organizations in achieving sustainability performance and success:

- Identify nonfinancial sustainability initiatives (including environmental and social trends) that will affect the company's ability to create stakeholder value over time

- Link business sustainability challenges to the company's strategy, business model, operations, and performance

- Assess and explain the impact of these sustainability issues, including challenges and concerns

- Develop both financial and nonfinancial KPIs that support achievement of sustainability strategic and goals

- Apply management accounting tools and techniques including balanced score cards, scenario planning of natural resource availability, data analytics, life-cycle costing, and carbon foot-printing, to integrate sustainability into the decision-making process

- Produce integrated/sustainability reports that include data on sustainability impacts in all business decisions including supply chains, budgeting and pricing decisions, cost analysis, investment appraisals, and strategic planning

- Develop a sustainability reporting strategy that integrates all five dimensions of sustainability performance into strategic planning, decisions, and operations[34]

34   White, 2015.

8.13 Global collaboration and leadership for sustainability

The 2015 research conducted by *MIT Sloan Management Review*, the Boston Consulting Group, and the United Nations Global Compact indicates that an increasing number of companies collaborate with their suppliers, industry alliances, peers (even competitors), and government and non-government entities to become more sustainable.[35] The report promotes sustainability collaboration within the company (lead by tone at the top of robust commitment by the board of directors for the achievement of sustainability performance) and outside the company (industry leaders, suppliers, peers, and governments). This suggests there is a need for integrated efforts by all stakeholders to focus on achieving all five EGSEE dimensions of sustainability performance, address sustainability challenges, and create new product and market opportunities. The report suggests that sustainability has and will continue to occupy the center of business as evidenced by:[36]

- Of the companies that responded, 39% publicly report their sustainability efforts and expect them to increase by 15% in the next four years

- The number of companies that utilize financial and nonfinancial sustainability KPIs and effective governance structure toward sustainability has increased by 6% in the past four years

- The number of companies that consider sustainability a top management agenda item has increased substantially to 65% in 2014 compared with 46% in 2010

- The number of companies with no focus on sustainability has significantly decreased in the past four years

The study also looked at board engagement as a driver of sustainability success. Overall, 86% of respondents believe that the board of directors should play a strong role in driving their company's sustainability efforts. But only 42% of respondents see their boards as moderately or more engaged with the company's sustainability agenda. This disconnect affects performance: in companies whose boards are perceived as active supporters, 67%

35   Kiron *et al.*, 2015.
36   Kiron *et al.*, 2015.

of respondents rate collaborations as very or quite successful. In companies whose boards are not engaged, the reported rate of success is less than half that. The report also suggests that the type and extent of collaborations may vary among companies, but at the minimum can include:[37]

- Developing sustainability standards and promoting best practices of business sustainability

- Sharing information about best practices of sustainability to foster discoveries or communicate externally about sustainability performance

- Empowering all stakeholders to engage in business sustainability that creates value

- Sharing in investments to save costs or reduce risks and create value

In recent years, business sustainability has evolved from a focus on promoting ESG performance to initiatives that can drive revenue growth and high quality financial performance. Business sustainability practices demand the integration of sustainability strategies on sustainable financial and nonfinancial performance into the core business models. High profile global companies employ sustainability development to create opportunities for business growth, innovate through new products and services, and generate revenue. In 2013, sustainable products accounted for more than 21% of total revenue for some companies compared to about 18% in 2010, with a growth rate of six times the overall revenues.[38] The primary driver for focus on sustainable product initiatives and growth is customer demand for a focus on resource scarcity and climate change.[39]

8.14 Conclusions

In the past two decades, investors and creditors have shown increasing interest in nonfinancial sustainability information that impacts long-term viability and the well-being of the company in creating shareholder value. With the advent of social media and new technological developments, investors and creditors can easily obtain the necessary information they

---

37   Kiron *et al.*, 2015.
38   Singer, 2015.
39   Singer, 2015.

need beyond traditional financial reporting. The number of business organizations providing sustainability information regarding their financial and nonfinancial EGSEE performance is on the rise and might be an indication that the traditional financial reporting model should be more inclusive of relevant nonfinancial sustainability information disclosures. Business sustainability performance reporting, better known as integrated reporting, has extended the type and amount of financial and nonfinancial information that business organizations provide to their stakeholders regarding their EGSEE sustainability. This integrated reporting can provide the foundation for the communication of both financial and nonfinancial information to stakeholders.

8.15 Action points

- Make business sustainability, integrated thinking, and integrated reporting key components of your business strategy and strategic decisions.

- Director and executive commitment to integrated thinking, performance, and reporting is vital in creating sustainable value for all stakeholders.

- A balance between all five dimensions of sustainability performance can lead to competitive advantage and long-term and enduring value creation for all stakeholders.

- Sustainability reporting should reflect business organizations' sustainability performance in all five dimensions of economic, governance, social, ethical, and environmental (EGSEE) activities.

- External assurance on sustainability reports improves its reliability, credibility, and effectiveness in achieving the organizational objectives of creating value for all stakeholders.

- Tone at the top commitment to sustainability leadership requires organizations to define their sustainability mission, strategic objectives, and actions and integrate their processes to promote sustainability and its link to sustainable financial performance throughout the organization.

- Sustainability performance in all five EGSEE dimensions is an important driver for building a corporate environment of trust, retaining talented employees, satisfied customers, and rewarded shareholders.

- Business sustainability development enables organizations to integrate sustainability principles into everyday business operations and processes and performance.

- The success and effectiveness of business sustainability is determined by the integration of sustainability into all facets of business operations, measurements, performance reporting, and assurance.

Bibliography

AccountAbility (2003). *AA1000 Assurance Standard: Practitioners Note*. Retrieved from http://www.accountability.org/about-us/publications/aa1000-assurance-1.html.

Accounting Standards Board (1998). *Financial Reporting Standard 12: Provisions, Contingent Liabilities and Contingent Assets*. Retrieved from http://frc.org.uk/Our-Work/Publications/ASB/FRS-12-Provisions,-Contingent-Liabilities-and-Cont-File.pdf.

Adams, C. (2013). Integrated reporting – what it is – and is not: an interview with Paul Druckman. Retrieved from http://drcaroladams.net/integrated-reporting-what-it-is-and-is-not-an-interview-with-paul-druckman/.

Amato, N. (2014, September 24). Better reporting leads to improved decision-making, strategic clarity. *CGMA Magazine*. Retrieved from http://www.cgma.org/Magazine/News/Pages/201410986.aspx.

American Institute of Certified Public Accountants (1977). Statement on Auditing Standards No. 20: Requiring Communication of Material Weaknesses in Internal Accounting Control. *Professional Standards* vol. 1, Au Section 323,01. (August).

American Institute of Certified Public Accountants (1979). Exposure Draft: Reporting on Internal Accounting Control. Auditing Standards Board (December 31).

American Institute of Certified Public Accountants (2003). *Attest Engagements on Greenhouse Gas Emissions Information. Statement of Position 03-2*. New York: American Institute of Certified Public Accountants.

American Institute of Certified Public Accountants (2006). *The Auditor's Communication With Those Charged with Governance*. Retrieved from http://www.aicpa.org/Research/Standards/AuditAttest/DownloadableDocuments/AU-00380.pdf.

American Psychological Association (2015). Professional codes of conduct. Retrieved from http://www.apa.org/science/programs/research/codes.aspx.

Apple (2015). MacBook Pro and the environment. Retrieved from http://www.apple.com/macbookpro/environment.html.

Aravind, D., & Christmann, P. (2011). Decoupling of standard implementation from certification: does quality of ISO 14001 implementation affect facilities' environmental performance? *Business Ethics Quarterly* 21(1), 73-102.

Aspen Institute (2007). *Long-Term Value Creation: Guiding Principles for Corporations and Investors*. Retrieved from http://www.aspeninstitute.org/sites/default/files/content/docs/bsp/FinalPrinciples.pdf.

Association for Computing Machinery (2015). ACM code of ethics and professional conduct. Retrieved from http://www.acm.org/about/code-of-ethics.

B20 Panel of Six International Accounting Networks (2014). *Unlocking Investment in Infrastructure: Is Current Accounting and Reporting a Barrier?* Retrieved from http://www.bdointernational.com/News/Documents/B20%20Report%20-%20Unlocking%20investment%20in%20infrastructure%20(2).pdf.

Baker, P. (2014, December 18). U.S. weighs response to Sony cyberattack, with North Korea confrontation possible. *The New York Times.* Retrieved from http://www.nytimes.com/2014/12/19/world/asia/north-korea-confrontation-possible-in-response-to-sony-cyberattack.html?_r=0.

Beasley, M., Branson, B., & Hancock, B. (2015). *2015 Report on the Current State of Enterprise Risk Oversight: Update on Trends and Opportunities.* Retrieved from http://www.aicpa.org/InterestAreas/BusinessIndustryAndGovernment/Resources/ERM/DownloadableDocuments/AICPA_ERM_Research_Study_2015.pdf.

Bertoneche, M., & van der Lugt, C. (2013). *Director Notes: The Sustainability Business Case – A Model for Incorporating Financial Value Drivers.* Retrieved from https://www.conference-board.org/retrievefile.cfm?filename=TCB_DN-V5N12-131.pdf&type=subsite.

Boston Consulting Group (2012). Nearly a third of companies say sustainability is contributing to their profits, says MIT Sloan Management Review-Boston Consulting Group report. Retrieved from http://www.bcg.com/media/PressReleaseDetails.aspx?id=tcm:12-96246.

Boston Consulting Group (2013). Bridging the gap: meeting the infrastructure challenge with public–private partnerships. Retrieved from https://www.bcgperspectives.com/content/articles/public_sector_transportation_travel_tourism_meeting_the_infrastructure_challenge_with_public_private_partnerships/.

Brockett, A., & Rezaee, Z. (2012a). *Corporate Sustainability: Integrating Performance and Reporting.* New York: Wiley & Sons.

Brockett, A., & Rezaee, Z. (2012b). Sustainability reporting's role in managing climate change risks and opportunities. In J.A.F. Stoner & C. Wankel (Eds.), *Managing Climate Change Business Risks and Consequences: Leadership for Global Sustainability* (pp. 143-158). New York: Palgrave Macmillan.

Bruner, R., Eades, K., & Schill, M. (2013). *Case Studies in Finance: Managing for Corporate Value Creation* (7th ed.). New York: McGraw-Hill/Irwin.

California State Teachers' Retirement System (2013). *Corporate Governance 2013 Annual Report.* Retrieved from http://www.calstrs.com/sites/main/files/file-attachments/corporate_governance_annual_report_7-19-13.pdf.

Canadian Psychological Association (2000). *Canadian Code of Ethics for Psychologists* (3rd ed.). Retrieved from http://www.cpa.ca/aboutcpa/committees/ethics/codeofethics.

Carroll, A.B. (1999). Corporate social responsibility: evolution of a definitional construct. *Business and Society*, 38(3), 268-295.

Carroll, D. (2014, June 16). Taking the leap toward sustainability. *AICPA Insights*. Retrieved from http://blog.aicpa.org/2014/06/taking-the-leap-toward-sustainability.html.

CDP Worldwide (2013). Climate change reporting taxonomy (CCRT) due process. Retrieved from https://www.cdp.net/en-us/news/pages/xbrl-due-process.aspx.

CERES & Environmental Defense Fund (2009). *Climate Risk Disclosure in SEC Filings: An Analysis of 10-K Reporting by Oil and Gas, Insurance, Coal, Transportation and Electric Power Companies.* Retrieved from http://www.ceres.org/resources/reports/climate-risk-disclosure-2009.

CERES, Environmental Defense Fund, & Centre for Energy and Environmental Security (2009). *Reclaiming Transparency in a Changing Climate: Trends in Climate Risk Disclosure by the S&P 500 from 1995 to the Present.* Retrieved from http://www.ceres.org/resources/reports/reclaiming-transparency-in-a-changing-climate-1.

Cheng, D. (2011). Executive pay through a peer benchmarking lens. Retrieved from http://www.isscorporatesolutions.com/White_Paper_Request.

Chipotle (2014). Food with integrity. Retrieved from https://chipotle.com/food-with-integrity.

Christmann, P., & Taylor, G. (2001). Globalization and the environment: determinants of firm self-regulation in China. *Journal of International Business Studies*, 32, 439-458.

City Developments Limited (2014). *2013 Sustainability Report.* Retrieved from http://www.cdl.com.sg/sustainabilityreport2014/.

Climate Disclosure Standards Board (2012). *Climate Change Reporting Taxonomy: Taxonomy Architecture and Style Guide.* Retrieved from https://www.cdp.net/Documents/xbrl/CCRT-taxonomy-architecture-and-style-guide-v1-0.pdf.

Committee for Economic Development (2007). *Built to Last: Focusing Corporations on Long-Term Performance.* Retrieved from https://www.ced.org/reports/single/built-to-last-focusing-corporations-on-long-term-performance.

Committee of Sponsoring Organizations of the Treadway Commission (1992). *Internal Control: Integrated Framework – Executive Summary.*

Committee of Sponsoring Organizations of the Treadway Commission (2004). *Enterprise Risk Management: Integrated Framework.* New York: Committee of Sponsoring Organizations of the Treadway Commission.

Construction Sector Transparency Initiative (2013). *CoST Factsheet.* Retrieved from http://www.constructiontransparency.org/the-initiative?forumboardid=1&forumtopicid=1.

Core, J.E., & Guav, W. (1999). The use of equity grants to manage optimal equity incentive levels. *Journal of Accounting and Economics*, 38(Dec), 151-184.

Damall, N., & Sides, S. (2008). Assessing the performance of voluntary environmental programs: does certification matter? *Policy Studies Journal*, 36, 95-117.

Delaware Law Series (2013). DGCL amended to authorize public benefit corporations. Retrieved from http://corpgov.law.harvard.edu/2013/08/15/dgcl-amended-to-authorize-public-benefit-corporations/.

Delmas, M., & Toffel, M.W. (2004). Stakeholders and environmental management practices: an institutional framework. *Business Strategy and the Environment*, 13, 209-222. doi:10.1002/bse.409

Deloitte (2013, March 4). US SASB publishes exposure drafts on health care sector sustainability reporting. *IASPlus.* Retrieved from http://www.iasplus.com/en/othernews/united-states/2013/sasb-health-care-ed.

Dhaliwal, D.S., Li, O.Z., Tsang, A., & Yang, Y.G. (2011). Voluntary nonfinancial disclosure and the cost of equity capital: the initiation of corporate social responsibility reporting. *The Accounting Review*, 86, 59-100.

Dhaliwal, D.S., Radhakrishnan, S., Tsang, A., & Yang, G.Y. (2012). Nonfinancial disclosure and analyst forecast accuracy: international evidence on corporate social responsibility (CSR) disclosure. *The Accounting Review*, 87(3), 723-759.

Dodd-Frank Act (2010). Wall Street Reform and Consumer Protection Act of 2010 (pp. 111-203). Pub. L.

Druckman, P. (2013, June 17). Opinion: accountants at the forefront of change. *CGMA Magazine.* Retrieved from http://www.cgma.org/magazine/features/pages/20137566.aspx.

Edwards, D.O. (2010). An unfortunate "tail": reconsidering risk manager incentives after the financial crisis of 2007–2009. Retrieved from http://lawreview.colorado.edu/wp-content/uploads/2013/11/11Edwards-Final_s.pdf.

Ernst & Young (2010). *Action and Uncertainty: The Business Response to Climate Change.* Retrieved from http://www.ey.com/GL/en/Services/Specialty-Services/Climate-Change-and-Sustainability-Services/Action-amid-uncertainty--the-business-response-to-climate-change.

Ernst & Young (2014). *Cyber Hacking and Information Security: Mining and Metals.* Retrieved from http://www.ey.com/Publication/vwLUAssets/EY-Cyber-hacking-and-information-security/$FILE/EY-Cyber-hacking-and-information-security.pdf.

European Commission (2011). *Communication from the Commission to the European Parliament, the Council, the European Economic and Social Committee and the Committee of the Regions, Brussels, 25.10.2011, COM(2011) 681 final.* Retrieved from http://ec.europa.eu/enterprise/policies/sustainable-business/files/csr/new-csr/act_en.pdf.

European Commission (2014). Disclosure of non-financial information: Europe's largest companies to be more transparent on social and environmental issues. Retrieved from http://europa.eu/rapid/press-release_STATEMENT-14-291_en.htm.

Fama, E.F., & Jensen, M.C. (1983). Separation of ownership and control. *Journal of Law and Economics*, 26(2, Corporations and Private Property: A Conference Sponsored by the Hoover Institution), 301-325.

Fedération des Experts Comptables Européens (2002). *Discussion Paper: Providing Assurance on Sustainability Reports.* Brussels: Fedération des Experts Comptables Européens.

Financial Accounting Standards Board (1975). *Statement of Financial Accounting Standards No. 5.* Retrieved from http://www.fasb.org/jsp/FASB/Document_C/DocumentPage?cid=1218820126761&acceptedDisclaimer=true.

Financial Reporting Council (2014). *The UK Corporate Governance Code.* Retrieved from https://www.frc.org.uk/Our-Work/Publications/Corporate-Governance/UK-Corporate-Governance-Code-2014.pdf.

Global Auditor Investor Dialogue (2009). *Enhanced Disclosure Working Group: Guidelines for Enhanced Disclosure to Assist Directors, Audit Committees, Shareowners and Investors.* Retrieved from http://pdf.standardlifeinvestments.com/exported/pdf/CG_Guidelines_For_Enhanced_Disclosure/CG_Guidelines_For_Enhanced_Disclosure_09.pdf.

Global Initiative for Sustainability Ratings (2013). *GISR Standard Consultation Process: Principles.* Retrieved from http://ratesustainability.org/wp-content/uploads/2013/10/GISR_StandardsDevelopment_PublicComments2013.pdf.

Global Reporting Initiative (2002). *Sustainability Reporting Guidelines on Economic, Environmental and Social Performance.* Amsterdam: Global Reporting Initiative.

Global Reporting Initiative (2006). *Sustainability Reporting Guidelines, Version 3.0.* Retrieved from https://www.globalreporting.org/resourcelibrary/G3-Guidelines-Incl-Technical-Protocol.pdf.

Global Reporting Initiative (2011). *Sustainability Reporting Guidelines, Version 3.1.* Retrieved from https://www.globalreporting.org/resourcelibrary/G3.1-Guidelines-Incl-Technical-Protocol.pdf.

Global Reporting Initiative (2012a). A complete listing of organizations currently providing sustainability reports. Retrieved from http://database.globalreporting.org/.

Global Reporting Initiative (2012b). GRI G3 and G3.1 update: comparison sheet. Retrieved from https://www.globalreporting.org/resourcelibrary/G3.1-Comparison-Sheet.pdf.

Global Reporting Initiative (2013a). *G4 Sustainability Reporting Guidelines.* Retrieved from https://www.globalreporting.org/standards/g4/Pages/default.aspx.

Global Reporting Initiative (2013b). Frequently asked questions about the G4 Exposure Draft and the second G4 Public Comment Period. Available at https://www.globalreporting.org/resourcelibrary/G4-FAQ.pdf.

Global Reporting Initiative (2013c). *The External Assurance of Sustainability Reporting.* Retrieved from https://www.globalreporting.org/resourcelibrary/GRI-Assurance.pdf.

Global Reporting Initiative (2014). About the Sustainability Disclosure Database. Retrieved from http://database.globalreporting.org/pages/about.

Global Reporting Initiative & Carbon Disclosure Project (2010). *Linking up GRI and CDP: How do the Global Reporting Initiative Reporting Guidelines match with the Carbon Disclosure Project questions?* Amsterdam & London: Global Reporting Initiative & Carbon Disclosure Project.

Grant Thornton (2014). *Sustainability Goals and Reporting.* Retrieved from https://www.grantthornton.com/~/media/content-page-files/advisory/pdfs/2014/ADV-sustainability-reports.ashx.

Grinblatt, M., & Hwang, C. (1989). Signaling and the pricing of new issues. *Journal of Finance*, June, 393-420.

Guthriea, J., & Parkerb, L.D. (1989). Corporate social reporting: a rebuttal of legitimacy theory. *Accounting and Business Research*, 19(76), 343-352.

Hill, D. (2014, June 11). Chilean Patagonia spared from US$10 billion mega-dam project. *The Guardian.* Retrieved from http://www.theguardian.com/environment/andes-to-the-amazon/2014/jun/11/chilean-patagonia-spared-10-billion-mega-dam-project.

Hiller, J.S. (2013). The benefit corporations and corporate social responsibility. *Journal of Business Ethics*, 118, 287-301.

Holland, L., & Foo, Y.B. (2003). Differences in environmental reporting practices in the UK and the US: the legal and regulatory context. *The British Accounting Review*, 35(1), 1-18.

Hong Kong Stock Exchange (2015). *Appendix 27: Environmental, Social and Governance Reporting Guide.* Retrieved from http://www.hkex.com.hk/eng/rulesreg/listrules/mbrules/documents/appendix_27.pdf.

Institutional Shareholder Services (2013). *2013 US Proxy Season Review (Environmental & Social Issues)*, ISS (October 17, 2013).

International Auditing and Assurance Standards Board (2009). Draft Assurance Standard ISAE 3410, assurance on a greenhouse gas statement.

International Federation of Accountants (2010). *International Ethics Standards Board for Accountants.* Retrieved from http://www.ifac.org/system/files/downloads/IESBA_Fact_Sheet.pdf.

International Federation of Accountants (2011). International Standard on Assurance Engagements (ISAE) 3000 Revised, Assurance Engagements Other than Audits or Reviews of Historical Financial Information. Retrieved from https://www.ifac.org/publications-resources/international-standard-assurance-engagements-isae-3000-revised-assurance-enga.

International Federation of Accountants (2012a). *Basis for Conclusions: ISAE 3410, Assurance Engagements on Greenhouse Gas Statements.* Retrieved from https://www.ifac.org/publications-resources/basis-conclusions-isae-3410-assurance-engagements-greenhouse-gas-statements.

International Federation of Accountants (2012b). *Investor Demand for Environmental, Social, and Governance Disclosures: Implications for Professional Accountants in Business.* Retrieved from http://www.ifac.org/publications-resources/investor-demand-environmental-social-and-governance-disclosures.

International Integrated Reporting Council (2011). *Towards Integrated Reporting: Communicating Value in the 21st Century.* Retrieved from http://theiirc.org/wp-content/uploads/2011/09/IR-Discussion-Paper-2011_spreads.pdf.

International Integrated Reporting Council (2012). Governance. Retrieved from http://www.theiirc.org/wp-content/uploads/2011/02/IIRC-GOVERNANCE-2012-04.pdf.

International Integrated Reporting Council (2013a). *Consultation Draft of the International <IR> Framework*. Retrieved from http://www.theiirc.org/consultationdraft2013/.

International Integrated Reporting Council (2013b). International integrated reporting framework. Retrieved from http://integratedreporting.org/wp-content/uploads/2013/11/COUNCIL-20131205-ITEM-3b-DRAFT-FRAMEWORK-1.pdf.

International Organization for Standardization (ISO) (2009). ISO 31000: risk management – principles and guidelines. Retrieved from http://www.iso.org/iso/home/store/catalogue_tc/catalogue_detail.htm?csnumber=43170.

International Organization for Standardization (ISO) (2010a). ISO 26000: social Responsibility. Retrieved from http://www.iso.org/iso/home/standards/iso26000.htm.

International Organization for Standardization (ISO) (2010b). ISO 9001 certifications top one million mark, food safety and information security continue meteoric increase. Retrieved from http://www.iso.org/iso/pressrelease.htm?refid=Ref1363.

International Organization for Standardization (ISO) (2011). ISO 26000: social responsibility. Retrieved from http://www.iso.org/iso/home/standards/iso26000.htm.

International Organization for Standardization (ISO) (2012). *Sustainable Events with ISO 20121*. Retrieved from http://www.iso.org/iso/sustainable_events_iso_2012.pdf.

International Organization for Standardization (ISO) (2014). *ISO/TC 207/SC 1: Revision of ISO 14001 Environmental Management Systems, Updated July 2014*. Retrieved from http://www.iso.org/iso/1n1000_iso_14001_revision_information_note_update_july2014.pdf.

International Organization for Standardization (ISO) (2015a). ISO 9000: quality management. Retrieved from http://www.iso.org/iso/iso_catalogue/management_and_leadership_standards/quality_management/iso_9000_essentials.htm.

International Organization for Standardization (ISO) (2015b). ISO 14000: environmental management. Retrieved from http://www.iso.org/iso/iso_catalogue/management_and_leadership_standards/environmental management/iso_14000_essentials.htm.

International Organization for Standardization (ISO) (2015c). ISO 20121: sustainable events. Retrieved from http://www.iso.org/iso/home/standards/management-standards/iso20121.htm.

International Organization for Standardization (ISO) (2015d). ISO/IEC 27001: information security management. Retrieved from http://www.iso.org/iso/home/standards/management-standards/iso27001.htm.

International Organization for Standardization (ISO) (2015e). ISO 31000: risk management. Retrieved from http://www.iso.org/iso/home/standards/iso31000.htm.

Ioannou, I., & Serafeim, G. (2010). What drives corporate social performance? International evidence from social, environmental and governance scores. Harvard Business School Working Paper No. 11-016. Retrieved from http://www.hbs.edu/faculty/Publication%20Files/11-016.pdf.

Ioannou, I., & Serafeim, G. (2011a). The consequences of mandatory corporate social reporting. Unpublished working paper, Harvard Business School.

Ioannou, I., & Serafeim, G. (2011b). The consequences of mandatory corporate sustainability reporting. Harvard Business School Working Paper No. 11-100. Retrieved from http://ssrn.com/abstract=1799589.

IRRC Institute (2013). *First Comprehensive Study on State of Integrated Reporting in United States*. Retrieved from http://irrcinstitute.org/projects.php?project=63.

IRRC Institute (2014). *IRRCi Research Report: The Alignment Gap Between Creating Value, Performance Measurement, and Long-Term Incentive Design*. Retrieved from http://irrcinstitute.org/pdf/alignment-gap-study.pdf.

IRRC Institute & Sustainable Investments Institute (2013). *Integrated Financial and Sustainability Reporting in the United States.* Retrieved from http://irrcinstitute.org/pdf/FINAL_Integrated_Financial_Sustain_Reporting_April_2013.pdf.

Jensen, M.C. (2001). Value maximization, stakeholder theory, and the corporate objective function. *Journal of Applied Corporate Finance*, 14(3), 8-21 and *European Financial Management*, 7(3), 297-317.

Jensen, M., & Meckling, W. (1976). Theory of the firm: managerial behavior, agency costs and ownership structure. *Journal of Financial Economics*, 3, 305-360.

Jiao, Y. (2010). Stakeholder welfare and firm value. *Journal of Banking and Finance*, 34(10), 2549-2561.

Kassinis, G., & Vafeas, N. (2002). Corporate boards and outside stakeholders as determinants of environmental litigation. *Strategic Management Journal*, 23, 399-415.

Khanna, M., & Anton, W.Q. (2002). Corporate environmental management: regulatory and market-based pressures. *Land Economics*, 78, 539-558.

Kim, Y, Park, M.S., & Wier, B. (2012). Is earnings quality associated with corporate social responsibility? *The Accounting Review*, 87(3), 761-796.

Kiron, D., Kruschwitz, N., Haanaes, K., Reeves, M., & Goh, E. (2013a). The benefits of sustainability-driven innovation. *MIT Sloan Management Review*, 54(2), 69-73.

Kiron, D., Kruschwitz, N., Haanaes, K., Reeves, M., & Goh, E. (2013b). *The Innovation Bottom Line: How Companies That See Sustainability Both a Necessity and an Opportunity, and Change Their Business Models in Response, Are Finding Success.* Retrieved from http://csbf.org.nz/wp-content/uploads/the-innovation-bottom-line.pdf.

Kiron, D., Kruschwitz, N., Haanaes, K., Reeves, M., Fuisz-Kehrbach, S., & Kell, G. (2015). *Joining Forces: Collaboration and Leadership for Sustainability.* Retrieved from http://marketing.mitsmr.com/PDF/56380-MITSMR-BGC-UNGC-Sustainability2015.pdf?cid=1.

Kollman, K., & Prakash, A. (2002). EMS-based environmental regimes as club goods: examining variations in firm level adoption of ISO 14001 and EMAS in U.K., U.S. and Germany. *Policy Sciences*, 35, 43-67.

KPMG (2013a). Beyond quarterly earnings: is the company on track for long-term success? Retrieved from http://www.kpmg-institutes.com/institutes/aci/articles/2013/07/beyond-quarterly-earnings.html.

KPMG (2013b). *GRI's G4 Guidelines: The Impact on Reporting.* Retrieved from http://www.kpmg.com/Global/en/IssuesAndInsights/ArticlesPublications/Documents/g4-the-impact-on-reporting-v2.pdf.

KPMG and United Nations Environment Programme (2006) *Carrots and Sticks for Starters.* Retrieved from http://ec.europa.eu/enterprise/policies/sustainable-business/corporate-social-responsibility/reporting-disclosure/swedish-presidency/files/surveys_and_reports/carrots_and_sticks_-_kpmg_and_unep_en.pdf.

KPMG, Unit for Corporate Governance in Africa, Global Reporting Initiative and United Nations Environment Programme (2010). *Carrots and Sticks: Promoting Transparency and Sustainability – An Update on Trends in Voluntary and Mandatory Approaches to Sustainability Reporting.* Retrieved from https://www.globalreporting.org/resourcelibrary/Carrots-And-Sticks-Promoting-Transparency-And-Sustainbability.pdf.

KPMG, Centre for Corporate Governance in Africa, Global Reporting Initiative and United Nations Environment Programme (2013). *Carrots and Sticks: Sustainability Reporting Policies Worldwide – Today's Best Practice, Tomorrow's Trends.* Retrieved from https://www.globalreporting.org/resourcelibrary/carrots-and-sticks.pdf.

Kuehn, K. (2010, April 13). Five Ways to Convince Your CFO that Sustainability Pays. *GreenBiz.* Retrieved from http://www.greenbiz.com/blog/2010/04/13/five-ways-convince-your-cfo-sustainability-pays.

Kugel, R. (2013). International integrated reporting framework takes shape. Retrieved from http://robertkugel.ventanaresearch.com/2013/04/23/international-integrated-reporting-framework-takes-shape.

Kumar, R., & Honick, D. (2014). *IQ Insights: SSGA's Active Ownership Process on ESG Risks and Opportunities Facing Investee Companies*. Retrieved from https://www.ssga.com/investment-topics/general-investing/2015/SSGAs-Active-Ownership-Process-on-ESG-Risks-Opps-Overview.pdf.

Lazo, J.K., Lawson, M., Larsen, P.H., & Waldman, D.M. (2011). United States economic sensitivity to weather variability. *Bulletin of the American Meteorological Society*, 92, 709-720.

Leuz, C. (2004). Proprietary versus non-proprietary disclosures: evidence from germany. In C. Leuz, D. Pfaff, & A. Hopwood (Eds.), *The Economics and Politics of Accounting* (pp. 164-197). Oxford, UK: Oxford University Press.

Maxwell, J.W., Lyon, T.P., & Hackett, S.C. (2000). Self-regulation and social welfare: the political economy of corporate environmentalism. *The Journal of Law and Economics*, 43, 583-619.

Miller, K., & Serafeim, G. (2014). Chief sustainability officers: who are they and what do they do? In R. Henderson, R. Gulati, & M. Tushman (Eds.), *Leading Sustainable Change: An Organizational Perspective* (pp. 196-221). Oxford, UK: Oxford University Press.

MIT Sloan Management Review & Boston Consulting Group (2011). *Sustainability: The 'Embracers' Seize Advantage*. Retrieved from https://www.bcg.com/documents/file71538.pdf.

Murphy, K. (1999). Executive compensation. In O. Ashenfelter, R. Layard and D. Card (Eds.), *Handbook of Labor Economics* (vol. 3, pp. 2485-2563). San Diego, CA: North Holland.

National Environmental Policy Act (1969). *National Environmental Policy Act of 1969: Public Law 91-190, as Amended Through December 31, 2000*. Retrieved from http://www.epw.senate.gov/nepa69.pdf.

Nidumolu, R., Simmons, P.J., & Yosle, T.F. (2015). *Sustainability and the CFO: Challenges, Opportunities and Next Practices*. Retrieved from http://www.corporateecoforum.com/wp-content/uploads/2015/04/CFO_and_Sustainability_Apr-2015.pdf.

Novartis (2014). *Novartis Corporate Responsibility Performance Report 2013*. Retrieved from http://www.novartis.com/corporate-responsibility.

O'Rourke, D. (2003). Outsourcing regulation: analyzing nongovernmental systems of labor standards and monitoring. *Policy Studies Journal*, 31, 1-29.

Organisation for Economic Co-operation and Development (2003). Guidelines for multinational enterprises. Retrieved from http://www.oecd.org/corporate/mne/.

PricewaterhouseCoopers (2014a). Sustainability goes mainstream: insights into investor views. Retrieved from http://www.pwc.com/en_US/us/pwc-investor-resource-institute/publications/sustainability-goes-mainstream-investor-views.jhtml.

PricewaterhouseCoopers (2014b). *Corporate Performance: What Do Investors Want to Know?*, July 2014. Retrieved from http://www.pwc.com/en_GX/gx/audit-services/corporate-reporting/publications/investor-view/assets/pwc-investors-survey-apms-july-2014.pdf.

PricewaterhouseCoopers (2014c). *Tomorrow's Corporate Reporting: A Critical System at Risk*. Retrieved from http://www.tomorrowscorporatereporting.com.

PricewaterhouseCoopers (2014d). *Learning from Early Adopters of Integrated Reporting: Five Themes to Drive Improvement*. Retrieved from http://www.pwc.com/en_GX/gx/audit-services/publications/assets/pwc-learning-from-early-adopters-of-integrated-reporting.pdf.

Protiviti (2015). *Executive Perspectives on Top Risks for 2015: Key Issues Being Discussed in the Boardroom and C-Suite*. Retrieved from http://www.protiviti.com/en-US/Documents/Surveys/NC-State-Protiviti-Survey-Top-Risks-2015.pdf.

Public Company Accounting Oversight Board (2004). Auditing Standard No. 2: an audit of internal control over financial reporting performed in conjunction with an audit of financial statements. Retrieved from http://pcaobus.org/Standards/Auditing/Pages/Auditing_Standard_2.aspx.

Public Company Accounting Oversight Board (2007). Auditing Standard No. 5: An audit of internal control over financial reporting that is integrated with an audit of financial statements. Retrieved from http://pcaobus.org/Standards/Auditing/Pages/Auditing_Standard_5.aspx.

Reich, R. (2008). The case against corporate social responsibility. Goldman School of Public Policy Working Paper No. GSPP08-003. Retrieved from http://ssrn.com/abstract=1213129.

Rezaee, Z. (2007). *Corporate Governance Post-Sarbanes-Oxley: Regulations, Requirements, and Integrated Processes.* Hoboken, NJ: John Wiley & Sons.

Rezaee, Z. (2009). *Corporate Governance and Ethics.* Hoboken, NJ: John Wiley & Sons.

Rezaee, Z., & Elam, R. (2000). Emerging ISO 14000 environmental standards: a step-by-step implementation guide. *Managerial Auditing Journal,* 15(1), 60-67.

Rezaee, Z., & Ng, A. (2014). Business sustainability and cost of capital. Working paper, the University of Memphis.

Sarbanes-Oxley Act (2002). The Public Company Accounting Reform and Investor Protection Act, Pub. L. no. 107-204.

Securities and Exchange Commission (1977). Securities Exchange Act Release No. 13185 (January 19).

Securities and Exchange Commission (1978). Notification of Enactment of Foreign Corrupt Practices Act of 1977. Accounting Series Release No. 242 (Release No. 34-14478, February 16, 1978, 43 FR 7752).

Securities and Exchange Commission (1979). Statement of Management on Internal Accounting Control. 17 CFR Parts 221, 229, 240, 249; Release No. 34-15772, File No. S7-779 (April).

Securities and Exchange Commission (2010). 17 CFR Parts 211, 231 and 241 Commission Guidance Regarding Disclosure Related to Climate Change; Final Rule. Federal Register Vol. 75, No. 25.

Sethi, S.P. (1975). Dimensions of corporate social performance: an analytical framework. *California Management Review,* 17(3), 58-64.

Shaw, W.H. (1999). *Business Ethics.* Belmont, CA: Wadsworth.

Shearman & Sterling LLP (2011). Corporate governance of largest u.S. public companies: director and executive compensation. Retrieved from http://corpgov.shearman.com.

Singapore Exchange (2011). SGX introduces sustainability reporting guide to support listed companies. Retrieved from http://investorrelations.sgx.com/releasedetail.cfm?releaseid=589149.

Singer, T. (2015). *Driving Revenue Growth Through Sustainable Products and Services.* The Conference Board in collaboration with the Investor Responsibility Research Center Institute (IRRCI). Available at https://www.conference-board.org/sustainability-innovation/.

Singh, R. (2013, April 16). Consultation launches on integrated reporting framework. *AccountancyAge.* Retrieved from http://www.accountancyage.com/aa/news/2261369/consultation-launches-on-integrated-reporting-framework.

Social Investment Forum (2009). *2009 Annual Report.* Retrieved from http://www.ussif.org/files/Publications/2009_SIF_Annual_Report.pdf.

Society for Research in Child Development (2007). Ethical standards in research. Retrieved from http://www.srcd.org/about-us/ethical-standards-research.

Soyka, P.A., & Bateman, M.E. (2012). *Finding Common Ground on the Metrics that Matter.* Retrieved from http://www.irrcinstitute.org/pdf/IRRC-Metrics-that-Matter-Report_Feb-2012.pdf.

Spurgin, E.W. (2001). Do shareholders have obligations to stakeholders? *Journal of Business Ethics*, 33(4), 287-297. Retrieved from http://www.jstor.org/stable/25074611.

Starik, M., & Kanashiro, P. (2013). Toward a theory of sustainability management: uncovering and integrating the nearly obvious. *Organization & Environment*, 26(1), 7-30.

Starr, M. (2012). Remarks to the IFRS taxonomy annual convention. Retrieved from http://www.sec.gov/news/speech/2012/spch042512ms.htm.

Sustainability Accounting Standards Board (2013). *Conceptual Framework of the Sustainability Accounting Standards Board*. Retrieved from http://www.sasb.org/wp-content/uploads/2013/10/SASB-Conceptual-Framework-Final-Formatted-10-22-13.pdf.

Tilling, M.V. (2004). Refinements to legitimacy theory in social and environmental accounting. Commerce Research Paper Series No. 04-6, ISSN 1441-3906.

Tonello, M. (2011). Assessing pay for performance. Retrieved from http://corpgov.law.harvard.edu/2011/10/20/assessing-pay-for-performance/.

Topazio, N. (2014a). *Integrated Thinking: The Next Step in Integrated Reporting*. Retrieved from http://www.cgma.org/Resources/Reports/DownloadableDocuments/integrated-thinking-the-next-step-in-integrated-reporting.pdf.

Topazio, N. (2014b, October 6). Six tips for integrated thinking. *CGMA Magazine*. Retrieved from http://www.cgma.org/magazine/features/pages/201410895.aspx.

Toronto Stock Exchange & Chartered Professional Accountants of Canada (2014). *A Primer for Environmental and Social Disclosure*. Retrieved from https://www.cpacanada.ca/en/business-and-accounting-resources/financial-and-non-financial-reporting/sustainability-environmental-and-social-reporting/publications/a-primer-for-environmental-social-disclosure.

United Nations (1987). *Report on the World Commission on Environment and Development: Our Common Future*. Retrieved from http://www.un-documents.net/our-common-future.pdf.

United Nations Environment Programme Finance Initiative (2005). *A Legal Framework for the Integration of Environmental, Social and Governance Issues Into Institutional Investment*. Retrieved from http://www.unepfi.org/fileadmin/documents/freshfields_legal_resp_20051123.pdf.

United Nations Environment Programme Finance Initiative (2013). *How Investors are Addressing Environmental, Social and Governance Factors in Fundamental Equity Valuation*. Retrieved from http://www.unpri.org/viewer/?file=wp-content/uploads/Integrated_Analysis_2013.pdf.

United Nations Global Compact (2013). *Global Corporate Sustainability Report 2013*. Retrieved from https://www.unglobalcompact.org/docs/about_the_gc/Global_Corporate_Sustainability_Report2013.pdf.

United States Environmental Protection Agency (2015a). Introduction: environmental enforcement and compliance. Retrieved from http://www.epa.gov/region9/enforcement/intro.html.

United States Environmental Protection Agency (2015b). National priorities list. Retrieved from http://www.epa.gov/superfund/sites/npl/index.htm.

United States Environmental Protection Agency (2015c). Summaries of environmental laws and EOs. Retrieved from http://www2.epa.gov/laws-regulations/laws-and-executive-orders.

United States Government Accountability Office (2010). Superfund: EPA's Estimated costs to remediate existing sites exceed current funding levels, and more sites are expected to be added to the national priorities list. Retrieved from http://www.gao.gov/products/GAO-10-380.

United States Green Building Council (2012). *LEED 2009 for New Construction and Major Renovations*. Retrieved from http://www.usgbc.org/ShowFile.aspx?DocumentID=8868.

United States Green Building Council. (2015). LEED. Retrieved from http://www.usgbc.org/DisplayPage.aspx?CMSPageID=1990.

US SIF Foundation (2012). *Report on Sustainable and Responsible Investing Trends in the United States 2012*. Retrieved from http://www.ussif.org/files/publications/12_trends_exec_summary.pdf.

Wheeler, D., Colbert, B., & Freeman, R. (2003). Focusing on value: reconciling corporate social responsibility, sustainability and a stakeholder approach in a network world. *Journal of General Management*, 28(3), 1-28.

White, S. (2015, January 6). How management accountants can lead their organizations towards sustainability success. *CGMA Magazine*. Retrieved from http://www.cgma.org/Magazine/News/Pages/201511533.aspx.

Woll, L. (2009, July). Social Investment Forum. Retrieved from http://www.sec.gov/comments/4-567/4567-20.pdf.

World Commission on Environment and Development (1987). *The Brundtland Report: Our Common Future*. Oxford, UK: Oxford University Press.

World Economic Forum (2013). *Strategic Infrastructure: Steps to Prepare and Accelerate Public–Private Partnerships*. Retrieved from http://www3.weforum.org/docs/AF13/WEF_AF13_Strategic_Infrastructure_Initiative.pdf.

XBRL (2013). An Introduction to XBRL. Retrieved from https://www.xbrl.org/the-standard/what/an-introduction-to-xbrl/.

Ziobro, P. (2014, September 3). CVS renames itself CVS Health as it ends sale of tobacco products. *The Wall Street Journal*. Retrieved from http://www.wsj.com/articles/cvs-renames-itself-cvs-health-as-it-ends-sale-of-tobacco-products-1409716801.

About the author

Zabihollah Rezaee is the Thompson-Hill Chair of Excellence, PhD coordinator and Professor of Accountancy at the University of Memphis and has served a two-year term on the Standing Advisory Group (SAG) of the Public Company Accounting Oversight Board (PCAOB). He received his BS degree from the Iranian Institute of Advanced Accounting, his MBA from Tarleton State University in Texas, and his PhD from the University of Mississippi. Dr. Rezaee  holds ten certifications, including Certified Public Accountant (CPA), Certified Fraud Examiner (CFE), Certified Management Accountant (CMA), Certified Internal Auditor (CIA), Certified Government Financial Manager (CGFM), Certified Sarbanes-Oxley Professional (CSOXP), Certified Corporate Governance Professional (CGOVP), Certified Governance Risk Compliance Professional (CGRCP), Chartered Global Management Accountant (CGMA) and Certified Risk Management Assurance (CRMA). He is currently serving as the 2012–14 secretary of the Forensic & Investigative Accounting (FIA) Section of the AAA.

Professor Rezaee has published over 200 articles in accounting and business journals and made more than 210 presentations. He has also published eight books: *Financial Institutions, Valuations, Mergers, and Acquisitions: The Fair Value Approach*; *Financial Statement Fraud: Prevention and Detection*; *U.S. Master Auditing Guide* 3rd edition; *Audit Committee Oversight Effectiveness Post-Sarbanes-Oxley Act*; *Corporate Governance Post-Sarbanes-Oxley: Regulations, Requirements, and Integrated Processes*;

Corporate Governance and Business Ethics and *Financial Services Firms: Governance, Regulations, Valuations, Mergers and Acquisitions,* and contributed to several other books. Three of these books are translated into other languages including Chinese, South Korean, Spanish and Iranian. His book on *Corporate Sustainability: Integrating Performance and Reporting,* published in November 2012, won the 2013 Axiom Gold Award in the category of Business Ethics.

Index